"Her Name is Happiness"

The Inspirational Account of the Life of Happiness Emejuru

By: Douglas S. Anderson

PRESS

www.xulonpress.com

Ciara -
Trust in the Lord with all
your heart! Prov 3:5

Remember Ciara,
"It is finished" Matt. 19:30
Have faith in God.

DEDICATION

To my wife Laura whose unending support and encouragement continues to bless me;

to my children Paul and Christina who I will always cherish;

and to a man I have never met in this life, but I hope to meet in the life to come, Mr. Dick Azundah Hekerem ("D.A.H.") Emejuru: a man of complete integrity and unwavering faithfulness to God; a man whose bonds of family love were so strong as to reach across an ocean to a daughter a continent far away, and to a man much like who I aspire to be.

AUTHOR'S NOTE

The life, struggles and blessings of Happiness Emejuru are all true. However, I have applied a certain amount of literary license in telling her story. Although I have used the actual names of all of Happiness' immediate family, to avoid unnecessary embarrassment, or unwanted publicity, I have used fictional names for some of the other individuals. Moreover, while I sought to not stray too far from the realm of nonfiction, I have exercised some liberties in how I chose to tell her story so that the sequence and details of some events have been altered to provide greater clarity.

ACKNOWLEDGEMENTS

This book could never have come about had it not been for the help and assistance of some amazing people.

Though she would never take the credit, my wife Laura was incredible, patiently reading each and every draft of the manuscript. No one could be asked to give more assistance than she did. Her candid and sometimes difficult assessments of the writing, that only a loving wife could give, provided me with much needed, and excellent, direction.

Additionally, I wish to thank a man I greatly respect and admire, Pastor Tony Hall, who encouraged me to start this project when I was hesitant to do so. Also, I am grateful to Pastor Brenda Hall, who despite a busy schedule of children, grandchildren and church responsibilities, kindly agreed to read the first draft, and despite its initial roughness, gave me mercifully kind compliments and words of encouragement that kept me pursuing the project. That meant a lot.

I would be greatly remiss if I were not to acknowledge the invaluable contributions of Julia whose endless hours of review and work on this manuscript brought its quality to a higher level than I could have ever reached on my own.

Finally, I wish to express my deepest and fondest gratitude to the gracious subject of this book, Happiness Emejuru. Without her fortitude of spirit and determination to cling to her Lord, this story would never have come to pass. I cannot adequately convey the emotional pain it must have been for her to recall so many difficult memories of her past she had once hoped to forget, as I probed mercilessly for every last detail to better tell her story. Yet through it all, she demonstrated extraordinary patience. As I hope this book reveals, she is truly a remarkable woman with a remarkable story to tell. My prayer is that I was able to tell her story in a manner that is worthy of her life.

Thank you Lord for giving me the opportunity to tell the extraordinary account of your hand of destiny on this woman. Otito dili Chukwu! (To God be the glory!)

CONTENTS

❧

INTRODUCTION

❧

"Shew me thy ways, O Lord; teach me thy paths."
– Psalm 25:4

Destiny is a curious thing. It is both unique to each person, yet common to all. The story that follows is the story of heavenly destiny upon one woman, and how God raised her up, protected her through the howling winds of life's adversities, and then released her into her ultimate life purpose. Her particular story is unique. But, like heavenly destiny, the woman in this story has much in common with us. We too, have a destiny God has set before us that is bigger and greater than ourselves, if we will surrender our will to His and let Him direct our steps.

But God's path to our life purpose is not always easy. Ask Joseph, who was given his divine purpose in a dream as a child, only to be sold into slavery, falsely accused of rape, and faced cruel injustice for untold years in a rat-infested dungeon. Ask King David, who received his divine assignment as a youth when anointed as the future king of Israel, only to be envied by the current king, and forced to flee for his life, living as an outcast in the mountains and caves of his future kingdom. Though no doubt tempted, neither man allowed bitterness or anger toward God to divert them from their heavenly destiny. Instead, they each allowed God to use those hardships and heartaches to mold their character, to mature them, and prepare them. Only by determining to take God's path for their life, regardless of the difficulties or the price to be paid, were they able to reach the pinnacle of their heavenly calling.

That is what makes this particular woman's story so worthwhile. Throughout all her heartaches and overwhelmingly difficult circumstances, this woman never blamed God. When others would have cursed God, she never did. When others might have become bitter towards God, she never did. In the face of some of life's most ferocious storms, she never wavered in her love for God. Her trust remained unshakable and deeply rooted.

As a result of her determined hold on God, every attack of the devil upon her life was defeated; every effort by the enemy to destroy her life and her destiny failed. With each assault upon her life, she just became stronger. Adversity strengthened her far beyond what an easy, comfortable life could have. We may want the easy life, but God knows that to fulfill our calling, we often must be tested and tried by fire. The greater the testing, the stronger we become. When life hits us hard, that is the time to draw closer to God; hold tighter to Him, and trust He will take us through the fire.

We must not blame God. Instead, we must understand what this woman did; that while God is not the source of our hardships, He will turn those hardships around for our good, if we let Him. Allow yourself to see the bigger picture. Our heavenly calling has been purposely interrupted and harassed by the devil whose desires for our lives are just the opposite of our Creator's. While God seeks to give us an abundant life, filled with His glory, the devil comes to steal, kill, and destroy. While God loves us, the devil hates us. While God's purposes for our lives are always for our best, the devil's purposes are always for our destruction. If the devil can destroy your destiny and your life through drug or alcohol addiction, pornography, extra-marital affairs, incessant greed, uncontrolled anger, feelings of inferiority, shame, guilt or fear; he surely will. The devil loves to ruin whatever wonderful plans God has for you.

It is the devil, not God, that brings heartache, broken-ness and despair. He does so in hopes that we will blame God. If we respond in the wrong way, then we allow him to bring unforgiveness and bitterness upon us and those resulting wounds can become so deep, we may never fulfill our heavenly purpose. We can become permanently crippled soldiers whose time on the front lines fighting the good fight of faith is over. When that happens, God's heart breaks, and the devil grins broadly in cruel satisfaction. There is a spiritual war for each person's soul, and it is not too dramatic to declare that the stakes are high.

Today's church is weak because it is filled with permanently crippled soldiers who have lost the ability to confront the devil and the evil he brings to God's people. Unforgiveness, bitterness, and fear from facing a barrage of life's hardships have combined to effectively thwart the wonderful plans and dreams our heavenly Creator has for us. Moreover, such infectious wounds often fester into doubt and unbelief.

That is why this story is so important for the world to hear. It is the story of the devil's numerous, but failed, efforts to destroy a life of destiny. It is the story of a coura-geous woman overcoming those demonic attacks by not giving up on the God who created her, and despite difficult circumstances, continuing to place her trust in Him. As a result, her wounded life was healed to return to the front lines and to fulfill her heavenly calling. Now she is being used by God to transform the lives of many others. There is a lesson in this for us: We too must not become bitter or angry toward God when hardships come; we too must not let circumstances defeat us, and we too must trust God to restore and heal. Only then can we return to the front lines and fulfill the purpose He gave us the day we were so tenderly formed.

The woman you meet in the pages that follow is unique in the hardships she faced, but she is just like you and me in the fact that hardships of some type have been, are being, and will continue to be, faced in everyone's life. May you let her life's example inspire you in your difficult circumstances; may you see the true source of hardships without blaming God, and as you read the pages that follow, may you trust God to preserve or restore you to your divine destiny.

1

REFLECTIONS

The day after Christmas was no time to be standing in a graveyard, but that is where a distinguished-looking African woman found herself on that cold and rainy December day of 2007. A tear rolled down her cheek as she stood silently by a freshly dug American grave. She was in her mid-forties, smartly dressed, and holding a large umbrella. The other funeral attendees had left, allowing her one last moment to say her silent goodbye to the woman in the casket; Mrs. Atkinson, a lonely, elderly lady long-since abandoned by friends and family.

She stood amazed that the Lord had brought her all the way from Nigeria to the United States where, following a seemingly endless array of heartaches and struggles, she had recently been used by God to bless Mrs. Atkinson with sacrificial love and compassion during her last days on earth. Now for the first time in her life, while standing before this simple grave, God revealed how the previously disjointed puzzle pieces of her life fit together with the unifying life purpose she had been earlier shown.

As she laid a modest bouquet of roses upon the plain, unadorned casket above the open grave, she reflected on how God had allowed her to minister love to Mrs. Atkinson, ensuring the elderly woman had proper medical care, a place to live, and all the little things that mean so much. She had often and tirelessly rubbed the older ladies' sore shoulders and legs, spent hours listening to her, shared moments of laughter and tears, as the two ladies developed a special bond much like that of a mother and daughter.

Who but God could have orchestrated this farewell; a last embrace of love between two women whose origins, cultures, and ethnicity were so different? Who but God could have led her to this lonely gravesite to pay her last respects to another who the world had forgotten? Only the Master Conductor could have drawn together all the devilish instruments of her past, the discordant sounds of heartache, sorrow and brokenness, and used them to create a harmonious melody wrought by a tender heart of compassion; an instrument truly designed to bless.

This woman, who had traveled so far in life, knew Him well. He was her "invisible friend," the one who had never forsaken her, and the one who now was using this gravesite to show her the bigger picture of her life. It was now clear to her how she was fulfilling her heavenly calling to touch those in need, to heal the brokenhearted, and to embrace the forgotten. She had crossed a vast ocean to live amongst a strange people far from her child-hood home; yet every past struggle of her life journey had prepared her for this moment; to render respect and love to a life others had neglected. She knew it would be one of many such moments to come.

She could linger no longer; it was time to go. The dreariness of this day perfectly reflected the sadness that engulfed her deep inside as she mourned the loss of one so dear. Yet a surge of gratitude welled up in the woman's heart as she touched the casket in one last farewell, leaving the flowers while carefully shielding her suit and hair with the umbrella.

You think that I helped you, but really you have helped me, the woman whispered quietly as she turned to walk to her car. *God used you to show me real joy, real happiness, and the fulfillment of my life's purpose.*

2

A FATHER'S LOVE

❧

In the small town of Elele, heat waves were already distorting the patches of grass that dotted the dirt parking lot outside the Nigerian hospital. Summer is nearly year round in southern Nigeria, so this July day in 1962 was hardly exceptional in its temperature. The Niger River, which here split into thousands of tributaries on its way to the sea, created rich and fertile land along with unbelievable humidity.

Inside, an expectant father was oblivious to the heat. Instead he paced nervously along the corridor waiting for the news that would tell him that this particular summer day would be unlike all the rest. He shouldn't have been so nervous. It wasn't as if he had not experienced the joys of fatherhood before. Dick Azundah Hekerem ("D.A.H.") Emejuru was already the proud father of three young boys and a girl. But since the birth of his third son, Mr. Emejuru had faithfully and fervently prayed for another girl. His hopes of answered prayer were high, yet he nursed a strange uneasiness as he listened to his wife's moans from her room down the hall and contemplated what was to come. Sybel had been in labor for five hours—not too

20

unusual. But wasn't that too long for such an experienced mother? How long had it taken with his daughter Esther? *No, no*, he assured himself, *everything is fine.*

For him, waiting was always the toughest part. It was the uneasy time when the situation was out of his control and he had to trust in the Lord. While he was a man who trusted God more than most people he knew, he also was a man who was ready for God's answer. *"I wanted another girl so badly,"* Mr. Emejuru would later remember of that day. The desire that he felt for that particular child to be another daughter, more pronounced than any preference he had regarding the four that preceded her or the three that would follow, contributed to his irrational anxiety surrounding this birth. He tried to think of other things, but his mind kept returning to the baby whose birth was now taking too long.

As he stared at the tiles of the waiting room floor, his mind began to drift. He began to anticipate what it would be like to hold his little girl; to see her looking at him in innocence and trust, just as our Heavenly Father dreams of seeing us. He imagined what it would be like to see her first smile, or later to watch his little girl running and jumping in delight and to know he was going to be there to protect her. He smiled as he realized that his thoughts were again similar to those shared by our Heavenly Father towards us. A Father's love can be an amazing thing.

"Mr. Emejuru, Mr. Emejuru!" The voice startled him out of his deep thought. A nurse had just approached him, smiling broadly. *"Congratulations Mr. Emejuru; you have a beautiful baby girl. Both she and your wife are doing well. You may see them now, if you like."* Joy flooded his heart. Many nights of secret prayers were answered in that moment. Boys were prized for strength and their ability to carry on the family name, but his heart had long desired this daughter for reasons he could not explain. His

mind was racing, pondering the goodness of God to have answered his prayers.

He followed the nurse to the room where his wife and baby girl were waiting for him. He smiled at Sybel as he gently took his precious baby girl from her arms. As he held her, the brilliant sunlight streaming in from the window illuminated her tiny features. Her skin was smooth, her lips and nose perfectly formed. His heart instantly melted as the intensity of the moment caught him off guard. God had answered his prayers in such a powerful way that he had trouble containing his emotions. He couldn't help thinking, God had done well!

"Her name, Sir?" the nurse asked respectfully, interrupting his rapturous gaze. She held a clipboard with the medical records to record his decision. He looked up and answered instantly. *"Happiness; Her name is Happiness, since that is what she has brought me this day."*

As the nurse duly recorded the decision, an orderly drew the curtain for it was now midmorning and the sun was getting higher. A shadow fell momentarily over the infant's face and she squirmed in her father's arms. Years later, he would wonder if that shadow was an omen of sorrows yet to come. For now, though, his thoughts were fixed upon Happiness: the daughter of her father's joy. So with that pronouncement from an exuberant father, a new life had begun, touched by heaven with a destiny and purpose no one but God Himself yet knew.

We often minimize their significance, but names can be important. In the book of Genesis, the Bible records the account of Rachel, Jacob's wife dying in childbirth as she delivered her second son. With her dying breath, she named her little boy, "Ben-oni," which meant "son of my sorrow." How tragic that a mother sought to burden her son with her sorrow for the rest of his life through the use of a name. Fortunately, Jacob changed the boy's name to Benjamin and spared the boy of a constant reminder of his mother's misfortune.

Now God was doing something special with the use of a name. He had taken the prayers of a faithful father and used a father's gratitude to forever bless this little girl. By naming his little girl "Happiness," or "the daughter of my joy," this Nigerian father was giving her a permanent reminder of her father's love. Little did he realize that her name would become part of her destiny, and thus, the target of her spiritual enemy. Much of what would happen to her later in life would be the result of the devil trying his best to steal that joy of her father's love. But all that would be for a later time.

Mr. Emejuru touched his wife's forehead affectionately as she dozed off to sleep. His thoughts wandered reflexively to the large, dangerous world that his daughter would inhabit with the rest of his children. Specifically, he thought of the rumblings against the Ibos whose villages surrounded his own. Now that the British had left Nigeria, how much longer could the resentment of the Hausa-Fulani and the Yoruba be held at bay?

He looked again at his daughter and prayed silently, *"Lord, you are faithful. You promised to strengthen and protect us from the evil one. By all that I hold dear, I vow to You that I will do everything I can to protect this little one from all of his devices."*

—

Over the ensuing weeks and months, little Happiness had no trouble living up to her name. She brought joy to her mother and her siblings but to her father she was a special delight. Mr. Emejuru was a prominent man in their village who had been raised by British Christians when his own parents passed away. Unlike more traditional men, he had no trouble showing affection to all his children, especially his daughters. Years later Happiness would recall of him that *"his encouragement was almost endless."*

As she learned to speak, Happiness would call to him, *"Papa, Papa!"*

"What is it My Happy?" he would always ask.

"Mama made yams for dinner," she might answer.

"And do you like yams, Happy-mm?"

"I do, Papa. But I also like corn," she would say while giggling.

"Roasted corn?," lifting her onto his lap.

"Oh yes, roasted corn. Fire roasted corn!" she squealed with delight.

And more often than not, Happiness would find herself feasting on one of the treats she so loved a few moments later. Life was everything it should be for a growing little girl.

On one particular occasion, their regular interchange took a more serious note. *"Do you know what, Happy-mm?"* Papa asked tenderly as he looked into her big brown eyes. *"It is my heart's desire that you should know the meaning of your name."*

"Happiness! My name is Happiness Emejuru!" she responded as her eyes twinkled back at him.

"Yes, that is indeed your name. But do you know why your Papa has given you that name?"

"No, Papa! I do not know. Why, why, why?" she giggled, playing with the collar on his shirt.

"I gave you that name because of the joy you brought me when you were born, and the joy I knew you would bring to me all of my days on this earth. I want you to know that every time your name is called, you are to remember that you are God's great gift to me. You are the daughter of your father's joy."

"Yes, Papa!" she smiled, covering his face with kisses. *"Yes, I am the daughter of your joy!"* The delighted child basked in her father's love as he held her tightly in his arms. Reveling in the moment, Mr. Emejuru silently committed not only to show his little girl more of his love, but to teach her about the love of her Heavenly Father, for she truly was His joy as well. This faithful Nigerian father wisely understood that it would take the combined love of both an earthly and a Heavenly Father, to protect Happiness through the future storms in her life. Indeed, her life would soon demonstrate that there are few things in life more powerful than a father's love.

3

BUILDING A STRONG FOUNDATION

"No, Ogu, you will not go!" Once their father had spoken, it was hardly worth bringing it up again. There would be no more discussion of Ade Okoro's ceremonial transition to manhood or the village party that was to follow. Ogubuike, or "Ogu," as his family and friends called him, was Happiness' oldest brother. Even though he knew the rules of his father, Ogu was clearly disappointed in not being able to witness his friend's ceremony or partake in the festivities. Her other siblings knew the rules too: Esther, the second child and only other girl, Allswell and Christian, her other two older brothers, along with her two younger brothers, Johnson and Isaiah.

When Mr. Emejuru became a Christian he made a serious commitment, far stronger than many of his fellow villagers who merely added biblical sayings to a mixture of traditional beliefs. He had rejected the gods of his ancestors and all their associated rituals when he embraced the Gospel of Jesus Christ. He was proud to live in Nigeria and proud to be an Ikwerre, but he considered himself a man of

God before he was anything else. He also knew better than to take the rituals of his ancestors and his neighbors lightly.

Nigeria during the early 1960s when Happiness was born, had very few Christians. Of those who were there, many had allowed pagan influences to compromise their faith. It was a nation dominated by witchcraft, paganism and those who practiced satanic rituals. It was a place where a person could easily be swept up in the rising tide of the occult. The spiritual darkness from such pagan influences had the effect of a strong under current drowning its unsuspecting victims.

"False gods are not less seductive just because they are false," Mr. Emejuru explained to Ogu. *"Stronger boys than you have been tricked and deceived, even when their parents tried to teach them the Bible. You must guard your heart."*

There was much to guard against. No one dared speak of the evil things witch doctors did to placate spirits or create medicine for their "patients." Whether it was a meal left under a tree or a slaughtered goat or chicken, the gods in Nigeria were always hungry. What would happen if you didn't feed them? The typical villager did not want to find out.

Animal sacrifices were prevalent in that area, and the macabre remnants of such practices found in the morning were a constant demonstration of the culture of death and destruction wrought by the witches and pagans. Chicken and goat sacrifices were common. So too was the sight of a bowl of rice and a fully-cooked meal left under a tree for the gods to eat. As a result of paganistic beliefs, there were a multitude of taboos and occultic rituals practiced in the village where the Emejurus lived. The superstitious villagers were convinced that the gods had to be appeased, and their gods were not kind or merciful.

The Emejuru family was surrounded by Nigerian villagers who were deeply enslaved to the false gods they

served. To this day, Happiness recalls many stories of
the pagan rituals that she and her siblings were taught to
strictly avoid. When a chicken was sacrificed, villagers
would gather in a circle, cut off its head, and then swing
the chicken around, while chanting various prayers to their
gods. Afterwards they would eat the sacrificed animals in a
celebratory feast. Even though Mr. Emejuru would forbid
his children to take part in any of these rituals, Happiness
learned about them through stories she heard and by sometimes hiding in the crowd and peeking through the legs of
the people watching the ritual. She couldn't help it; sometimes curiosity just got the best of her.

That is how she witnessed the pagan ritual of boys
entering into "manhood," the party her brother had been
told not to attend. She had already heard warnings to stay
clear of pagan rituals and traditional "medicine" more
times than she could count. However, like her brothers
and her sister, she could not help but wonder what was so
dangerous about these mysterious happenings. What was
so terrible that they could not even go near? What was so
bad about Ade Okoro's party that Ogu, one of Ade's best
friends, could not even attend?

That afternoon, Happiness' curiosity seemed to grow.
Ogu was done pouting and decided to finish his homework. Esther was reading to Isaiah while the maid hung
out the washing. Even Christian and Allswell were preoccupied, kicking a ball in the yard when the sounds of the
party began to rise in the distance. Happiness could resist
her curiosity no longer. While her brothers were occupied
with their soccer match, she snuck away to the center of the
village, where the sounds were originating.

Although still quite young, Happiness was old enough
to be sent short distances on errands, to deliver a letter
or a basket to a neighbor. She had no trouble finding the
ceremony, as nearly all gatherings of such importance were

held in a similar spot. She immediately recognized what seemed like all the people from nearly every family she knew, gathered in a large circle. She shuddered as she realized that some were even from church, something she knew her father would never approve. Ade was there, adorned in a colorful costume as his relatives sang and undulated with delight around him.

Nothing so terrible, thought little Happiness. Then she heard shouting and saw someone carrying a skull. It was the skull of a goat, although Happiness could not recognize it as such. Ade was given a large stick by his father while the other villagers shouted encouragement; the boy struck the skull violently and howled. Happiness wanted to look away, but was captivated by the sight. On the fourth blow, he crushed the skull and the surrounding people shrieked and cheered with glee. Then the shouts grew louder and louder as the crowd seemed to writhe out of control.

Now Ade's uncle handed him a live chicken and a knife. Happiness thought she saw a tinge of fear in his eyes as he took the knife and raised it to cut the chicken's head off. This time Happiness looked away. She didn't want to see all the blood. But she heard the squealing of the chicken and the shouts of the crowd and she knew what had happened. Now the screams of the crowd rose to a fever pitch.

Suddenly an overwhelming fear seized her. She felt sick to her stomach and began to run home. All of a sudden, she understood why her father had always cautioned her to stay away from such places. She could feel something reaching for her heart, a dark power trying to draw her into its clutches and she wanted nothing more than to be safe in her father's arms again. Never again would she allow her curiosity to trick her into going somewhere she did not belong.

—

29

Being part of a handful of Christians in a nation dominated by Muslims to the north and pagan worship in the
surrounding areas meant that Mr. Emejuru had to set
himself apart. There could be no peaceful coexistence, no
approving tolerance. He knew how easy it was for some to
fall back into the old ways; visiting a witch doctor to heal a
mysterious illness or taking a second or third wife when the
first grew old or tiresome.

"We are not like other people," Papa would make clear,
before he opened the Bible to teach his children. *"God says
that we are not supposed to be. We are peculiar."*

"What is 'peculiar', Papa," Happiness had asked more
than once.

"It means different, set apart," her father explained.

Mr. Emejuru's passionate refusal to compromise
with village religious traditions earned him the nickname
"Bulldog" in their local Seventh Day Adventist church.
Happiness knew her father was different from other men
and she was proud of that. Her father was key to the protective spiritual foundation the Lord gave Happiness. Not
only was she placed in the home of a strong Christian
family, she was given a father who was, without doubt,
"God's man." He was an uncompromising pillar for God's
truth. Sitting with her mother and sisters on the women's
side of the church each Saturday, she knew that all her
siblings belonged to her mother, and that her mother was
Mr. Emejuru's only wife. Other friends she knew had
fathers with two or three wives, even if they did not bring
all of them to church. Even as a little girl she pictured her
wedding to a man like her father: a man who would make
her his only wife and make her very happy.

Happiness knew that none of the church members,
no matter how much her father might irritate them, dared
to question her father's rejection of the traditional ways,
for fear of being easily argued down by his commanding

knowledge of the Bible. Even the elders in the church were afraid of her father's reaction to any compromise in their own lives. They all remembered days when Mr. Emejuru had left service early upon hearing that a church leader had taken part in a ritual or taken a second wife. No one wanted to incur the Bulldog's wrath.

Of course Mr. Emejuru's bold convictions did not go unnoticed by his neighbors whose loyalty to other gods went beyond traditionalist sentiments. Several times occultists placed curses on some animal, sacrificed it to their gods, and then intentionally buried it within the Emejuru family compound to bring sickness or death upon the family. Like biblical villains of old, they bragged of their deed and demanded that Mr. Emejuru make a sacrifice to their gods before they would remove the curse from his family. He always refused, steadfastly telling them, *"I and my family are Christians; our God will protect us."*

On occasions when one of the Emejuru's would get sick, the pagan leaders would again tell him of his need to sacrifice to their gods. Their demands upon Mr. Emejuru were to no avail. His convictions were strong. He would not compromise. His opposition to the traditions many of his neighbors held dear did not make him popular, but it did earn him respect. Everyone knew what he believed and that his actions matched his faith.

That is the kind of unshakable conviction that Mr. Emejuru taught his children. Even as a little girl, Happiness was taught the importance of God in her life and the importance of living in a way that would be pleasing to the Lord. God's hand of protection over her life was obvious by virtue of the family and father He placed her with. To Happiness, her father was the complete package; he exuded an abundance of love, yet stood as a pillar of integrity. His character was unquestioned. Happiness believed him to be the most deeply-committed Christian in the entire village of Elele, and the whole community knew it. His love and integrity were the gifts he bestowed to each of his children, but especially to his second little girl. He had promised God to protect her as best he could, and he did so with a strong foundation of faith and trust in God. In retrospect, there is nothing more valuable her father could have given her.

The Bible reminds us of an enduring truth; the importance of building our lives upon a solid foundation. People, like buildings, must be able to weather the storms of life, for storms will surely come. The question is not whether we will face storms, but how we will respond to them? Without a sure foundation in Christ, we will be unable to stand tall against their howling winds. In Matthew 7:24-27 we are reminded of two competing foundations:

> *"Therefore whosoever heareth these sayings of mine (Jesus), and doeth them, I will liken him unto a wise man, which built his house upon a rock: And the rain descended, and the floods came, and the winds blew, and beat upon that house; and it fell not: for it was founded upon a rock. And every one that heareth these sayings of mine, and doeth them not, shall be likened unto a foolish man, which built his house upon the sand: And the rain descended, and the floods came, and the winds blew, and beat upon that house; and it fell: and great was the fall of it."*

It is foolish to build anything of importance upon a soft, compromising foundation; especially our lives. Christ must be the cornerstone in our lives and His Word must be the mortar. God made sure that Happiness would have both before life's storms came her way.

To this point in her life, Happiness' father had been true to his commitment to protect the special girl God had given him. By placing Happiness with this particular family and this particular father, God had made sure she would have a rock-solid foundation of faith in Christ and an under-standing of God's love for her. As a result, life thus far was good for this little Nigerian girl named Happiness. Indeed, given the circumstances, it was almost perfect. Her father, true to his vow, did all he could to protect the treasure that God had so graciously given him. Everything he had done, from the example he tried to set as a father, to the very name he gave her, was designed to prepare her. Somehow, he sensed his special daughter was going to need that preparation even more than his other children. Storms were coming her way and he wanted her to be ready.

4

STORM CLOUDS COMING

A charred body lay by the side of the road at the edge of the neighboring village. All that was visible now was the blackened skeleton, partially crushed by passing traffic. A neighbor, returning from an errand in a nearby village, had the misfortune of coming across the grisly discovery and knew it was an Ibo man. Ibos were being burned and buried alive as they fled the aggression of the Muslim Hausa-Fulani. Long despised as the "Jews of Africa," the educated, wealthy and largely Christian Ibos were being persecuted to the point of genocide.

The British had left Nigeria as promised and now a few years into its independence, the fledgling nation was descending into civil war. The Emejurus lived in the better educated and more affluent southeast region of Nigeria in the town of Elele, just outside of the great oil refining city of Port Harcourt, Rivers State. They came from a smaller group of Nigerians, largely Christian, called Ikwerre. Yet even though they were not part of the Ibo and Hausa-Fulani feud that was gripping the nation, Mr. Emejuru knew that the rising tide of violence would be unlikely to spare them as it swept across the Niger Delta. Life in their once peaceful village was becoming increasingly dangerous.

At the time, Nigeria was loosely segregated into three main ethnic groups. The Ibo (also called "Igbo"), were primarily Christian and dominated the eastern portion of Nigeria. Their high education levels carried them into the more influential positions in government and business. The Hausa-Fulanis were Muslim who dominated the north and largely retained their feudal tribal practices. Such out-dated practices led to wide-spread poverty, creating a rift of resentment at the success and prosperity of the modernized Ibo Christians. How much of that resentment was religiously motivated and how much was economically motivated is hard to quantify, but clearly the religious animosity of the Muslims toward the Christians was deeply rooted. The third major ethnic group in Nigeria at that time were the Yorubas who lived in the southwest portion of the country.

While each side of this brewing civil war had their own interpretation of the facts, no doubt the spark that ignited the war was fueled and fanned by ethnic and religious rivalry. In January, 1966, army officers staged a military coup led primarily by Ibos from the eastern part of Nigeria.

Happiness knew that some kind of trouble was brewing. Several days earlier, when she was struggling to fall asleep she had wandered into the hallway in the middle of the night. She stopped in her tracks when she heard her parents whispering.

"The Ibos staged a coup?" It was her mother's voice.

"Yes, a group of army officers from the east," her father answered. *"Major General Ironsi was appointed head of the new government. He has already announced the suspension of our Constitution and the formation of a federal military government."*

"But he is an Ibo! The others will think they are trying to take over Nigeria! They will say it is as they have always warned; that the Ibos have been hoarding away their gold and have long plotted this." Her mother sounded concerned.

"Likely you are right, my wife," her father answered soberly. *"Yet we must trust God. We will see what happens."*

The conversation, which she didn't understand, haunted Happiness for weeks afterwards. Her mother was right, as it turned out. The take over played into the religious and economic animosities of the more affluent Ibo and it ignited flames of hatred. Two months later General Ironsi appointed Ibo governors over each region of Nigeria. The fragile bonds which held the new nation together were breaking apart before their eyes. That summer a Hausa-Fulani militia staged a counter-coup, killing General Ironsi and many of his officers. Yakubu "Jack" Gowon became the new leader of Nigeria.

Now with control of the government in hand, the Hausa-Fulani planned, and began executing, the initial phase of their revenge against the Ibos. Some observers called it a "pogrom"; others called it a massacre, and still others used the word "genocide." It mattered little what semantic choice you made; it all meant murders of innocent people on a large scale. News reports circulated stories of Christian Ibos being killed in the streets, in the market-places and even in their places of worship.

Despite assurances by the Nigerian leader, General Gowon, to protect the Ibos and stop the violence, by September, 1966, attacks on Ibos had escalated to a crescendo, with reports of deaths as high as 10,000 to 30,000. Not believing their government would protect them, more than one million Ibos began to flee towards the southeast, a region known as Biafra. Besieged by militia

and vigilantes on all sides, on May 30, 1967, regional
governor Lt. Colonel Ojukwu announced Biafra's intention
to secede from the rest of Nigeria to form an independent
republic.

Happiness' father would have been keenly aware of
these reports. He was well-read, highly educated, and
closely followed current events. No doubt, reports of such
violence towards Christians, whether they were Ibo or not,
must have gravely concerned him. As the events unfolded
up north, Mr. Emejuru and his wife, began to pray and
make preparations. They too might need to flee, although
they hoped it would not come to that.

The Biafran decision to secede from Nigeria was
a move made out of desperation, not military strength.
Militarily, the 3,000 poorly equipped Biafran volunteers
(though they would increase in size, they would never
exceed 30,000 soldiers), were no match for the 85,000
well-supplied, foreign-supported, Nigerian federal army.
The civil war, known to the world as the Biafran War, had
officially begun.

Families, such as the Emejuru's, had to make a decision. Even though they were not Ibos or Biafrans, they
were Christians and they did live in the southeast region
that was now Biafra. They would be deemed enemies of the
Nigerian federal army. Reports were rampant of civilians
being forcefully conscripted to fight, with refusals punished
by death on the spot. No one was safe.

As the conflict dragged on, the Emejuru children began
to notice the changes around them. Each day, Happiness
and her siblings saw another stream of refugees passing
along the road in front of their home. They were traveling to camps set up outside the area where the bulk of
the fighting was anticipated and brought with them more
news of the escalating violence. The Nigerian army was

advancing. Their village was indefensible. Time was running out.

Mr. Emejuru knew what he had to do and he couldn't wait any longer. The journey would not be easy. His seven children ranged in age from thirteen to one and Mama was pregnant with number eight. His aging mother, too, would need to walk the twenty or more miles a day that lay ahead of them. A proud accomplished man, he was about to become a common refugee: powerless and living on the charity of foreigners. He gathered the family to explain his decision. As he prepared to inform the family, Mr. Emejuru's heart was torn between the need to ensure the safety of his family, and the agony of seeing them uprooted from their home.

As Mr. Emejuru looked into the faces of each of his children, knowing the hardships they were about to experience, he held a quiet assurance that God would not forsake them. He was entrusting his children to God's sovereign protection, for he knew that events were now well beyond his control. Each child was precious to him; each child he had dedicated to the Lord, and each child he had given a name that reminded him of their God-given purpose, destiny or character trait.

There was his oldest son, 13 year old Ogubuike (his western name was "Paul"), whose name meant "endurance." As his name implied, he had a tenacity to see things through, but he also was very smart, inheriting the intelligence of his father. His second child was his daughter Mamma (her western name was Esther), whose name meant "testimony". Even at her young age of 11, he was proud of the testimony God was already forming in her life. Their third child was 9 year-old Kemjika (western name "Allswell"). His name meant "what I have is more" referring to the extra blessing of a father holding a second male child, thereby securing acceptance in the Nigerian

culture. His next child was seven-year old Chikwere
(western name "Christian"), whose name meant "if
God agrees." Mr. Emejuru smiled at Chikwere fidgeting
against the wall, clearly annoyed at having to sit still to
listen to his father's announcement. Sitting still was not
an activity designed for little boys like him. Then Mr.
Emejuru turned his focus to his fifth child, five-year old
Wegwu (Happiness), whose name reflected the joy he felt
that day in the hospital when she was born. Wegwu meant
"celebration", the kind of exuberant joy experienced when
opening your presents at Christmas. She was definitely
the apple of his eye. Sitting next to his Mom was three-
year old Okechukwu (western name Johnson). His name
meant, "God's portion" and he truly was. Finally, his
youngest child, absent-mindedly sitting in his mother's lap
was Ubojiekere (western name "Isaiah" after his uncle).
Mr. Emejuru always had a special fondness for his name,
for it meant, "Destiny", or more specifically, "what God
has given you, no one can take away." Finally, his focus
turned to his wife, Sybel. They had been through so much
together. They were a powerful team, united in the goal of
raising their children to glorify the God who made them.
How would she handle the trip? He could only pray and
ask the God who had never let him down, to protect her
and give her the strength she would need.

At that moment, Mr. Emejuru wished time would stop.
He wanted to savor this slice of his life. Here in front of
him, sat his wife, seven children, and an eighth on the way.
They were his family, but even more, they were one of the
many physical evidences of the goodness of God upon his
life. Individually they each were treasured by him; corpo-
rately, there was something powerful about the impact they
had upon his emotions. He would do anything to protect his
family. Now it seemed, it was time to put that conviction to
the test.

No one recalls exactly what was said, but the gist was that they were in imminent danger if they stayed, less danger if they left for a refugee camp. He may have mentioned their need to trust God through this ordeal, but if not, he clearly believed it. Trusting in God is easy to say, more difficult to believe. But God had never forsaken him before. Mr. Emejuru had confidence that God would not forsake them now.

As for Happiness, she didn't really understand it all. The only thing that mattered to her was that she trusted her father. If he said they needed to leave their home, that was enough for her. She knew he loved her and she knew her father would never do anything to hurt her. She was convinced that whatever decision he made was for her best interest. Hers was a child-like faith. The kind of faith our heavenly Father longs for us to have in Him. Although she didn't realize it at the time, Happiness was learning a valuable life lesson: the importance of trusting God, through the trust she had in her father. Years later they would all remember the lesson that sometimes the path of suffering is really a path of protection from untold horror.

The decision to leave having been made, they quickly packed what belongings they could carry, buried some dishes, boxes of clothes and some valuables, and left the rest. With a sense of reluctant necessity, the Emejuru's headed out the back door to gather with members of their extended family at the large, covered gazebo in the back of their house. It was centrally located within the family compound and was surrounded by the homes of their uncles, aunts and cousins. This gazebo had been the place where the family had frequently gathered over the years to share precious family moments. It held special memories of pleasant conversation, laughter and tears. On its benches had sat nearly every family member at one time or another. It was a sort of family landmark, high on the sentimentality scale. Now, in the midst of fleeing refugees and the Biafran War, it was a place of last departure. Happiness glanced back at her house with sadness and confusion. Would she ever see its comforting sight again?

Mr. Emejuru led his children, and all their relatives, away and toward their place amidst the steady stream of travel-worn refugees along the road. He carried the largest pack, of course, and little Johnson in his arms. His wife walked beside him with Isaiah tied to her back. Like another patriarch over three millennia earlier, he was steadfast in his faith as he led his family in exodus to an unknown place for temporary refuge. His children saw nothing but resolve on his face, whatever torments might have been besieging his soul. He knew he had to be strong for his family. Somehow, God would get them through this.

Approaching the bend in the road that would take them beyond sight of their house, Happiness, along with Paul, Esther, Allswell and Christian, all turned to look back one last time, at the only home they ever knew. No words were spoken between them. None were necessary. They all shared a common sense of sadness. To Happiness, it seemed as if they were breaking an unwritten rule of Heaven; the one that said children and their homes were not to be separated. Well, if that were the case, at least they had not broken the other unwritten rule of Heaven; that children and their family were not to be separated. She glanced into the eyes of her brothers and sister, comforted by the knowledge they were all still together. None of them knew when they would be back, but they prayed it would be soon.

The family rounded the bend, while their house disappeared from view. In that process, they gained a new title: that of "refugee." They had officially joined the ever growing stream of countless other uprooted souls. Happiness would later recall the situation with these words:

"Many people fled their homes by foot, a few by transportation with only what they were able to physically carry with them to sustain them to an unknown fate and destination. They left behind family valuables, some buried in the ground while some were locked away in a room hoping to retrieve them when they returned from what they thought was going to be a temporary and very short escape from the noise and rumors of war fast approaching the town."

The long trek began. Every so often a car or jeep would pass by, but the vast majority of their new traveling companions were on foot as they were. Some wore shoes; more did not. Happiness had no real hope of being carried much of the way; Johnson was only three and little Isaiah was almost too big for their mother. Still her little legs kept up and she never complained. To the children it was a surreal experience but their parents' presence and calm reassured them that they would be safe. When they camped for the first night, all seven sandwiched between their mother and their father, they slept with remarkable peace.

For the Emejurus and their fellow fleeing refugees, the dangers they faced were real. Military pilots would often fly their planes low along the refugee-packed roads, taking delight in strafing them with a barrage of bullets. There were many reports of Nigerian federal soldiers shooting at unarmed women and children, along with other reports of looting and rape of the fleeing refugees by federalist soldiers. Happiness' "auntie," a young and attractive woman, disguised herself to look pregnant, in hopes of reducing her risk of being raped.

Refugee men were subject to capture by the soldiers at gunpoint and given the unenviable choice of being shot on the spot or to fight in their army. Happiness witnessed several men being captured in this manner and led away while their wives and children were left behind screaming, knowing they would likely never see their husband or father again. As traumatic as that was for her, remarkably she was shielded from witnessing the one thing that would have devastated her to the core; seeing her own father captured and taken away.

She would learn years later from her Mom that that is exactly what happened. Her own father had been captured and forcibly taken by renegade Federal soldiers on two separate occasions as they were fleeing to the refugee camps. How the family was able to keep Happiness from finding out is a mystery that has yet to be solved. By nothing short of the grace of God, Happiness' uncle Isaiah held a very influential position in the government and was able to obtain her father's swift release both times.

It was about the fifth day, after an early start, Happiness was startled by the sound of a fast-approaching aircraft flying very low. In an instant she felt herself pulled behind a bush on the side of the road surrounded by the sounds of panicked screams and the explosion of gunfire. Happiness covered her ears and began to cry. She was too scared to open her eyes, but she could feel that it was Esther that had pulled her off the road and that she was still next to her. Then she felt a strong arm lift her up and found herself nestled protectively beside her father. In a moment the sounds of the plane began to die away and the gunfire ceased. The federal military pilots loved to strafe fleeing refugees on their way to more important wartime excursions and the Emejuru family had had their first taste of this cruelty.

As the Emejuru family fled down dirt roads to a destination unknown, they saw for themselves more and more of the reality of the conflict around them. Real bullets were being fired, real military aircraft flew low overhead, and real bombs exploded in the midst of soldiers and civilians alike. As they fled with the other refugees, they came across many uniformed soldiers guarding various military check-points, looking menacing with their rifles. Along the road-side, they also passed by what no five-year old girl should ever have to see: decaying and charred bodies of dead corpses. Everyday was a new test of faith for the family and a new reminder of God's protection in the face of over-whelming adversity.

Many more miles passed. Happiness' legs were so coated with dust that her skin was barely visible now. Her parents stayed cheerful, praising the children's efforts to keep up with the quickening pace. Yet there was a new worry on her mother's face: grandmother was growing weaker. She had started the journey walking fairly upright despite her elderly status. Then she had begun leaning on Ogu, and now it was necessary for both Ogu and Esther to support her, one on each side. She was growing thinner too, often claiming that she was not hungry and insisting that the children should eat her share of the provisions. More than anything, as they passed the growing numbers of mili-tary check-points with menacing soldiers and saw more and more dead bodies by the side of the road, grandmother's heart was breaking.

Finally, one afternoon after six hours of walking, Happiness saw the sight they had been waiting for. In a flat area several hundred yards off the road, countless tents were clustered together. To Happiness it seemed like a strange dream. On the outer edges of the camp she saw foreign vehicles parked and large fires heating kettles. Laundry hung on a line stretched between two trees. It was discolored and ragged; it looked nothing like the fresh sheets and table cloths of pure white Happiness was used to seeing on her own clothesline, stirring gently when a waft of air decided to disturb them. The closer they got the more the camp seemed eerily quiet. There were hundreds maybe thousands of people, but very little movement. A few children chased each other, but many more sat vacantly, leaning against tents or one another. Grown-ups too moved very little. Some foreign workers circulated about, also looking tired and grim. Everything looked dusty and crowded. Was this to be their new home?

It seemed to be. They left the road for the first time in two weeks and started filing toward the camp with everyone else. Her father gave their names to the foreigners and Happiness saw a white woman write them down and shake her head. What could be wrong?

"We will have to move again tomorrow," her father explained as he returned to them. *"The woman says there are already too many here. Do not worry though, my children. It is only a little further; less than one more day's walk."* He smiled encouragingly and the children smiled back. Yet Happiness saw her mother lean into speak to him privately.

"Grandmother cannot go any further," Happiness heard her whisper. *"Can we not see if they can keep her here? She must see a doctor."*

"She could never bear to be parted from us," he responded. *"She would sooner have stayed home."* Again that night the family slept crowded together, this time at the edge of the camp in the dust. All the tents were full.

The next morning they rose with the sun, accepted a small ration of food for the family from the aid workers, and set out for the next camp. As Mr. Emejuru had promised, they reached the new camp when the sun was at its apex. It was similar to the first, but had fewer people and more trees providing welcome shade.

"Grandmother, we are here!" little Happiness called joyfully to the old woman, leaning against her father for support.

"That is good, my child," she answered wearily. *"You will be safe here. And when you return home you must work hard in school. You are clever and you will make us all proud."*

"Yes, Grandmother," Happiness answered, confused. Why was she talking like this? She saw her parents exchange a worried glance.

"Rest, Mother," her father said as he assisted her onto a mat in the tent where they would now live. *"We will eat after you have rested."*

So began the refugee life of the Emejuru family. To the rest of the world, the Biafra War was initially seen as a minor blip on a news cycle with greater priorities: namely another foreign conflict called Vietnam. The British Broadcasting Corporation (BBC) reported their opinion that the conflict in Biafra would likely be wrapped up in ten days. Instead, it became a 30 month long war that some journalists and historians would later describe as the cruelest in modern Africa. Before it was over, attention by the world's news media would become significant. Biafra would become a major news story and the whole world would be exposed to some of the most haunting images of human suffering imaginable.

The next morning, the war claimed its first casualty from the Emejuru clan. While the rest of the world saw thirty second clips of razed villages and bloody corpses on the evening news, Happiness and her family buried Grandmother at the edge of the camp. Her days on the run were finally over; her exhaustion relieved at last by rest and peace.

Mama and the children wept. From his well worn Bible, Papa read, *"The Lord giveth and the Lord taketh away. Blessed be the name of the Lord."*

5

LIFE AS A REFUGEE

ஓஒ

B iafran troops surprised everyone by advancing their positions despite having few soldiers and scarce ammunition. Undaunted, Federal troops began to increase attacks in the air, where the Biafrans had no answer. Days became months, and the world began to realize that the conflict would not end nearly as soon as everyone had hoped. News trickled into camp over the radio and from newly arriving refugees. The Emejurus now realized they needed to prepare for an extended stay.

Soon Happiness grew used to the sounds of her new home: the roar of military planes overhead, explosions in the distance that shook the ground, and the omnipresent staccato rhythm of gunfire. The camp itself was rarely attacked, so the sounds became a background noise, as the chirping of birds had been back home. The smells too, became familiar. Thin porridge cooking in a pot over a fire, the industrial quality soap the aid workers used to try to keep everything clean, and the smell of hundreds of people, breathing, sweating, urinating, trying to stay alive.

The camp was situated in a small, mostly abandoned, town. The new community, comprised mostly of Ibo, along with some Ikwerre like the Emejurus, began to piece together a routine. Empty buildings became schools and churches and Mr. Emejuru set to work teaching in the school, much like he had done back home. Happiness' older siblings began to wake each morning and gather their school things just as they had always done. Happiness helped her mother care for little Johnson and Isaiah and tidy up their small tent. And in the miraculous way that children do, she began to smile and laugh and play in spite of her surroundings. They may have been uprooted from their home, but Mr. Emejuru and his wife were grateful they were still together as a family.

However, the grave impact of war soon became apparent as Happiness began noticing that their three daily meals shrank to two, and the meals themselves became smaller. More and more of her mornings were spent waiting in long lines for food rations with other families. She began to feel hungry, even after she ate, but somehow knew that she shouldn't say anything.

"The federal soldiers have blockaded the entire region," her father explained to Mama one night. *"They are trying to starve us all so the Biafrans will give up."*

"What about the relief agencies and churches?" Mama responded anxiously.

"They will try to fly over the lines and bring supplies, but it will not be easy. Maybe some powdered milk, eggs, rice, cornmeal and okporoko [dried fish]."

"We will be content with what God provides," Mama resolved.

The rest of the world soon learned that Mr. Emejuru's suspicions were correct. The federal government was deliberately starving the Biafrans, including the refugees. Colonel Adekunle, leader of the Third Marine Commando Division of the Nigerian Federal Army, known also as "The Black Scorpion" bragged to foreign media, *"I want to see no Red Cross, no CARITAS, no World Council of Churches, no Pope, no missionary and no U.N. delegation. I want to prevent even one Igbo having even one thing to eat before their capitulation. We shoot at everything that moves. Then we shoot at everything, even things that don't move."* (Economist Magazine, September 7, 1968.)

He came very close to having his way. In August, 1968, Western journalists reported widely varying estimates of between 1,500 to 40,000 Biafrans and refugees who died of starvation every week. One British journalist recalled starting his news day with his cameraman helping to bury 8-9 refugee children. Another journalist showed video images of an emaciated Biafran boy around the age of 7 or 8, looking expressionless into the camera, and then walking away. His life was over and he knew it. The narrative, as the tape rolled, stated that the boy had died of starvation within an hour of his being filmed. Such scenes shocked the world and introduced the western world to the diabolical process of starvation, to which the children seemed to be most susceptible.

Happiness knew nothing of The Black Scorpion's plans, but she saw them come to fruition every day. The more meager the rations became, the more often she found herself in the interminable food lines with her mother, waiting to see what else was available. Outside the tents, children who had been playing a few weeks ago began to lay there, expressionless. Those in the worst shape began to develop distended bellies and bloated feet and legs, a phase of starvation known as "kwashiorkor." More than once Happiness saw a distressed mother trying to pour cornmeal into the mouth of such a child, only to have it spill out again and down the child's chin.

The starvation process of "kwashiorkor" was without mercy. Towards the end, the child would become listless, slowed by weakness, and then he or she would lie down to die. At that stage, even if they could have obtained food, their bodies would not be able to digest it. Their fate was sealed. Pictures of flies swarming around the faces of little children too weak to bat them away were common.

"Afo mmili ukwa!" some healthier children would call out, taunting the sick. Happiness flinched at the insult, which meant "big-bellied." Little did the tormentors know that the children's enlarged bellies were filled with gas, not food. A few days later those same "big bellied" children would no longer be there, leaving weeping mothers behind. As the blockade continued, the air was filled with the sounds of children crying and whining and the stench of corpses decomposing.

Through it all, God protected Happiness and her family. None of them came down with the dreaded kwashiorkor disease. In fact, comparatively speaking, they all stayed in good health. That fact would later prove crucial in keeping their family together. But for now, they were grateful for the health God gave them and the food they received. Today, none of the Emejuru children recalls any particular prayers by their father, but it is not unlikely that Mr. Emejuru found new significance to The Lord's Prayer and the plea to *"give us this day, our daily bread."* That plea would be answered each day by a God they came to trust as their provider.

Their provider would also bring them a new "treasure." Incredibly, within the midst of such overwhelming death, God brought forth new life to the Emejurus. Happiness' Mom, who had been four months pregnant when they fled their home, now gave birth to their eighth child. Mr. Emejuru named this son, "Asondu", which appropriately meant, "running for life." Even in the crowded stench of the camp, Happiness delighted in her new brother Asondu. Tiny little hands and feet always captivate their holders and she cooed over her new sibling daily.

As her older siblings went to school, Happiness noticed that her mother began to examine her for signs of kwashiorkor more often and more anxiously. She sat patiently as Mama looked at her eyes and felt her belly, wondering why she seemed so concerned.

Perhaps the emotions of this latest mouth to feed in the midst of lack impacted Mrs. Emejuru more than any of them realized. Maybe it was the typical "postpartum blues" so many women experience, although this was hardly a "typical" situation. Whatever the impetus, Happiness' mother began to become anxious that there was not enough food to feed their whole family. That meant all of them were at greater risk of contracting kwashiorkor.

Unknown to Happiness, her mother began to seriously consider the option of giving over her youngest daughter to one of the relief agencies who would take Happiness to a place where there was more food and greater safety. Mrs. Emejuru determined in her heart that the next time the Red Cross came to take away the children that were the most sick and malnourished, as they periodically did, she was going to see if they would take Happiness with them.

Not long thereafter, their daily routine of refugee camp life was interrupted by just such a visit from Red Cross volunteers. The Red Cross came to medically examine the children in the camp to determine who were the most malnourished and in need of greater medical attention. Once identified as the most needful, Red Cross volunteers would remove those children from the camp and re-locate them out of the war zone to places that offered greater safety and better care. Here was the opportunity Happiness' mother saw for removing her young daughter from the dangers of hunger.

Happiness does not recall whether her mom talked to her about what she was planning to do beforehand. It's not likely she did because Happiness remembers being taken aback by the incident. Mrs. Emejuru took Happiness by the hand and they walked together toward one of the Red Cross volunteers at one of the medical tents. Around them was a crowd filled with other mothers and their children. The children were crying from their hunger or diseased condition. Medical personnel were clearly overwhelmed, having difficulty keeping up with the volume of patients foisted upon them. It took awhile, but eventually Happiness and her mom made it to one of the volunteers. Mrs. Emejuru asked the young woman from the Red Cross if they would be able to take her daughter with them.

For a mother to reach such a point of desperation, the danger of starvation and hunger had to have been extreme. She loved her daughter and hated the thought of sending her away, but in her mind, it seemed like the only hope for Happiness to survive. Nonetheless, it took all the courage she could muster to hand her daughter over to the Red Cross medical staff to see if her daughter would be accepted for removal from the camp.

If it was hard for the mother, it was even harder for Happiness. She was too young to understand why her mother was doing this. Being torn away from her home had been hard enough. But the thought of leaving her father, mother, brothers and sister, was even worse. Happiness was horrified at the thought and devastated by what her mother was proposing. Her family was all she had left. Now she was about to lose even that. How could her mother send her away with strangers? What if she was never able to re-unite with them? She might never see them again.

Happiness stood frozen with fear as her mom approached one of the aid workers and began whispering something to her. She strained her ears to hear what her mother was saying.

"She is weak. She is only a little girl," Mama explained to the relief worker.

"We will have to examine her," the lady explained.
Happiness looked about desperately for her father, who was
teaching at the school, while her mother handed her over
to the aid worker. Tears began rolling down her cheeks as
the trembling little girl was led over to one of the doctors.
He pressed a stethoscope to her chest and listened, felt her
belly, and looked in her eyes. She tried to cry quietly, but
she felt miserable. In fact, she had never felt more sad and
scared than she did at that moment. Her world was crashing
in on her as never before. She would much rather be hiding
in the bushes in danger with her family than to be sent off
to safety with strangers. When the cursory exam was done,
she ran back to her mother as fast as she could and clung in
fear to the cloth wrap skirt around her mother's legs.

Soon an aid worker approached them holding a clipboard. She smiled apologetically and said, *"Mrs. Emejuru,
we have examined your daughter and find that she is in
fact relatively healthy. While she is quite thin, she is not
malnourished. We are only able to take the really sick children. I am sorry."* The woman said goodbye quickly and
rushed back to the medical tent overflowing with other
mothers and children. Mrs. Emejuru said nothing. She held
Happiness' hand tightly as the little girl wept with relief.
Her mom had done what she could; now she would need to
trust in God to get them through. In fact, it may have been at
this point that her mother realized that God had been doing
that all along. Surely He would continue to do so now.

Meanwhile, Happiness was visibly shaken by this entire
incident. Certainly she felt waves of relief flooding over
her. Yet, at the same time, she was struck by the horrific
realization of how close she had come to being taken away
from her family. Given the chaos of war, she might never
have seen them again. She shuddered to think about it.

In retrospect, a fair question to ask is why. Why, out of
all of the children she had at this time, did Mrs. Emejuru

choose Happiness to be the child sent away? Happiness was no longer the youngest. By now, Happiness had three younger brothers. Why not seek to send them away for their protection? If it was food consumption her mom was most concerned about, then why not offer up one of her older brothers? Why was Happiness, the fifth of eight children, the one offered up? We may never know the answer to that question, but its one that can haunt a person if you are the one being offered to go. Perhaps, the incident was orchestrated by the devil's minions as another way of separating Happiness from her father's love, the one foundation and source of protection the devil could not penetrate. If so, it would not be the last time the devil tried to separate this girl from her father, and in so doing, separate her from her heavenly Father. Regardless of the reason, one thing was clear: God had truly spared Happiness of a fate she was not sure she could have handled.

Months wore on and the Emejuru family entered their second year of life at the refugee camp. Ogu, Esther, Allswell and Christian diligently continued their studies. Johnson, Isaiah and Asondu managed to grow as well, despite dwindling food rations. Happiness began to learn at home, looking over Esther's shoulder as she studied until her sister relented and taught her the alphabet. She loved to read, although there were hardly any books to come by. To placate her, Ogu and Esther would trace words in the dirt for her.

News continued to come in over the camp radio and then travel quickly by mouth through the camp. Rarely was it good. The refugees had no love for the federal army, but mostly they wanted everything to be over.

"The Biafrans are isolated in the southeast," Mr. Emejuru remarked to her mom one night. *"They cannot hold out much longer."* Mama said nothing, but nodded. Everyone hoped silently that the end might be near. They

sympathized with the Biafran forces, knowing that they believed their attempted succession to be the only alternative to genocidal slaughter. Yet they had known from the start the effort would prove hopeless. The radio confirmed their suspicions.

"They are issuing one round per man," her father shook his head one night, after returning from the center of the camp where he often picked up news.

"What?" her mom asked in disbelief.

"One bullet each when they are taking up defensive positions," her father explained. It was almost funny. *"Two bullets per gun when they are on the attack."*

"God have mercy," her mother said, almost laughing. *"Will they fight with stones and clubs when their bullet is used up?"*

Her father smiled. *"No my wife, but they will hold out as long as they can. They are certain they will all be killed if they surrender. Who knows? They may be right."*

Mercifully, on January 13, 1970, roughly two and a half years after its inception, the war officially ended. The effects of the war had been devastating. While estimates varied widely, the estimated number of dead from hostilities was approximately 400,000; from disease and starvation, about 1.5 million.

Of all the "participants" in the Biafran War, none were more relieved the fighting had ended than the refugees. When Happiness heard the news, and she realized she and her family would be able to return to their home, she was filled with a multitude of emotions. Certainly joy and relief that they could finally leave a place of hunger, disease and death, but she also was filled with a renewed hope that all could return to normal. There was a lot to be said for normal! After what they had been through for the last two and a half years, she desperately wanted to experience that feeling again. Now seven years old, Happiness had almost forgotten what such life was like.

Going home was much easier than their long hikes by foot to the refugee camps of an unknown location. This time the family was able to travel by car, at least over the last half of the journey, headed for a sure destination! The excitement amongst each member of the Emejuru family could not be contained, nor did they try. Pent-up emotions were flowing out of each of them; their exuberance was almost limitless. The thought of going home brought unspeakable joy to Happiness and her family. Nothing else mattered now. Not the hunger, not the sight of death and disease; only home and family.

The Emejurus trekked the last few miles to their home. The children sang songs of rejoicing while their parents were secretly wary about what they would find upon their return. Happiness' joy was complete when she caught the first glimpse of her house, seeing it just as she had remembered it. At last it seemed, she had finally awakened from a bad dream.

"Some high-ranking military officer was living here," she heard her father remark as the family approached the door together.

"Another man was living in our house?" Ogu asked. *"Does the army just barge in and live wherever they please?"*

"I suppose we can thank God he did. Otherwise the place might have been flattened by shells and mortar," Mr. Emejuru observed wisely. It was true. Their home was relatively untouched. A glance into the yard revealed that all the family dishes, clothes, and other valuables they had buried had been dug up and stolen. While certainly disappointing, they all realized it was a small price to pay to be safely back in their home.

While many families mourned the loss of children to famine and pestilence, the Emejurus found themselves blessed beyond measure. Soon maids were scrubbing clean the walls and windows, and a new housekeeper was preparing delicious meals and snacks. Later that year, Mama gave birth to their ninth child, her seventh son, Obuokam, which means, *"it's not my saying or my doing,"* a reference to the idea that man had nothing to do with this blessing. It was God's doing and His alone. Indeed, only God could have brought forth the blessing of joyous life from the midst of so much recent death and suffering.

Shortly after settling back into their home, Mr. Emejuru found himself watching his little girl playing outside the window with her brothers and sister. He watched her as she played in the yard, no longer a refugee but a child once more. She giggled uncontrollably as Christian kicked the soccer ball toward the homemade goal, missing it badly in his haste. His heart sighed with relief to see her suffering over and her innocence restored.

After all they had been through; Happiness had not lost her sweet innocence of childhood. That was more a testimony of God's miraculous protection than anything he had done, although he had done all he could. *Thank you God,* he prayed silently as he thought back to the vow he made to God several years ago when he first held his little girl. He reflected on his commitment to protect her and give her a foundation of God's love that would allow her to be unshakable in the storms of life.

Happiness had already seen and experienced more by the age of seven than many people experience their entire lifetimes. She had seen death up close, watched people starving and felt the pain of serious hunger herself. She had been uprooted from her home, hid in bushes while planes strafed bullets upon the road she had just walked, watched her grandmother die needlessly, and nearly been given away to strangers by her own mother. Through it all, she was still okay, for she knew she had the love of her family and, more specifically, the care and protection of her father. He was still there for her; he still adored her; and he still did his best to keep the silent vow he had made to God years earlier.

6

"BOYS ARE BAD NEWS"

❧

"*A*m *I really to go with the big children?*" Happiness asked with delight.

"Yes, my Happy," her mom answered with a smile. *"Your father might have sent you last year had we not been in the camp. But I am sure you will find that you are ahead of the other children your age. Your brothers will be there to watch over you, and two of the Dike* (pronounced "Dee-kay") *girls will be there to keep you company.*" Her mom was referring to the daughters of one of the most prominent families in the village. They were close friends of the Emejurus due to the strong Christian faith they shared.

After the war, the Emejuru family worked hard to return to life as it was before the conflict. That meant, among other things, returning their children to school. Having been raised by a British family when his own father passed away, Mr. Emejuru had been exposed to western culture and values. He had come to appreciate the importance of a good education as one of the keys to success. It was only natural that this would now be his prime focus of restoring order to his family.

As a result of having a father who valued education and demanded excellence, Happiness was always a top-notch student. Of course, she was highly motivated, driven by the desire to not disappoint her father. Even though his expectations were high, she knew they were in her best interest. However, there was added pressure on Happiness to succeed in elementary school since her father was more than just a concerned parent; he was the school principal. As if that were not enough, her father was also instrumental in establishing the school. His fingerprints of excellence were all over it. It was not surprising then, that many people in their village considered it one of the finest elementary schools in the country.

Principal Emejuru made sure that grades were emphasized. At the close of each of the three semesters throughout the year, students assembled in the auditorium for a school-wide awards ceremony. Parents were always invited. At the conclusion of the announcements and welcoming comments, the teacher of each class in each grade would stand up and announce the names of his or her students in order of achievement from number one in the class to last.

Happiness' father had made it abundantly clear to each of his children that being number two was not good enough. He knew they were capable of being ranked first in their class and anything less was his indicator they were not giving their best effort. Some might say he was too demanding. On the other hand, his attitude could be said to reflect a refreshing spirit of excellence rarely demanded elsewhere. Regardless, each of his children understood the standards their father expected of them, and each did his or her best to meet that standard.

For Happiness, she loved school and the opportunity to learn about new things. Her favorite class was Religious Studies where they taught a new Bible story every day. She looked forward with great anticipation to hear the stories

she was so familiar with from church; those of David
and Goliath, Noah and the Ark, and all the great Bible
heroes with the challenges they faced. She excelled in her
Religious Studies class with relative ease.

Her other classes required greater effort. While easily
one of the better students, she was not always the best.
That distinction frequently belonged to Amadioha, a
boy that Happiness pegged as the smartest student in her
class, and one who competed against her in the semester
rankings throughout her elementary school years. Every
semester either Amadioha or Happiness would be the first
name announced in the teacher rankings, and the other
student's name would inevitably be second. Sometimes
they even tied for the top ranking. It was quite a rivalry,
yet amazingly, both students held no jealousy toward
the other. There was a genuine feeling of mutual respect
between them. Happiness could have taken great pride in
knowing she was the only student to ever beat Amadioha
academically, but she didn't. She knew that when she
failed to beat him, she had to deal with the feeling she had
disappointed her father.

She still recalls the first time her name was announced
second. *"Mr. Uchechukwu's class,"* called the school
secretary that announced the rankings. Mr. Uchechukwu
stood up in front of the assembled students in the auditorium and began to read: *"First, Amadioha Okala. Second,
Happiness Emejuru. Third...."* Happiness felt sick to her
stomach. Second place! She tried anxiously to catch a
glimpse of her father, who as principal was sitting in the
front row of the assembly. Sitting several rows back, she
strained to read his facial expression. How upset would he
be? What would he say?

His face was completely expressionless.

It was times like this she wished she could be a mind
reader. Then again, maybe it was best she was not. Was he

61

really disappointed in her, or was he just trying not to show favoritism towards his daughter in front of the school? She couldn't tell. Not knowing was the worse part. She didn't know whether to be relieved or anxious. Reflexively, her mind chose anxiety.

When the presentations were over and the assembly concluded, Mr. Emejuru went to his office to complete some work, so Happiness walked home with Christian and Johnson. When she got home her mother greeted her warmly. Immediately her mom suspected what was wrong, but she didn't say a word. She kissed all her children as the maid gave them their snacks. Happiness ate in silence while Johnson kicked Christian under the table, and Isaiah, still not school-aged, ran in to join the fun.

"Papa is at the gate," Mama said softly as she looked out the window. Happiness jumped up, dropped the cookie she was eating and ran to the back of the house. Looking around anxiously, she hid herself beneath an old blanket that was used mostly for picnics. Second place! She felt overwhelmed with shame. She knew her father's academic standards and she had failed to meet them. Surely he would be upset. She would just hide here forever, safe in the dark, away from her father's disappointment.

Minutes passed and she heard her parents talking in the other end of the house. She thought she might have even heard them laugh, but she was unsure. The sounds of her siblings playing happily in the yard traveled through the open windows as Happiness considered what to do. The darkness under the blanket was beginning to feel lonely and stifling. Her stomach growled and she thought of the cookies she had left unfinished. Maybe hiding forever wasn't such a good idea after all. Finally, summoning all her courage, she threw aside the blanket and went to greet her father.

She peeked around the door to the kitchen where her parents were talking. Her father caught a glimpse of her out of the corner of his eye, and to her shock, he smiled broadly. With warm affection, he embraced her. *"Very good job Happiness,"* were the only words she remembered her father saying. He didn't yell or show any sort of disappointment; only acceptance. She was so grateful. It made her silently promise to try harder next time. Nonetheless, even though he did not say so, Happiness felt that deep inside, she had disappointed Papa. The thought of doing so hurt her deeply. It would be a thought that propelled her to always do her best. Later, as she grew older, it would be the same thought that propelled her to seek to please her Heavenly Father. Even though she knew He loved and accepted her, she didn't want to let Him down, anymore than she did her earthly father.

Growing up in Nigeria was more than just school and studies, although those were highly regarded in the Emejuru household. Likewise important however, was family time, and the family gathering place was the large gazebo in the middle of their family compound. The Emejuru's followed the Jewish week in which the Sabbath began at sundown on Friday night and continued until sundown on Saturday. There would be no cooking or lighting the fire in the fire pit that evening or following day. Instead they would eat pre-prepared meals for the Sabbath or pick the ripe bananas, mangoes and oranges from the fruit trees in their yard. The extended family would gather at the gazebo and the adults would tell old folklore stories; each one having a happy ending or containing a good strong moral. Often the stories made Happiness laugh; always they made her content to listen. Sundays would bring more family time at the gazebo. Adults would sit and relax, and when not listening to the story telling, the kids would be playing.

Holidays were spent in similar fashion, only with lots of cooking over the fire pit. In the fall, they would celebrate harvest festival, a holiday similar to Thanksgiving in the United States. The Emejuru's, and their extended family in the compound, would gather at the fire pit near the gazebo and roast corn on the cob. If they had dried out the cob before-hand, then the corn would pop into puffs of popcorn they ate right off the cob.

A popular fruit they liked to eat with their corn was called a "pear" or "ube'", but it wasn't at all like pears in the States. While it was growing on the tree, it was a green seed, but it would turn blue when it became ripe. They also ate what they called "yams" or "ji" but those too were different than their namesake in America. On the outside, they were tan in color, white on the inside, and they grew in the ground much like a potato. They were oblong in shape, often growing as large as a medium-sized water melon. As you might suspect from all these descriptions of food, eating was an important part of their celebrations, but so too was visiting with family and friends. The weekends were known to their friends and neighbors as a time to invite yourself over in a casual, relaxed atmosphere of fellowship and camaraderie. People would drop by and talk for hours, in no rush to leave.

During the week, after school, the children did their homework. The television was not a big focal point, nor was it permitted until all schoolwork was done and even then, only with permission from Mr. Emejuru. He was very particular about what they watched. When their homework was completed, the children often played board games, including Scrabble, or they would play hide and seek in the dark outside in the compound. They also enjoyed going out to the gazebo and talking with their cousins. Even today, that gazebo brings back fond memories to Happiness. It was, in her words, *"a loving place and a sharing place"*

64

where there was no arguing; only joy, laughter, and relaxation.

Happiness recalls being close with all her brothers and her sister. Rarely was there any bickering, fussing or fighting between them. However, her older brother Chickwere or "Christian," would sometimes take advantage of the special relationship Happiness had with her Father, by using Happiness as a protective buffer. He would often ask Happiness to get him an extra portion of a snack or larger cash allowance given out to all of them, or conversely, would have Happiness break any bad news to their father if Chickwere received a bad grade or had done something wrong. His strategy was brilliant, since it almost always worked.

Years well spent seem to fly by, especially to Mr. and Mrs. Emejuru as they watched their little children grow into young men and women. The oldest four were away at boarding school most of the time now, and Ogu had graduated and gone away to a university in the United States to study to become a doctor. Esther had grown into a young woman studying to be a teacher in Rivers State. Allswell was a quiet and mild-mannered young man, and Christian, known to use his creativity to fix just about anything including nursing sick chicks back to health, continued in his more adventurous ways, while the little ones enjoyed elementary school.

Happiness studied hard, preparing to apply to secondary school. She was beginning sixth grade, after which she would leave home and go to boarding school or "college" like her older siblings. The Dike children too had distinguished themselves by gaining entrance to fine schools. Sonny, the oldest, was actually studying medicine and rooming with Ogu in the States. The two families respected each other greatly and the children understood their parents expected the best from them. As would be the case time after time, Mr. Emejuru had nothing to worry about, for his youngest daughter would not disappoint him.

There were no separate junior high or senior high schools in Nigeria as it is in America, so boarding school was the only way to become educated past the sixth grade. Entrance exams were extremely tough and Happiness wanted to gain admittance to the highest ranked school possible. She knew if she did so it would be completely based on her grades and exam scores, not her father's money or influence, like so many of her richer friends.

Even though Mr. Emejuru had a comfortable income from other sources, such as rental income, contracts with his poultry farm business, and the sale of raw materials derived from his rubber plantation, he never prided himself on how wealthy he was. He lived a very humble and simple life, frequently denying himself for the sake of his children. His focus was primarily on his children's education, which he insisted they earn themselves.

"I know some of your friends' families are willing to buy their way into the best schools," Mr. Emejuru remarked one day.

"Yes, Papa," Happiness answered quietly. She had heard this speech before when it had been given to each of her four older siblings.

"I will never give a dime to influence anybody for anything, just as I will never receive a bribe from anyone for any favor. Do you understand that my Happy?"

"I understand, Papa," she responded quietly. She knew she had a lot of work to do, and her gaze returned to her geography text book.

"There is another thing, my Happy," her father added with a strange tone in his voice.

"What is it, Papa," she asked, looking up again from her book.

"My Happy, you are getting to the age now where boys are going to become interested in you. Do you understand what I am talking about?"

"Yes, I think so."

"Esther is so much older than you, and you have mostly brothers, so probably you think you know all about boys," her father said, almost to himself.

"Oh, is there so much to know, Papa?" she laughed.

"Well, it is not that there is much to know but what there is to know is very important," he answered solemnly.

"What is it I must know then, Papa?" Happiness responded with equal solemnity. To this day, his words to her at this point still echo clearly in her mind: *"My Happy, boys are bad news. They will promise you anything you want and tell you anything they think you want to hear. But you must promise me that you will ignore them."*

"I will, Papa," she promised. Inside she wanted to laugh. Why was Papa being so serious? Did he really think she was so foolish as to believe such a silly promise?

"If they try to give you a gift, refuse it and remind them your father can afford to give you that and more," Papa continued. *"If they write you any notes or poems, I want to see them; do you understand?"*

Happiness nodded. She had already seen some of the boys trying to give gifts and notes to older girls and she had noticed how silly some of the girls seemed to behave in response. Was Papa afraid that she would become like one of those silly girls?

Not long after, Mr. Emejuru's command was put to the test. Happiness received her first love note in school. After she read it, true to her promise, she gave it to her father. The boy was very nice, and from a good family, and so she was certain her father would not be too upset.

To Happiness' dismay, her dad read the note and was furious. He crumpled up the paper in his hands, and

marched directly over to the boy's house. Happiness
followed him, mortified at the thought of what he might
do. Oh, why had she shown him the letter? Surely no harm
would have come if she had simply ignored it! Mr. Emejuru
arrived at the boy's house as Happiness hid herself behind a
small clump of bushes. She could see her father on the porch
of the house and could hear him asking the boy's family to
speak with him. The family responded immediately, for Mr.
Emejuru was a well-respected man. The family all gathered
together outside the front door; father, mother, siblings and
even an elderly aunt that lived with them.

*"What is this note that your son has given my daughter,
asking her to be his only love?"* he demanded. Happiness
felt paralyzed with embarrassment.

"Mr. Emejuru," the boy's father began, *"I can assure
you that my son meant no harm."*

*"This is a blatant violation of the rules I have laid
out for my daughter and a gross disrespect to me as her
father!"* Papa was fuming, but under control.

*"I offer my sincerest apologies on my son's behalf.
He will be severely punished,"* the father responded
deferentially.

*"Very good. He is also to have absolutely no further
communication with my daughter whatsoever. Is that
clear?"* Papa said calming down.

*"Yes sir. I assure you Mr. Emejuru, that it will be so.
Again, I offer my apologies. Ade,"* he added, turning to his
son, *"do you promise to do as this gentleman has said?"*

"Yes, sir," the boy answered, looking at the ground. *He
meant no harm*, thought Happiness. He was only imitating
what all his friends were doing. Surely no one else's father
had reacted so angrily to such a demonstration of affection.

Within hours, news of the confrontation had reached
the outermost edges of the community. So this was the
"Bulldog's" latest decree? Poor Ade's story became

legendary, and he was teased relentlessly in school. Happiness, an unassuming but beautiful child, found that her name was now on everyone's lips: the girl who was too good for any boy in the village. As her father would have hoped, most boys kept their distance for fear of incurring his wrath. However, as many an innocent girl learns, forbidden fruit seems so much sweeter, and the more daring boys began to find her irresistible. Some waited along the path where she walked home when they knew her father was working late at school, hoping to catch her alone. Happiness chose wisely to ignore them and focus on school work and her future.

7

OFF TO COLLEGE

In Nigeria, the process for getting into secondary school or "college" was extremely formal and competitive. Every school in the country had an objective, well-publicized ranking that was known by all. Placement in the schools was primarily by merit based on grades from elementary school and the results of an entrance exam, though it was not uncommon for some families to use bribes to get better placements for their children. Raised under her father's strict standards of excellence, Happiness didn't need to rely on bribes to get into a fine secondary school. Her grades were superb and her entrance exam score was quite high.

It came as no surprise that, when the official notifications were mailed out, Happiness had been accepted by each of the top three schools in Rivers State, all of which were highly ranked nationally. *"Shall I go to ACMGS Elelenwo, Papa?"* she asked as she held her acceptance letters, savoring the reward for all her hard work. Archdeacon Crowder Memorial Girls School was located in Port Harcourt, Rivers State, Nigeria. It was about 35 miles away from home and had the best academic reputation of the three schools to which she had applied. It was also an all-girls school, where opportunities for the girls to mingle with boys were extremely limited.

"That would be a wise choice, my daughter," her father smiled, relieved to know his daughter was not seeking the best sports school as many students did. *"Books are more important than sports. No one ever went to university because their college had the best track team!"* Happiness laughed. Her father was right, of course.

As the day for her big departure neared, Happiness packed her clothes and other belongings with mixed emotions. There was certainly an excitement about going off to college. She had watched four of her siblings do so with great success. Yet her heart trembled at the thought of the great unknown that lay before her. What would her new schoolmates be like? She had played with the same girls in Elele for what felt like an eternity. This would also be her first time away from her family. All these thoughts swirled around in her head as she rode in the car to her new school.

Happiness' heart leaped when she saw her new school for the first time. The ACMGS Elelenwo campus consisted of five academic buildings and nine single-story dorm buildings. Each dorm held about thirty girls who slept on bunk beds which were lined in rows in a single large hall. Seniors had the luxury of their own twin beds. The school was located on the outskirts of Port Harcourt, one of the major cities in Nigeria, situated on the Bonny River in the Niger Delta. Happiness immediately noticed how much quieter and peaceful it seemed from the city itself, and how fresh the air was, throughout the immaculately kept grounds. It was like a little oasis from city life, surrounded by beautiful trees, a fence, and an ornamental wrought iron gate entrance guarded at all times.

Her mom and dad located her dorm room and helped her settle in. They folded her clothes carefully in one cabinet and another they filled with the provisions her mom had brought: cornflakes, cookies, oranges, bananas, and various kinds of personal supplies. They would be welcome reminders of the comforts of home in the weeks to come. Happiness heard her father clear his throat several times as they prepared to leave their littlest girl on her own. She wanted to cry, but knew she must not.

"Do not worry, my Happy," Mama said gently. *"You are a big girl now."*

"Yes, Mama," Happiness replied, bravely holding back the tears.

"And Papa and I will return in a month when they have visiting days," Mama said brightly. *"Then we will bring you new provisions. Do you want fresh mangos next time? I will bring a great sack of them!"*

"Thank you, Mama," she nodded, nestling her head against her mother's chest one last time as they embraced.

"Goodbye, my Happy," Papa said, gruffly. *"I know you will make us proud."*

Happiness found that her father's strict upbringing had prepared her well for college life. Each day's activities were tightly scheduled. Mornings began with the dreaded ringing of bells to wake up the girls to start their day. They were given 45 minutes to shower, iron their clothes and dress before arrival for breakfast in the dining room. Then the students would grab their books and head off to one of several academic buildings for classes that would last from 9:00 a.m. until 12:00 noon. Lunch in the dining room followed, after which students took a two hour "siesta" before study hall from 3:00 to 6:00 p.m. It took all of study hall and more to complete assigned home work, review prior lessons, and obtain extra teacher assistance when necessary.

Saturdays were inspection days. Senior student inspectors, along with a professor or matron, would check beds to ensure that sheets and bedspreads were without wrinkles. Student cabinets had to be tidy and clean, as must the windows and floors.

Classes too were run strictly. Students could not leave the classroom without specific permission from the designated senior posted to monitor the class. Even if a student was sick, she was not allowed to remain in the dorm room, or return to her parents, without obtaining a doctor's permission slip. If a student was caught in the halls or outside the building without permission, she would have to report to the Senior Prefect, a senior in charge of all underclassmen and the one responsible to report student misbehavior to the school administrators.

Happiness had no trouble with such rules, of course, having become accustomed to obeying her father and never daring to misbehave in a school he himself ran. She shuddered, however, when she saw other girls test the boundaries. Chisaro, an immature girl from a village even farther away than Happiness', often got in trouble for giggling in class or walking the halls without permission. She would be forced to sit on her knees with her arms over her head, until the senior monitor said she could get up. *Why would she be so foolish?* Happiness wondered. Chisaro was almost always allowed to kneel on the grass, because the seniors knew she wasn't a bad girl, just childish. Girls who demonstrated more rebellious attitudes would often be forced to kneel on the hard pavement, and for much longer periods of time, or scrub the dorm room floors on their knees with a scrub brush. An older girl, whom she did not know well, was punished by having to mow the grass around the campus with a machete.

Each first year student was assigned a senior girl as a mentor. While the first year student was required to do the senior mentor's chores, the senior was to provide leadership, guidance and counsel in return. Happiness

73

was assigned a senior girl named Siobu Nwoka, whom she knew from her village back home. She would wash Siobu's plates after every meal, fetch her water in a bucket each morning, clean Siobu's room, and do all her other chores. Happiness did not mind the tasks, as she was used to helping her mother when the maid had a day off and she appreciated being close to an older girl who reminded her of home.

It was also beneficial to have someone of whom to ask advice. In particular when the dreaded love letter issue resurfaced in Happiness' life, she decided to speak with Siobu. Her parents were due again for a visit in a couple of weeks, and the thought of reigniting her father's wrath cast a terrible shadow over her joyful anticipation of their biannual visit.

"What is it, Happy?" smiled Siobu, as she invited the younger girl to sit next to her on the edge of her bed.

"Oh, it is a silly thing," she answered, trying to sound unconcerned. *"It is only that a boy from back home has written me a letter, in which he says he loves me. I know he means no harm, and yet I know that it is wrong for him to say such things to me. I am too young yet for a suitor and he has not even spoken to my father."*

"Ah, I see," said Siobu gently. She too knew Mr. Emejuru's reputation, and could easily understand why Happiness was concerned. *"Do you have the letter with you?"*

"Yes," Happiness answered, producing it from her book bag.

Siobu looked at the letter from the boy, *"Happy,"* she said gently, *"you are in college now. This is a normal thing. Do not let it distress you. Boys are going to write you and they are going to want to be your friend. You don't need to take every letter to your father. Just let them know that you are not interested."*

Happiness was relieved. She could certainly ignore the letter, which would make it clear she did not return his affection. That seemed like the mature thing to do; and it would maintain her honor, while not unleashing her father's wrath.

Happiness was becoming more assured around boys, but she was still wary of them. She had seen many of her friends take the occasion of being away from home as an opportunity to challenge the old Nigerian customs which held strong taboos against young men and women dating without the approval and supervision of their parents. Despite the fact that there were only two school-wide socials each year with their "brother school," some of her classmates found ways to sneak out and meet older boys. As they threw off the traditions of their parents, it became common for the girls to fool around with the older boys. Inevitably, some girls not ready for the responsibilities of motherhood, found themselves in out-of-wedlock pregnancies. It was just as her father had always said: boys were bad news. The more Happiness grew up, the more she realized that not everyone's father had explained this important lesson. During her five-year stay at ACMGS Elelenwo, she received many letters similar to the one she had shown to Siobu. However, she never replied to a single one.

As Happiness grew from a child into a young woman, her youthful exuberance was replaced by a quiet confidence, born out of a strong spiritual foundation. Her father's influence was beginning to show in her. It gave her a quiet assurance of who she was and what was truly important in life. While other girls sought assurance and confirmation through others, Happiness already had it from God and her family. Perhaps, as a result, Happiness often felt out of place with her fellow students who were much more "worldly" in their focus and desires.

Besides, she was uncomfortable with how many of the girls liked to flaunt what they had, seeking after treasures that didn't last. Although her father was a prominent man in Elele, many of her new classmates were city girls from very wealthy families. She often heard them bragging about their fine clothes, new jewelry and fancy vacations to faraway places. Happiness refused to be impressed. Deep inside, she knew what counted most. Having the finest clothes and largest diamonds could never bring greater joy than she felt in the strong relationship she had with her family, or knowing that God, her "invisible friend" as she often called Him, was always there for her. Let the others seek their temporary pleasures; she preferred the pleasures that count for eternity.

It wasn't long after starting classes at ACMGS Elelenwo, that Happiness spotted a notice posted on one of the school bulletin boards inviting people to visit the Student Union ("SU"). The description made it seem like the meeting had something to do with God, but it was clearly not a church, for the meeting would be right there on campus. Happiness decided to visit. Although she faithfully attended with the other girls the boarding school-approved Catholic church nearby, she missed the close knit environment of her home church.

The afternoon of the SU meeting, she combed her hair and took her Bible for the short walk across campus. She heard singing as she approached the designated room. She was delighted to see the room filled with dozens of girls of similar interest. They smiled at her, and she felt she would immediately fit in. She stayed for the rest of the meeting which included singing, hearing a short lesson from the Scriptures, and praying together.

Happiness was elated with her new group of friends in the SU. For the first time, she found students who shared her strong convictions. No one was obsessed with status or wealth; they just sought to please God in everything they did. At last she felt she could be herself. These girls were nicknamed "Rigteou" or "righteous" by the other students, which was just fine with Happiness. While she had been prepared to live out her standards alone if necessary, it was much more pleasant to do so in the company of likeminded friends. In this group, there was no pretense, just genuine acceptance. She felt at home.

The huge academic load caused the months to pass quickly. Soon it was time to visit home for the holidays and then to return just as fast for the spring semester. Happiness was a stellar student, but she missed home terribly. Her visits were over far too fast, and her little brothers were growing up so quickly. Mr. Emejuru had been promoted to Inspector of Schools in his district, which kept him quite busy, and although she knew she was always his Happy, she sensed in her heart that her days as his little girl were over.

Although her Christian friends brought her great comfort, there was an ache in boarding school that could never be completely assuaged. Happiness had no way to call home, no way to hear her parent's voices. Letters came frequently at first, but then less often as she grew older. Life was changing so quickly and she felt that she was being made to live as an adult when she still wanted to be a little girl. She was certainly independent in one sense; she was easily able to keep up with her schoolwork on her own and stay out of trouble. Yet she had not developed the same attachment and loyalty to the school that many of her classmates had. The brightest moments of her school days remained the times each semester when her parents were allowed to visit her. Although she wanted to go on to a university, it was still hard for her to imagine that she would ever be happier than she was when she was at home in her father's house.

The worst day of boarding school came midway through her time at ACMGS Elelenwo. She woke up knowing it would be a bad day because she had received a letter three days earlier explaining that for the first time, her parents would not be able to come see her on Family Day. Since students were not allowed to leave the school during the school year, these parent visits were the only opportunities for family interaction. She did her best to take the news in stride, but it seemed too much to ask of a sixteen-year-old. She ate her breakfast in silence, failing to return the smiles of her classmates as she normally did. She returned to her room, intending to read the history assignment she had to learn for an exam in two weeks, but found herself unable to concentrate.

Outside she could hear the joyful noises of her friends, chatting with their parents and squealing with delight over the snacks they had received. She even smelled the delicious puf-pufs, a popular pastry similar to donuts, through the open windows. It was as if they were deliberately taunting her. Her provisions had run out five days ago, just before she got the dreaded letter. There would be no food for her until the designated lunch in the dining room.

She spent the rest of the morning sulking miserably on her bed, staring at her history text book. She skipped lunch, deciding that it was better to go hungry than to eat alone in the dining room and face the humiliation of being with just one or two girls whose parents had not come to visit. Girls bustled into her dorm to put away their new possessions: new uniforms, new stockings, and of course, new provisions. They hurried out again to rejoin their families, hardly noticing Happiness studying on her bed. The afternoon seemed like it would never end. Happiness put aside the history book and tried to pick up mathematics. Her stomach began to growl and now she regretted her foolish decision to skip lunch.

Her eyes darted to the cabinets along the wall, all stuffed with snacks except for hers. She knew she could take one of her classmate's snacks without anyone seeing or knowing about it. Today she can no longer remember what it was she actually took; what specific snack it was she could not do without. Whatever it was, it wasn't worth the trouble. No sooner had she swallowed the last bite, that she felt condemned with the reality of her wrong. She could see her father's stern face. He had instilled a strong appreciation for the Ten Commandments and she knew, better than most, that what she had done in stealing from a classmate, had just broken one of those Commandments.

As she walked back to her bed, the Eighth Commandment, which she had memorized so many years ago, rang in her ears: *"Thou shalt not steal."* She climbed up onto her bunk bed and there she began to reflect on what she had done. She felt sick in her stomach. All her life she had shared and confided her deepest thoughts and dreams with "her invisible friend," the Holy Spirit. She had leaned on Him so many times before and He had always been there for her. He was her one true friend. With no earthly friend had she been so close. As with her earthly father, her desire was to do nothing that would cause her Heavenly Father to be disappointed in her. Now she realized that her "invisible friend" knew what she had done, even if no one else did. Nothing can be hid from God. She did her best to forget about the whole thing, to suppress it into the deepest reaches of her memory. Her efforts did not work. She became more and more condemned.

That night she was unable to sleep. Her agony was tearing at her conscience without mercy, refusing to leave her alone. Throughout the next day it continued. She could think of nothing else. Relentless guilt was consuming her. The second night she laid in her bed sobbing; she had to do something.

What could she do? Briefly, she entertained the thought of confessing her sin to her classmate. Perhaps she would find relief, as she had that day so long ago when she emerged from the blanket after taking second place in school. Oh, but how her classmates would scold her, call her a thief and a hypocrite: Happiness, the righteous one, whose daddy said she was too good for any boy, was nothing more than a common thief. Then she thought of what the school would do. She would be disciplined of course, probably harshly. That did not frighten her. But then she knew that they would have to write her father and notify him of what his little Happy had done. She could not bear to imagine the look on his face when he received that notification. No, there would be no "Good job, Happy" this time. There would have to be some other way.

Finally she began bargaining with God. It wasn't the most theologically sound prayer she had ever prayed, but she was young and desperate. Her prayer reflected both. Between the sobs, she began to pray:

"Oh Lord", she cried, *"you know me. You know I didn't mean to do wrong. I know I need your forgiveness, but I beg you to spare me and my family this humiliation. If only you can prevent anyone from finding out! Oh God, I will do anything, endure anything, and stay faithful to you always if only You will protect me from getting in trouble for this."* Then, true to her sixteen year old heart, she ended the prayer with the deepest desire of her heart. *Only I ask that I might be married to a rich and loving man and that you will give me four children, two girls and two boys.* Again, while not a recommended way of dealing with your sin, if you are going to "cut a deal" with God, you might as well be specific about the terms.

Sometime later, the theft was discovered and reported to the Senior Prefect of the dorm who called a mandatory gathering of all the girls in that dorm. The Prefect stood in the center of the large hall and announced the theft, demanding that the perpetrator step forward and identify herself. Happiness, still filled with shame, stood silent amidst the gathered students. She understood that the next step in the discipline process, if she were to be identified as the culprit, was the reporting of her name to the school principle, notification to her parents, then discipline. These matters were not treated lightly. She was filled with unbelievable shame. She couldn't bear the thought of embarrassing her father. So Happiness remained quiet, hoping God would show mercy and agree to her attempted "bargain" with Him.

The Prefect repeated the demand several times, and then exasperated, she dismissed the girls. Happiness, silently relieved, returned to her bed to study. Despite the heat, she hid herself beneath her blanket, and read under the covers. As night came, she prayed again for the darkness to cover her shame. Mercifully, God had granted the first part of her request; sparing her the embarrassment of going forward with her theft and forgiving her sin. Her peace returned. The second part of her request God would deal with later.

8

AN ARRANGED MARRIAGE

৬৯

Happiness would graduate from ACMGS Elelenwo girl's school with honors, continuing her strong record of making her father proud. She was now ready for her next adventure. At eighteen years of age, she was young, smart and pretty; she had a bright future seemingly awaiting her. The small-town girl had already conquered the challenges of big-city life; now she was prepared to conquer the challenges of a new profession. She applied to, took the rigorous entrance exam for, and was accepted into, the School of Nursing in Port Harcourt.

Her choice of nursing as a profession was made more by default than by dreams and desire. At the time, a woman in Nigeria who sought to be a professional had few choices. The fields primarily open to women were catering, nursing and education. Happiness may have been drawn to nursing subconsciously because she had seen the mother of their close family friends working as a nurse. Rebecca Nwoka-Aku Dike owned her own maternity clinic in Elele, where Happiness grew up. She was a practicing mid-wife who was very generous toward the poor; giving much of her time and money. She had a solid reputation as a Christian role-model. As a result, Happiness had great respect and admiration for Mrs. Dike. Happiness also knew her children well, all except their eldest boy Sonny, who had left Nigeria in 1977 and who she had never met.

While awaiting her exam results from ACMGS Elelenwo, along with the results of her application and entrance exam to nursing school, Happiness enrolled in a three-month course at the School of Basic Studies, also located in Port Harcourt. It was a common means of improving an applicant's chances of being accepted in the various professional schools, such as the School of Nursing. It was at the School of Basic Studies that she was re-united with one of her close child-hood friends, Edna Dike, one of Rebecca's daughters.

It was also where Happiness first met a young man, about her age, by the name of Noble Onyeka. She was temporarily living with her uncle Isaiah and his family in a house owned by Noble's father. Noble had noticed Happiness, and was immediately interested in getting to know her better. He began to make sure he was "around" with friends when she would leave and return to the house. He sought her attention at every opportunity, yet he tried not to be too obvious about it.

Noble evidently was an enterprising young man, managing to find out where Happiness was going to school and enough of her class schedule to meet her and her friend Edna as they came out of class together. Over time, his efforts to befriend Happiness began to pay off. She came to trust him enough to one day "grant him an audience" alone with her. It was the first time she felt comfortable spending time alone with a young man. That initial visit blossomed into a routine. Noble would show up each afternoon when he did not need to work for his father and escort Happiness on a walk, walks which became gradually longer as the days passed by.

Through their talks, Noble was able to learn of her values and character and the more he learned, the more he was drawn to her. She thought about her prayer for a loving and rich husband. Noble was the son of a local chief and prominent businessman, but he was also kind and loving. Not only was he from a well-established family, he was also pursing an advanced degree, which spoke well for his future prospects. Happiness could see that he was a man who would treat her well, as Papa had always treated Mama.

"Happiness," Noble asked her one afternoon when they were on a typical walk.

"Yes," she smiled.

"I must tell you something that is of great concern to me," he said with noticeable difficulty. Happiness' heart dropped. What could this possibly mean? He continued, *"I must leave in two months to continue my studies in London."*

"I see," Happiness responded evenly. So this was it; he was just amusing himself before leaving her to go abroad. How could she have been so foolish?

"But before I go, I must ask you something." Now her heart jumped from the depths of disappointment to the heights of anticipation. *"I love you, Happiness, and I want more than anything for you to be my wife. Would you be agreeable if my family approached yours with a proposal of marriage?"*

It took all her self-control to contain her joy. *"Yes, Noble, I would be quite pleased if you should do so. I am sure my father will receive the proposal with warmth."*

"Then it is settled. My parents will begin preparation of the appropriate gifts," Noble said with excitement.

"Have your parents no need to meet me?" Happiness asked with surprise.

"My father saw you that first day," Noble explained. *"And they know of all your accomplishments. Of course your father is known to them as well. And,"* he added with a smile, *"they have heard all I have said and described about you. They need no other assurance."*

"I am honored by their trust," Happiness said modestly. It all seemed so perfect, especially with a name like Noble for the suitor and a name like Happiness for the intended bride. How could anything go wrong?

At the time of Noble's offer of marriage to Happiness, rumors and expectations had been circulating for months that the eldest son of the Dike family would marry Happiness. Since the Emejuru and Dike families were so close, there had long been an unstated assumption that Happiness would marry one of the two Dike boys. The younger Dike boy, who was actually closer to Happiness' age, had already begun seeing another woman, so that left the eldest Dike boy as the logical choice for Happiness in the minds of the two families. Nothing had come of these rumors however, and Happiness did not feel compelled to wait for such a rumor to come to pass. She wanted to marry Noble and Noble wanted to marry her. Such a seemingly simple arrangement soon became complicated by an unexpected occurrence.

Whether her friend Edna told her parents about Noble pursuing Happiness, or whether her parents merely decided now was the time to act, was never determined. In either event, the Dike family asked Happiness to come over for a visit at their house. Such an invitation was not unusual as Happiness would frequently go to their house on their invitation. But this visit was not like the others.

Upon arrival at their house, Happiness was escorted into the sitting area. Both Mr. and Mrs. Dike began to speak to Happiness about their love and affection for her, and then they did something she wasn't expecting, at least not yet. She had also been aware of the rumors of their intentions along this line, but the suddenness of it all still caught her off guard. The Dikes proposed marriage between her and their eldest son, Sonny. While such an action was not unusual in Nigerian culture at the time, what was unusual was the fact that the man they were proposing her to marry she had never met! Nevertheless, Happiness respected the Dike family and considered the proposal a high compliment. She knew she had to think about this for awhile, especially in light of Noble's intentions toward her which she hoped he would pursue further. She was gracious to them, thanked them, and promised to consider the offer.

Sonny had completed his undergraduate studies in Alabama with her brother Ogu, and was now attending medical school in Monterey, Mexico. At 30 years of age, the Dike's son was a significant twelve years older than Happiness. He was the oldest of a family consisting of six girls and two boys. While Happiness had not yet agreed to the arrangement, and really preferred to marry Noble, it wasn't long before her family and the Dike family began acting as if she had. Everyone in the village seemed to be excited about the idea, even though Happiness still had some major misgivings. Unfortunately, the two families began to take steps to "protect her" and "fence her off" from other suitors.

Such apparent well-meaning steps of protection by these two families would cost Happiness a chance at the marriage proposal she strongly preferred, that made by Noble. There is an old saying that "timing is everything." That certainly proved true for Happiness' hopes of marrying someone else; someone she actually had met, knew, and liked. Now that Noble had determined Happiness was interested in marrying him, and not knowing of the subsequent proposal by the Dike family, Noble and his parents made arrangements to meet with the

Emejuru for the purpose of proposing marriage. As was consistent with Nigerian custom, they brought gifts with them, along with some bottles of wine, including a native wine, an English wine, and another special type of wine for this occasion. Noble and his parents formally asked Mr. and Mrs. Emejuru for their daughter's hand in marriage.

Noble had done everything right, but he had two factors against him in his pursuit of Happiness' hand in matrimony. First, he was up against a close family friendship in the Dike's and the expectations of marriage between their children that the friendship brought with it, and second; the Dike's had beaten him to the punch. Noble therefore suffered the misfortune of being from the wrong family and coming at the wrong time.

Happiness would never know until years later that Noble had come with his parents to formally propose. She would never know that his heart had been broken and his parents humiliated as Mr. Emejuru turned them down, informing them that she was already engaged to Sonny Dike. So even though Happiness had not said yes to the Dike marriage proposal, her father not only refused Noble's proposal, but he did not even inform Happiness it had been made!

Sadly for both Noble and Happiness, he had waited too long. Now as he made attempt after attempt to see and speak with Happiness, the Emejuru and Dike families sabotaged his every effort. What was worse, Happiness was not informed of all his efforts to see her. The families had decided she was to marry into the Dike family, and they weren't about to let any other suitor interfere with those plans.

When it was time for Noble to leave for London, he made one last attempt to see Happiness on his way to the airport. The Dike family, learning of his departure date and his desire to see Happiness, sent Happiness to visit her sister in law without telling her that Noble was seeking to visit her. When he arrived, he was told that Happiness was not available. Reluctantly, and with great sadness, Noble left her home for the last time. Happiness would never see him again, nor even know until much later that he tried so hard to see her.

Once in London, Noble made one last effort to connect with Happiness. He sent her some gifts in hopes that Happiness would see that he was still interested in her. These too, were intercepted by her family before Happiness could see them or even find out about them. Perhaps, had she been able to meet with him, she might have rejected the Dike proposal for marriage and thus have been spared what awaited her. But in fairness, it might not have made a difference. Happiness respected her father too much and she also respected the Dike family too much. Pleasing them was becoming more important than pleasing herself. So, despite the tantalizing option of marrying Noble, Happiness was left with the proposal from the Dike family for a 30 year old man she had never met.

As the days went by, the pressure on Happiness intensified. Both families sought to convince her to agree to the marriage proposal. She was still unsure and she needed counsel, but finding objective advice was difficult. She sought out her uncle's wife. Happiness told her of the insecurities she was feeling, her doubts about the marriage, and her concerns, including the 12 year age difference. Adding to these concerns were all the rumors she had heard that her proposed husband was secretly married to someone else, and that, unlike the Dike family, he was no longer following his Christian faith. According to the rumors, Sonny was not the same person his family thought he was. Unfortunately, her uncle's wife provided unwise counsel; stating her opinion that those who told Happiness of these rumors were just envious of the opportunity Happiness was being provided. She too encouraged Happiness to marry the man.

The Emejurus were also convinced it was a good
opportunity. They were persuaded by several factors, but
all represented false priorities. Nigerian culture tended
to base their judgment of individuals largely on family
reputation. The Dike family had a reputation as strong,
committed Christians, and certainly that was an important
factor. But how strong was the Christian commitment of
their son who they had not seen since 1977 when he left
for the U.S., now roughly five years ago? It was good and
right that the Emejurus were looking at the factor of faith
and belief, but they ignored the faith and belief of Sonny,
the proposed husband.

The other priorities were understandable, but also led
to a reliance upon the wrong criteria. The Emejuru's were
swayed by the prominence, influence and strong community reputation of the Dike family. The father had a high-
level position in the Nigerian government. Along with
influence, they also had wealth, which would help ensure
the Emejuru's daughter would be well taken care of. But
monetary protection would be the least of Happiness'
upcoming problems. In hindsight it is clear to see that the
Emejurus were persuaded too much by the faith, status,
and prominence of the Dike family and failed to give
sufficient focus to the faith, status, and prominence of
their prospective son-in-law. Certainly Mr. Emejuru knew
better, yet he too was taken in by the wrong focus. He
failed to see the foreboding signs of warning that God was
trying to make so obvious.

One of those signs of divine warning Happiness
noticed right away. She found it odd, and indeed it was,
that throughout this period following the families' marriage
proposal, that the prospective groom made no effort to
contact his hoped-for bride. Maybe she wasn't "hoped-for"
by the one person who counted, since Happiness never
received any letters, gifts or telephone calls from Sonny. He

made no effort to communicate with Happiness at all. She had seen a picture of him at his parent's house, but that was the only connection she had with him. The Lord could not have sent a much more obvious warning that danger lied ahead if He had screamed it in her ear.

If only her father had seen what Happiness was beginning to see. She trusted her father and she had always sought to please him. Now, in her time of great need for a father's discernment and protection, the devil seemed to have blinded Mr. Emejuru to the obvious warning signs God was sending. Had her father conveyed any misgivings about the marriage proposal, Happiness would have turned it down long ago, with a great sigh of relief. Yet his apparent desire for her to marry this man weighed heavily in her mind, ultimately becoming the deciding factor. Not wanting to disappoint her father, coupled with the pressure placed on her by both families, Happiness began to suppress the serious misgivings she was feeling about this marriage proposal. She sought temporary relief from this emotional agony by burying herself into her clinical work and studies at the school of nursing, but she couldn't escape. In the meantime, the Dike family continued to shower her with gifts, adding to the pressure.

One day in late February or early March, 1982, Happiness was told that Sonny had arrived home for a visit. His family had arranged for Happiness to come to their house for a family gathering. She had come to dread this moment, but now she could no longer avoid it. She knew this would be when the marriage proposal would be officially made and her acceptance would be expected. The night before she was to leave the school in Port Harcourt to travel back home to Elele and meet Sonny, proved to be a night of deep reflection and inner turmoil. She recalled finding a quiet, secluded corner of the hospital where she had been doing her clinical work to think about what she was going to do. Her emotions inside were churning. She hadn't felt like this since she was a little girl in the refugee camp listening to her mother try to give her away to the Red Cross representative.

The more she reflected on this arrangement, the more convinced she was that it wasn't right. Yet, she also believed she had no choice. Emotionally, she was on a runaway train with no brakes. As much as she longed to do so, she felt there was no way to slow down or stop this locomotive. It was bound to crash and there was nothing she could do about it. So, in that quiet corner of a Port Harcourt hospital, Happiness made her decision. In deference to her parent's wishes, and the Dike family who had befriended her, she chose that night to accept the marriage proposal and do her best to act happy about it. It was a decision she made to please everyone but herself. It was a decision made because, in her words, *"all odds were against me."*

The next morning, a driver arrived to take her the 35 miles or so back home to Elele to meet her proposed husband and accept the proposal of marriage. This marriage was what her family wanted for her. She had accepted the Dikes' presents, lived with their daughter, and had no other suitors who were pursuing her openly. She would keep her doubts and misgivings to herself and accept the proposal as everyone expected her to do. As the car brought her closer to her new future, she still harbored a secret hope that Sonny himself would call it off. For the first time in her life, she wanted to be rejected. As she rode alone in the backseat of the car, time was her only remaining ally, and she had very little of it left. She felt trapped; caught in a decision that was not of her choosing.

There was a large crowd of family and friends that had gathered around the car as it pulled up to the Dike house. The driver opened the door for her, and everyone seemed to smile with delight as she exited the car. She did indeed look beautiful, in her new dress, and with her hair freshly done; a fitting bride for a future young doctor. She was led over to the one man who she did not know, Sonny Dike, the man she was expected to marry.

As she was introduced to him, he seemed extremely casual and uncaring toward her. He made no effort to charm her, please her, or even to befriend her. In fact, he seemed completely without passion or emotion towards her. It was all so odd and more disappointing than she had anticipated. Again, God was doing His part to protect her, giving her another giant warning sign, but by now, Happiness was not listening. Indeed, at this point, no one was listening. She, and everyone else, had already determined that this marriage was going forward. She would do her duty. Through it all, Happiness played along like a grateful bride was expected to act. Her thoughts drifted to the image of herself as nothing more than a marionette on a string, with the two families controlling her every movement. She was no longer her own. She felt as if she had lost her identity, as well as her freedom. She could not even hear the voice of her Heavenly Father, warning her of impending danger.

Over the next month, Happiness and Sonny spent the time visiting relatives, while their families prepared for the wedding. Throughout this time, she continued to hear rumors about Sonny's wild life style and propensity to fool around with other women. It really didn't matter, for in her mind, it was already too late. Absent her family changing their mind, she would be marrying this man against her will for the sake of her family. Indeed, at this point, she seemed to have no will of her own.

Most women imagine their wedding day to be a day in which all is right in life. It is the one day in which story-book romance is supposed to intersect with reality. For Happiness, her wedding day would be neither a dream nor fantasy. It wasn't even preceded by a romance, let alone

one found in the storybooks. Her engagement period was completely devoid of joy, hope or dreams of happy endings. Instead, it was a tortuous march of a prisoner trapped in the shackles of family expectations.

When her wedding day arrived, April 4, 1982, it was little more than a joyless date on an impersonal calendar. To an outside observer, the wedding was splendid. Both families had put a great deal of time, attention and money into the ceremony and reception; sparing little expense. They even had a military band playing at the reception.

But for Happiness, none of that mattered, and none of that could diminish the emotional pain of marrying a man she did not love, did not trust, and a man she wasn't even sure she liked. She was caught in the midst of celebration and revelry while consumed with a sense that she was in a nightmare that would not end. To her, this marriage was not a voluntary act, it was a duty to her family, her husband's family, and their community reputations. So on the outside, the bride was beautiful that day, smiling and acting the part of a radiant woman on her special day. But this view was false. On the inside, this bride was nothing more than an insincere actress, playing a role she detested, in a play she had no control over. Sadly, this play would not have a happy ending.

9

LEAVING HOME

ꙮ

On a scale of most miserable days of her life up to this point, Happiness would probably rank April 12, 1982 as second, only behind her wedding day, on the misery index. This was the day she would leave her family and travel to Mexico with her new husband. Two Greyhound bus-loads of relatives, one for her in-laws and one for her family, accompanied her to the airport. This family separation was not going to be easy on her. It would require an even more stoic theatrical performance than she displayed on her wedding day. Still, she was determined to bury her emotions and show strength and determination. Again, it was a decision to please her family rather than herself. They all seemed so happy for her she did not want to spoil it for them by letting her true feelings show. Amazingly, many of her family and friends voiced their belief of how lucky she was. She did her best to appear grateful, but it was only a show.

The plane that would carry her and Sonny away from her family stood on the tarmac a short distance from the airport terminal. Happiness did her best to keep her emotions in check as she said her goodbyes to her family, gave her mother and father one last hug and kiss, and turned to walk out toward the plane that awaited her. As she walked across the tarmac, climbed the portable stairs, and found her seat on the plane, the overwhelming sensation of separation began to engulf her. Up until now, her family, and especially her father, had been her security blanket; one filled with much comfort and love.

Now she looked out the window at her family still waving goodbye to her. She sought to take one last "memory snap shot" of the scene, but specifically of one person in particular: her father. Even today, as she reflects back on that day, Happiness cries. The pain remains deep inside as she forces herself to remember a day that was externally filled with blue sky, billowy clouds and radiant sunshine, yet internally, was one of the stormiest of her life. Just nine days into her marriage she had cried more tears than she remembered crying in her entire life. Now she felt herself being torn from the people and the land that she loved. When asked to describe what she felt, she still struggles with the emotion of it. She had been so close to the love of her father, both emotionally and physically. Now everything that had meant so much to her was being taken away. Although painful, the torch of her earthly father's love was being passed to her Heavenly Father. She would need to lean on that love to get her through what was to come.

As the flight lifted off Nigerian ground and left Nigerian airspace, the separation was complete. Throughout the rest of the flight to the United States, Happiness felt dead inside. The marionette on strings was all that was left. During the flight, Sonny remained aloof, doing nothing to assist her in her emotional loss, and apparently oblivious to it. He seemed preoccupied and uncaring.

Their flight took them initially to Houston, Texas, where they were met by a friend of Sonny's, with whom they would live for the next two weeks, before departing for Sonny's home in Monterrey, Mexico where he was attending medical school. After an all day drive through Texas, they crossed into Mexico around midnight. It was not until early the next morning when they arrived in Monterrey where, after much searching for a vacancy at that hour, plopped their fatigued bodies on the beds of a run-down motel room. The next day, after a day-long search, they found a one-bedroom apartment that matched, if not exceeded, the dilapidated condition of their motel room of the night before.

Happiness was becoming more and more distraught. She had been used to a much higher standard of living back in Nigeria. Indeed, that higher lifestyle, complete with maids and the best of accommodations, was one of the reasons her father had agreed to the marriage, thinking his daughter would be well taken care of. Now, as Happiness was swirling with the magnitude of changes hitting her all at once, she remembered the "guarantee" by the Dike family that she would not suffer if she married their son. Their son, they told her, "was a good man."

Too bad they didn't know their son as he had turned out to be. They would have been shocked. Sonny treated her more like an unwelcome inconvenience than a wife. He was impatient with her efforts to talk with him, rarely talked to her, and showed no desire to help her adjust to her new surroundings. It was also unfortunate that she had no way of communicating with her parents. She and Sonny had no phone and, even if she found a pay phone somewhere, she didn't know how to use it to make an international call. Happiness began to turn inward toward the only one she had left, her "invisible friend," who had upheld her through every prior difficulty.

That first evening in their new apartment, Sonny decided, without explanation, that they should take a drive. He rebuffed the efforts Happiness made to find out where they were going or what his plans were. Since he had never consulted with her on any of his decisions up to this point, she was "learning" not to question him and just follow along. They arrived at a location unknown to Happiness somewhere within the vast reaches of Monterrey, a large city in the northeast portion of Mexico, with a metropolitan area of roughly 3.8 million people.

As Sonny got out of the car, he told Happiness to remain until he returned, still not telling her where he was going or how long he would be gone. It was already dark and Happiness was in an unknown, unlit place, surrounded by an unknown culture. Those facts alone made her uncomfortable, but not knowing any Spanish made it even worse. She couldn't have asked for help, even if she wanted to. Feeling extremely vulnerable, Happiness began to pray, asking the Lord to protect her.

Three hours later, she was still waiting, all the while wondering if she would be assaulted by some stranger who meant her harm. Sonny did not return to the car until after mid-night, and when he did so, it was without any explanation of where he had been. In retrospect she should have been angry, but she wasn't sure how he would react. Besides, after spending three hours in the dark expecting to be accosted at any minute at an unlit location, her overwhelming emotion was relief that she had not been harmed. That fact was attributable solely to the grace of God who had protected her when her own husband had clearly not.

Sonny never did explain to her where he had gone that night or why he left her alone. It was as if he felt she wasn't entitled to an explanation. As the days went by, Sonny was frequently moody and angry towards her, showing flashes of temper she had not seen before. She tried to pass the time by reading the Bible, praying, or watching television. Even as she did so, her mind was filled with questions. Where were all his medical school books? Who had he gone to see their first night in Monterey and why could she not come in with him? Where had he lived before they got married and why had she never seen that place? He seemed to be bringing his clothes and other belongings from somewhere. Were the rumors she had heard about him true? She dared not ask anything, or he would surely lose his temper.

She lived a lonely life, afraid to complain or otherwise provoke her husband to anger lest she lose the only English speaker she had. A pattern developed where she was told to stay in the apartment while he left for the day, presumably to attend classes at medical school, though she was never quite sure. With the exception of buying her one introductory Spanish language book, Sonny did little for her. He never took her with him to see the city or try to show her around, or otherwise help her to adapt to her new environment. She remained isolated in Mexico, with him as her only tie to the outside world. *It is so stupid that I am here,* she thought more than once. *He clearly doesn't want me; he is only doing this to placate his parents, even as I am only doing this to placate my parents. Oh, why can't he just reject me and send me home to my father?*

For three months this pattern continued, while Sonny continued to claim he was spending all his time attending medical school. One afternoon, that pretense was exposed. While watching television in their bedroom, Happiness heard a knock at the door, which her husband answered. Through the thin walls of their apartment, she overheard him speaking to someone in Spanish in a loud and angry tone. *"Cayate, Marisol! Cayate!"* Sonny kept repeating, as Happiness peeked out from the bedroom doorway. She saw a young Mexican woman holding a baby in her arms. Before Happiness could pull back from the door, the woman caught sight of her and pushed past Sonny. The sight of Happiness coming out of the bedroom sent the woman into a deeper frenzy of rage. She moved toward Happiness, screaming directly into her face. Seeing that Happiness could not understand, the woman dropped the crying baby on the bed and returned her angry focus toward Sonny.

As the Mexican woman and Sonny continued arguing, Happiness picked up the baby who was crying louder now, and squirming very close to the edge of the bed. As she did so, she noticed the baby looked just like Sonny. *Now I understand why the Mexican woman is so angry,* she thought to herself, as the other two voices quieted and they both sat down.

"This woman is trying to say that I am the father of her baby, Sonny tried to explain. *They do this all the time to foreigners. They become pregnant by anyone and then try to pick someone rich to blackmail. She thinks I can get her into America."*

Despite knowing her husband was lying to her, she was filled with an overwhelming compassion for the welfare of the baby, still resting comfortably in her arms. *"Does this woman want to leave the baby?"* Happiness asked. *"I will care for her if she does."* The Mexican woman seemed to read Happiness' meaning in her eyes, for she stood up, grabbed the baby and quickly left.

For what seemed like a very long time, there was complete silence between Happiness and Sonny. She now realized that she could not trust her husband, that the rumors she had heard about him back in Nigeria were true, and that neither her father nor family could make things right. She was stuck and she knew it. Even if her family wanted to come help her, they didn't have a visa to enter Mexico. She was on her own. She would need to draw closer to God and trust Him for everything. It would be her only hope.

A few days later, the same Mexican woman returned. This time she was calmer, but clearly not pleased as she spoke with Sonny. They exchanged a brief conversation and then she left. Happiness had deduced that the lady had been living with her husband in Sonny's other apartment and was upset to learn she was "sharing" Sonny with this Nigerian woman. Shortly after this latest incident with the Mexican lady, Sonny informed Happiness they needed to go to the Nigerian Embassy in Mexico City to see the Ambassador. As was typical of him, he didn't provide any further explanation. Happiness suspected it had something to do with the Mexican lady.

They drove all night and arrived at the Embassy the next morning. When the car came to a halt in front of the Nigerian Embassy, Sonny showed their passports and handed a letter to the guard. They were warmly received, and soon they found themselves ushered into a richly furnished sitting area awaiting the ambassador himself.

"Mr. and Mrs. Dike, welcome to Mexico City," the ambassador said warmly as he entered. He was a tall, strapping man, wearing a dark western style suit. They exchanged the proper pleasantries. The relief Happiness felt to be somewhere that seemed familiar made it easy to play the part of the happy newlywed, despite her fatigue.

"Mrs. Dike," the ambassador continued. *"I understand that you are the daughter of Mr. Dick Emejuru, is that right?"*

"Yes, Sir," Happiness replied.

"Ah, that is good news. My wife knows your sister Esther quite well. She will be delighted to talk with you at dinner tonight."

That evening they dined on all the finest Nigerian food, and were waited on by servants just like at home in Elele. Happiness felt comfortable and welcome for the first time since leaving her country.

After an hour of pleasant conversation, the ambassador turned to them and spoke in a serious tone, *"I am sorry, Mr. Dike, to be the bearer of bad news, but it is important that you know of a communication I have received through*

*my staff. It is because of this communication that I have
summoned you here."*

Happiness and Sonny nodded and leaned forward to
listen.

*"I am very sorry for the sordid nature of what I am
about to say. I say it only because it is imperative that
you know what is going on. A week ago, a local woman
in Monterrey called the Embassy, informed us that she
had a child by a man named Mr. Sonny Dike and that she
had been living with this man for some time. She said he
then returned from a trip with a new wife, whom he kept
hidden from her. She made it clear that she would not allow
another woman to take him away from her. She conveyed
very explicit plans to kill this new wife."* He paused to
let the significance of his words sink in. Happiness shuddered to think that someone wanted to kill her! *"We know
a woman of such admittedly loose morals can hardly be
considered credible,"* the ambassador continued, *"but we
have determined that the threat is a serious one and that is
why we brought you here for your own protection."*

What Happiness was not told, but she would find out
years later, was that the Mexican woman was already pregnant by Sonny with a second baby girl.

Happiness, concerned that she was the object of a
death threat, and devastated by the confirmation of her
worst fears about her husband, at least had the diplomatic
comforts of a week at the Embassy to soothe her battered
mind. Her time there was far better than anything she had
experienced in the preceding few months. Yet she knew that
the fairytale must end sometime; they could not possibly
stay there forever. Nothing could be worse, she thought
than returning to Monterrey, and yet she feared to think
what could be next.

Following a week of pampered living in the Embassy,
Sonny told Happiness he had decided they were moving to

the United States; specifically, San Bernardino, California, to be near his sister. Happiness received this news with joy and relief. California! People spoke English there. She would be able to find her way around and meet people. Perhaps she could even resume her studies. She almost felt warmth toward her husband, despite his cruel and uncaring ways.

"Sonny," she said, uncharacteristically breaking her silence.

"What is it?" he asked, annoyed.

"I am pregnant," she answered.

"I see. Well, it will be better to have the baby in America anyway. You should see the hospitals here. They are mostly disgusting." Such a small indication of his care struck Happiness as being one of the nicest things he had yet said to her.

Without even returning to Monterrey for the few things they had left behind, Happiness and Sonny left Mexico City and began driving north toward California. They drove all night, arriving at his sister Evelyn's house in San Bernardino the next morning. Sonny had been able to call from the Embassy, so they were expected, and Evelyn came running out of the house to greet them with excitement. She looked like such a kind, generous woman, genuinely excited to see both of them. *She cannot know how he really is,* Happiness thought. *She is a good woman. She would be mortified to learn how her brother behaves.*

San Bernardino was a world apart from Monterrey. The house was modest but clean and well furnished. Evelyn had heard only wonderful things about Happiness from her mother and shared the family's delight that her brother had married such a beautiful and accomplished young woman. They had much in common to talk about: both were pregnant, Evelyn was a nurse, just as Happiness hoped to be, and Evelyn's husband was also studying to be a doctor.

It wasn't long thereafter that Happiness and Sonny were able to move into their own apartment in San Bernardino, a much nicer one than their first apartment in Mexico. For the first time since she was married, Happiness was able to begin getting some of her life back. So, despite the obstacles of being an expectant mother, she enrolled at San Bernardino Community College, taking some prerequisite classes for a degree. While there, she met Celeste, a Mexican-American classmate who took an instant liking to Happiness. They became close friends in short order. Happiness appreciated that she didn't seem to have many of the silly stereotypes some of the Americans had toward her African background. Her friend also became an enthusiastic supporter of her pregnancy; both planning and offering to host a baby shower. Celeste introduced Happiness to her family, the Canelas, who also showed her genuine love. They treated her as if she were part of their family; in fact, they made it clear, they were informally "adopting" her.

On April 17, 1983, just over a year after she had left Nigeria, Happiness gave birth to her first child, a lovely daughter she named Queenette Nwoka-Aku, meaning "a child is greater than wealth." Rita Canela, her newly adopted "mother," was thrilled that she was now an "abuela." Likewise, her adopted "sisters" from the Canela clan treated the baby like their own niece, even introducing her as such wherever they went. Sonny remained Sonny, but Happiness now had enough warmth in her life to survive, even under the pressures of new motherhood.

10

DETAINED AT THE BORDER

It was late summer, 1983 when Happiness realized it was time to update her visa status. To do so, she had to go to the Immigration and Naturalization Service (INS) office in Los Angeles, about an hour and a half drive west from their San Bernardino home. With uncharacteristic civility, Sonny agreed to take her. Upon arrival, they met with an INS official who reviewed her documents, checked her status in the system and prepared a document for her.

"You must take this and temporarily leave the U.S." the official explained. *"Just go south to Mexico; it is very simple. When you reenter, show them this document, and your immigration status will be automatically updated in the system."*

Indeed it did sound simple.

"Oh, we can go to Tijuana and buy Queenette some new clothes," Mrs. Canela said with delight when she heard of the plan. *"She is growing so fast! There is a little restaurant where I must take you. They make the best pollo asada and we will eat our fill for less than two dollars each!"* To Happiness' surprise, Sonny expressed a willingness to go when he learned Rita's husband would also be

going. Although she wasn't sure of the cause for this more pleasant response from Sonny, she definitely wanted to enjoy it while it lasted. The four of them, along with baby Queenette, left for Tijuana, Mexico immediately across the border from San Diego. When they arrived at the U.S. - Mexican border, Happiness showed the agent her document and he waved her through without incident.

They all enjoyed a wonderful day of shopping, along with a relaxing lunch, just as Mrs. Canela had said they would. Sonny was the perfect gentleman, laughing and joking in Spanish and English. When the day was spent and Queenette exhausted, they headed back to re-enter the U.S. at the same border checkpoint they had crossed just hours ago. They presented their documents to the agent and waited to be waved through. Happiness watched the agent confer with an assistant and then return to their car.

"There is a problem with one of these documents," the border agent explained. *"We need you to pull over."* After a few minutes waiting inside their parked car, another agent approached them. Happiness could tell from his expression that something was wrong. He asked a few more questions of Sonny, who had been driving, and looked at their documents once again. Then he made a pronouncement none of them were expecting. *"All of you are fine to reenter the United States except for Happiness Dike. We need to detain her for further questioning."* Happiness' stomach dropped. She was being taken into custody! How could this be happening? Her mind was reeling as she found herself ordered out of the car. Sonny began arguing on her behalf with the border agent, and the Canelas were shouting in Spanish that there had to be a mistake.

No amount of arguing by her husband or the Canelas had any effect on the border agent; they were told they were released and needed to leave. Happiness would not be allowed to see or talk to them while being held in custody.

His mind was made up. The Canelas assured Happiness they would take care of Queenette until they were able to re-unite with her, and they tried to encourage her that everything would be alright. To her dismay, Happiness found herself handing her three month old daughter to Mrs. Canela while she was led away to a temporary detention room.

The sound of Queenette crying for her rang in her ears as she was led into a small, poorly lit room, furnished only with a government-issued metal desk and a couple of chairs. Once again, Happiness felt the painful sting of being separated from those she loved, specifically the pain of being separated from her treasured baby girl. The thought of little Queenette crying for her mommy, with no understanding of what was happening, tore at her from the deepest part of her emotions.

She was left alone with no explanation of when anyone would come in to see her or question her further. She became afraid, allowing her mind to give in to the horrible scenarios that could happen to her while alone in a holding area, removed from outside observance. Anxieties of not being able to see her baby again flooded her mind, as did a myriad of other equally horrible thoughts.

As she sat there all alone, with no one to comfort her, she began to think about how things once were in Nigeria before she had left the comfort of a family who loved her and a lifestyle that she had been secure with. She began to second guess everything about her life. Perhaps God was punishing her. Although she couldn't think of anything she had done to warrant this renewed suffering, she began to repent of every sin she could think of, even asking God's forgiveness for anything she didn't know about. Maybe the pagan gods of her village back home were punishing her for not serving them. She was confused. Her whole world was turning upside down again. *Why does this keep happening to me?*

Whether intentional or not, the border agents kept
Happiness waiting alone in that small room for several
hours. Finally, as it was getting close to dark, a border
agent came in, asked a few more questions, and then told
her she would not be allowed to re-enter the United States.
She would be released back into Mexico. She was devastated, shocked and scared. Again she wondered to herself
how all this could be happening? With no apparent concern
for her safety at night alone, the border agents released her.
She had only one direction she was allowed to go; south,
away from her home, family and security.

The outskirts of Tijuana were in the distance about a
mile away and she was now walking along the side of the
freeway, strewn with empty plastic bottles, cigarette butts,
and a wide assortment of other debris. For no apparent
reason, she turned to look north. There in the distance she
could see the lights of San Diego. How she longed to be
walking towards those lights. They were so close, yet not
for her. Within moments she had to turn her head away.
Why torture herself with thoughts that were not to be?

On she walked toward Tijuana, away from the direction she wanted to go. She could see the last remnants
of light from a sun that had already gone down over the
Pacific Ocean. The scene of growing darkness in the sky
was a perfect reflection of what she was feeling inside.
With no one to translate for her, and completely alone, she
wandered the streets of Tijuana in a state of hopelessness.
It was as if she was "lost to the world." Hungry and full of
emotional pain, she regretted she had even been born. She
felt as if she couldn't go on.

She doesn't recall how long she wandered the streets
in a daze of despair, but she finally awoke out of her stupor
long enough to find a pay phone and call her husband who
was now back home. Sonny then called their friends, the
Canelas, who made arrangements for someone to meet

Happiness at her location. Happiness was told to stay where she was. A few hours later a Mexican man approached her. He spoke very little English, but enough to let her know his name was Pedro and that he had been sent by the Canela family to help her. What Happiness did not learn until later, was that Pedro was a professional border crossing "assistant" the Canela family hired to sneak Happiness illegally across the border.

The first priority at this late hour was to find Happiness a place to spend the night, a task made more difficult since Happiness had no money. They approached a local hotel, and Pedro went inside for a moment. Happiness waited outside, and observed an older man peek out at her through the blinds. She saw him turn to Pedro and nod.

It seems her new-found "assistant" was able to negotiate accommodations for her at a local hotel, but there was a "catch." Since she had no money to pay for a room, Pedro had cut a deal with the hotel manager to let her spend the night, in exchange for her sharing the manager's room and bed with him. Not knowing the language, the explicit expectation of sexual favors was not explained to Happiness, but it didn't take her long to figure it out.

Pedro broke the news to Happiness, in his best broken English. *"We go here,"* Pedro explained. *"You go him."* He pointed toward the manager and gave her an apologetic look. The manager took her by the hand and smiled. The room she was taken to was small, dirty, and poorly lit by one uncovered light bulb in the middle of the ceiling. There was only one double bed in the room that looked more like a storage room than a bedroom. Happiness' stomach stung with anxiety. *So this was to be the price of one night's lodging.* The nightmare seemed never to end.

She looked at the manager with dreadfulness and curled up on the bed in a fetal position. Fearing what was about to happen, she turned to her only hope. She prayed for God to protect her. He had been her source of protection all her life; surely He would not let her down this time. She was praying in earnest, putting God to the test. *Oh, God, you promised me that you would protect me. You said that no weapon formed against me would prosper. I need to see your protection now, Lord. Oh Lord, please spare me of this humiliation.* As she continued to fervently pray, tears flowed down her cheeks. *Oh, God please don't let him touch me.*

The manager climbed into bed and curled up next to her as if she were his wife. She continued to pray, and wait. Her heart pounded and her palms were drenched in sweat. She felt his hot breath on her neck and reflexively curled into a tighter ball as he reached his right arm around and placed it on her hip. Her prayers became louder as she began to sob. He removed his hand. The muscles in her body remained tense as she remained in her fetal position, continuing to sob and pray. After a few minutes, it was apparent he was not making any further overtures. Perhaps his heart was not made of stone. Perhaps he thought he was going to bed with a prostitute, not an innocent young wife and mother. Twenty minutes later, he got up and went to sleep on the floor in the far corner of the room. He never sexually touched her! God had once again answered her prayers. Happiness was filled with relief as she began to relax little by little and eventually managed to fall asleep.

Late the next morning, Pedro brought her some lunch and then they boarded a bus headed toward the outskirts of town. From there, they walked to an abandoned, run-down warehouse where they met up with about thirty Mexicans. They all waited there for several hours. Throughout the waiting, Happiness was filled with unease as she was in the midst of strangers who looked like criminals. While the Mexicans all seemed to know what was going on, she did not. She still didn't realize she was about to be snuck across the U.S.-Mexican border. The hours wore on and all she could do was wait. Dinner didn't seem to be part of the plan.

Sometime after dark Pedro signaled that it was time to depart. The group left the warehouse and began heading, trotting actually, into the open terrain heading north. It was hard to see in the dark the further they got from the city, but Pedro seemed to know every rock and pebble by heart. As her eyes adjusted, Happiness noticed they were on a narrow, dirt trail with thick bushes on either side. It was a well-worn path, but wide enough for only one person at a time. She also noticed several other parallel paths, filled with other Mexicans all moving northward behind their leaders. Happiness was young and healthy but she found the pace exhausting. Still, the fear of losing Pedro and being left behind gave her strong motivation to keep up.

Their journey would take them over ten miles across heavily shrubbed terrain, and across the Mexican-U.S. border into California. Happiness' legs were scratched by the bushes, and her feet were sore, but she kept up. Along the way, they stepped over countless discarded food containers and empty bottles left behind from others who had preceded them. Happiness caught her breath as she noticed human bodies among the discarded waste. Her mind flashed back to the charred bodies of the Ibos from her childhood that she had tried so hard to forget. Happiness kept pushing herself through the growing fatigue, asking God to give her the strength she needed.

By early the next morning, the group had reached a spot where a train was waiting for them. Her fellow travelers all seemed to scatter instantaneously, leaving just her and Pedro. The two of them would be the only ones boarding the train. Her legs felt numb as they sat down, traveling farther north as the sun rose. Her thoughts began to wander as she dozed in and out of her fatigue-induced stupor, and the train swayed and clattered rhythmically against the tracks. *Why did this happen? I only did what they told me to do. How could such a simple-sounding plan have gone so wrong?*

Happiness could tell from the surroundings as the train pulled to a stop and they disembarked, that they were back in California. American-style houses dotted the landscape. Pedro took her to an apparent transition house where other "travelers" were eating and sleeping, clearly fresh off the road like she was. He disappeared without a word. He knew he would get paid and he had other groups to escort.

Happiness, feeling strangely safe, even amongst new strangers, took a shower, gratefully accepted a plate of tamales from her hostess, and then fell asleep on a nearby couch. What a terrifying and strange three days it had been. It was as if she had made some terrible enemy who was trying to destroy her at all costs.

Shortly after dark, Sonny and Mr. Canela arrived and gently woke her up from a deep sleep. Seeing their familiar faces brought her instant relief and comfort. Even though she wasn't yet home, she already felt much safer. They would be taking her back home, that is if they could get her through the checkpoint on the U.S. side of the border. As their car approached a small, rural border control check-point, the men told Happiness to scrunch down low, pull a hat down over her face, and pretend she was asleep. The border patrol agent stopped their car, shining his flashlight into the faces of the car occupants. After asking a few ques-tions and searching the trunk, he let them proceed. They had made it. After three nightmarish days, Happiness was safely back in the United States!

It wasn't long before they arrived back in San Bernardino. At her apartment, Mrs. Canela came rushing out to greet her, holding Queenette. Queenette squealed with delight at the sight of her mommy. *"Oh, my little treasure!"* Happiness cried, as she held her baby close. Queenette grinned broadly while tears began to flow down the cheeks of an exhausted, yet grateful mother. Despite all she had been through, Happiness was overwhelmed with gratitude. She held Queenette tightly while thanking and praising God for getting her through another major storm in her life, in fact, several storms. She and her Lord had been through a lot together. She marveled that her "invisible friend" had protected her once more.

11

ENDURING A HUSBAND'S ABUSE

❧

Oh God, please help my husband. I feel as if he would rather be free to roam around the streets as he once did in Monterrey. He hates me for disrupting his life. He does not even appear to care for our child. Dear Lord, what am I to do? Daily he insults me. Daily he is angry, and I have done him nothing but good since we have been married. Everyone thinks we are the perfect couple; what would they say if they saw how he treats me?

Lord, always he is asking where I went, who I saw and why I was gone so long. Even at church he forbids me to speak to certain people. He would happily keep me prisoner in the house all day, while he ran around and did whatever he wanted. Oh God, I thought nothing could be worse than our first few weeks of marriage, but this is worse. He is becoming crueler by the day. If You do not sustain me, I don't know what I will do.

So confided a desperate woman in her Lord, as she could not tell anyone else. She could not tell Evelyn, who loved Sonny dearly and thought the world of her older brother. She could not tell anyone who lived around her, for

fear of what her husband would do if he found out. Every
so often she imagined her father rushing in from Nigeria
to save her. Sometimes, in her daydream, her father would
hear Sonny yelling at her and he would break down the
door. He would grab Sonny by the shoulders and demand to
know why he thought he could treat his precious Happiness
that way. Then Papa would throw him out of the house and
tell Happiness that she and Queenette were coming home
with him. She would smile, imagining this heroic scene,
and then a door would slam or the baby would cry or some
other sound would disturb her lovely fantasy.

"Where have you been?" Sonny would demand when
she returned home from an errand. He would speak as if
she had been gone past midnight when it was in fact 6:00 in
the evening.

*"At the store. I needed diapers for Queenette and we
needed more groceries,"* Happiness would respond quietly.

"You left at 4:45. Why were you gone so long?" It was
as if she was a suspect in a criminal investigation.

*"I had to go to two stores. I buy the rice at the Asian
store because it is cheaper there. I buy the diapers—"*

"Shut up!" Sonny would interrupt. *"You are nothing
but a lying nwatakiri. The baby cried the entire time you
were gone. I have to study and I couldn't get anything
done."* Happiness had never understood how Sonny could
have left his medical studies in Mexico so suddenly. He
grumbled about needing paperwork sent from Mexico to
prove he was a doctor. With nothing to prove his training,
he found himself working as a nursing assistant in the local
convalescent home.

Queenette was asleep when I left, thought Happiness to
herself. Outwardly she said nothing. There was nothing to
say.

The mental abuse Sonny had foisted upon Happiness
from the inception of their marriage began to rise in inten-

sity and frequency. Not only was he demeaning to her, he became controlling of her every move. Sonny made it clear she was not to visit anyone outside their home and he even restricted who she could talk to at church. When she had to run errands, he demanded to know where she was going and how long she would be gone. It got so bad, that whenever she left the house to run an errand, he would time her. If she returned later than the time he thought appropriate, he interrogated her like she was a suspect in a major crime.

Discovering the reasons for his control would require the considered opinion of experts, but much of it boiled down to pure, unadulterated, selfishness. Sonny resented having to watch their baby while she was gone. Not only did he not care about developing any meaningful relationship with his little girl, he saw babysitting as a task that inhibited his pursuit of his selfish desires. Sonny had a family, but he was no "family man." His rule of marriage was simple: no restrictions for himself; no freedom for his wife. Happiness was kept on a short, tight leash, and Sonny held the end of it.

Happiness needed to tell someone how she was being treated, but she was very selective in who she confided in. She didn't want her own family to know. She continued to have a good relationship with her sister-in-law, Evelyn and her husband Onyema, who they had lived with for a few months when they first arrived in California. Both were strong Christians and Happiness had special respect for Evelyn, having grown up hearing of her excellent reputation. Happiness also knew Sonny's other brother, Daniel very well from growing up together in Nigeria. Daniel was now also living near San Bernardino. Although she had to be careful in not disclosing everything, she did share some things. As such, these three people became Happiness' allies in a war in which she was otherwise completely outnumbered.

It was some consolation, albeit small, to at least be able to receive encouragement from them. When Happiness confided in them about the derogatory Nigerian name, *"nwatakiri,"* that Sonny frequently used against her, both Sonny's sister and brother became upset. Such a derogatory word, meaning "young child", was one of the worst insults a Nigerian man could utter to a grown woman. They both made a point to talk to him about it; scolding him about calling his wife such a name. However, as Sonny was their oldest brother, there wasn't much more they could do about her situation. Although they were living in California, the tie to their Nigerian upbringing, which honored the eldest son, was still strong.

Unfaithfulness to his marriage vows was another of Sonny's proclivities. He loved the pursuit of women, and he engaged in such pursuits repeatedly. Happiness became suspicious when various women her age befriended her and came by the house under the pretext of seeing her. Their timing always coincided with Sonny being at home. When such "friends" came to visit her, Sonny invariably came up with some errand he needed done that required Happiness to leave the house for awhile. Adding to her suspicion was the fact that these were the only times Sonny didn't seem to mind her being gone, nor did he get upset if she were late returning. No doubt he was timing these errands, as it gave him occasion to commit more mischief.

This pattern of female visitation became the rule rather than the exception and its conclusion was predictable. Happiness would typically find her "friend", who had come under the ploy of seeing her, suddenly needing to make an early departure as soon as Happiness returned from the errand. Happiness could only imagine how well her husband had "entertained" the company while she was gone. Happiness tolerated these visits as she had everything else in her marriage, feeling that she had no real proof with which to accuse him. One night, however, that changed.

"What is it my little darling?" Happiness ran to her daughter's bed. Something in Queenette's cry told her this was not an ordinary nightmare. Sure enough, as the young mother picked her up, her flesh felt startlingly hot. She quickly grabbed the thermometer and found her temperature to be nearing 101 Fahrenheit.

Sonny was working the night shift as a nursing assistant at a local convalescent home in San Bernardino, so Happiness immediately called him at work.

"I need to speak to Sonny Dike right away. It is an emergency," Happiness told the woman who answered the phone.

"I am sorry, he is not here," she replied matter-of-factly. *"It is his night off."*

"Are you sure?" Happiness asked sharply.

"Of course I am sure. I have the schedule right here and I have not seen him all night," the woman answered.

The anxiety over her daughter's illness compounded the anger that began to rise in her heart. So this was what her husband chose to do instead of working, while his daughter lay ill. How could she have been so naïve to have trusted him? She took Queenette to the bathroom and began putting towels soaked in cold water on her back and forehead to lower the fever as she had seen her mother do with her little brothers when they became ill. She stroked her daughter's back and did her best to give her comfort, but her own anger was simmering as her resolve began to harden.

The next morning, Sonny walked in the door dressed in his nursing uniform, yawning as if he had just worked a full shift. His ability to deceive without flinching was amazing. *Here I tortured myself over a stolen snack when I was girl and this man lies as easily as he breathes,* she thought as she watched him.

"Queenette is sick, and she was running a very high fever last night," Happiness informed him calmly. *"I called you at work to let you know, but you weren't there."*

"What do you mean, I wasn't at work?" he asked innocently as he slipped off his shoes. *"I mean that your office checked your schedule when I called and said that last night was your night off. So where have you been?"* Happiness had prepared herself for a violent explosion. Indeed she almost wanted one, imagining what she might say in response this time. For Sonny, being caught in this latest lie did not seem to stir up his conscience. There was nothing he could say. So he chose to ignore her, heading straight to the bedroom to get some sleep, leaving her to contemplate how anyone could be so shameless.

The cycle of abuse heaped upon Happiness by her husband extended beyond the mental abuse and blatant unfaithfulness that exemplified his complete disdain for her as a wife. Sonny now found new ways to demean her, adding physical and sexual abuse to his repertoire. Sexually, he would force her to do things she didn't want to do, when she didn't want to do them. He demanded her sexual attention without regard for her, as if she didn't count. He treated her as property to be abused, not as a wife to be cherished. At a time when many states were beginning to recognize a new legal theory recognizing that a husband could be guilty of committing rape upon his wife, Sonny was making that legal theory a reality. The marital bed, designed by God as a place of intimacy and mutual enjoyment, was transformed into a place where Happiness found utter debasement and shame.

Physical abuse was the capstone upon this spousal abuse pyramid. Pushing her was common and hitting her soon became routine. Yet, by far his favorite means of intimidation over his wife was to raise his fist and start to swing it at her. He would do this while standing over her and he would take obvious delight in watching her flinch in fear. When she instinctively did so, he would smile smugly, satisfied that he had showed her who was "in charge." It was one of the ways he demeaned her, mocked her and, in a very real sense, enslaved her to his authority. By forcing her to cower beneath him, he fed his insatiable need to bend her will to his and demonstrate that his control over her was absolute. He was like a typical bully, intimidating on the outside, but cowardly on the inside.

—

Oh, Lord. How long must I endure this man? How long must I be humiliated worse than a dog with which he appeases his basest of appetites? Will you not deliver me, Oh God?

After returning home from church one Saturday, as was her habit, Happiness let it slip that she had been talking to a lady at church that Sonny had previously warned her not to talk to.

"What?" Sonny demanded. "*I told you to stay away from that woman! She is a busybody and a gossip.*"

By which you mean that she can see through your act. She suspects what you really are, Happiness thought. She had let it slip that she had spoken to one of the many people on the "list" of individuals her husband considered of unsavory character.

"*Yes, of course. I had forgotten you do not like her,*" Happiness answered quietly.

"*Well you must not forget again!*" Sonny said, his voice rising. "*You are a foolish woman and you do not need to be made more foolish by others!*" He was standing up now. Queenette began to cry.

"*You are upsetting your daughter!*" Happiness answered back, her voice rising as well.

"Who are you to tell me what I am doing? She is upset because her mother is a disobedient fool who does not honor her husband properly!" He was yelling now. He followed her to the bedroom where she had hung up her dress in the closet and set out her regular clothes.

"How can I honor a man who is dishonorable?" Happiness asked, looking him straight in the eyes.

CRASH! Sonny had pushed her violently, knocking her down.

Happiness' head throbbed as it smacked violently against the floor. She was stunned by his reaction to such a simple matter. Dazed she tried to make it to her feet. As she was getting up, Sonny moved towards her, fists ready to strike. She could tell by his demeanor, this would not be a mere threat. She saw his eyes. He looked like a man possessed. Without thinking, she grabbed Queenette, and ran out of the bedroom and out the front door, wearing nothing but her underwear.

Her neighbor, an elderly Vietnamese woman, responded to her pounding by opening the door. Upon seeing Happiness and Queenette, she immediately brought them inside and bolted the door. Something in her silent reaction revealed an immediate understanding of their plight. The neighbor brought her a robe and invited her to sit down. Happiness did so, still clutching Queenette for dear life. She tried to calm down and gather her thoughts.

The police will not care, she thought to herself, considering more about how such issues would be handled in Nigeria than in the States. *What can I do? I have no money. He takes my paycheck as soon as it arrives. I don't even know how to use a bank,* she lamented. Sonny had effectively prevented her from learning anything that would help her become independent.

For a moment her mind traveled back to her home village. She sipped the tea her neighbor brought her and thought of how wonderful it would be to go back there. She and Queenette could be happy there, in her father's house. *But no, they would be so ashamed. Their daughter: a terrible wife, with a failed marriage. And the Dikes have been so good to me: they would be heartbroken to learn what their son has become.* Her neighbor patiently sat quietly, allowing Happiness to regain her composure.

She asked if she could use the phone; not to call the police, but to call her sister-in-law Evelyn, who was at least a partial sounding board. While she knew her sister-in-law would not do anything, Happiness wanted her to know what was going on. Happiness felt she needed to keep her one main ally aware of everything. Besides, she needed a witness in case Sonny later tried to lie about her.

Sonny was careful to protect his public image of a loving husband, even if he knew it was a lie. Not only did his reputation demand it, but so did the reputation of his family back home in Nigeria. Were they to know the truth, they would have been appalled, angry, and embarrassed. So Sonny lived a double life. In private, when there were no witnesses, he inflicted physical and emotional pain on his wife. In public, he put on the charm. Periodically, he would even join Happiness and Queenette at church, portraying himself as a nice, loving husband. Friends would often remark how they seemed like such a perfect couple, telling Happiness how lucky she was. If they only knew how wrong they were!

In looking back on this stage of her life, it is easy to identify all the classic signs of spousal abuse: controlling domination, humiliation, isolation, intimidation, and justification of the abusive behavior. Amazingly, when exposed, an abuser often "makes excuses for the inexcusable," finding ways to blame the victim. They use fear, guilt, shame, and intimidation to dominate and control their spouse.

According to most experts of such matters, the abuser's goal is to gain and maintain total control over the victim. They have a need to feel "in charge," and they expect total submission and unquestioned obedience. As a result, a husband who abuses his wife, can come to treat her like a child at best, or a slave at worst. He will do all he can to humiliate her through insults, and other derogatory comments designed to undermine his wife's confidence and self-esteem. He will use a variety of means to intimidate, such as threatening looks, or gestures, or smashing things in front of her to make sure she knows there will be violent consequences to not submitting. The abuser frequently hurts and threatens his wife emotionally, or physically, is excessively controlling, often forces her into sex to the point of rape, constantly checks up on her, and isolates her from her friends and family.

It is hard to conceive of any type of spousal abuse Sonny did not subject Happiness to. He engaged in the full gamut of mental, emotional, physical, and sexual abuse towards a woman who was trying desperately to hang on for the sake of her family. Happiness spent most of her time when she was alone, crying. She was trapped and she didn't know how to end the nightmare. Her common plea to God was "Why?" He had always been there for her, but where was He now, when she needed Him so much? She began to question Him, even to doubt some of His promises in the Bible, the book she had been raised to hold so dear. If she had not been so well grounded, she might have given up on God and His Word altogether at this point in her life.

The logical question everyone could be expected to have at this point is, why; why would anyone stay in such an abusive relationship? For Happiness, part of the reason was due to the effectiveness of Sonny's ability to intimidate her.

"I could not complain to anyone because I did not want to find out how life could be tougher than it already was. My husband made sure that I knew ahead of time that no one would come to my rescue and if I dared to embarrass his good image, I would pay greatly for it."

In short, as Happiness succinctly expresses it, *"I was afraid of him."* That is certainly understandable.

However, there was one final reason that prompted Happiness to stay in this abusive situation and not tell her parents or family. It is a reason much more difficult to understand, at least for those not familiar with a culture where family reputation is so highly valued. Happiness does her best to describe it.

"I was trying to protect my families' reputation and the Dike family name. I didn't want my parents to worry and suffer. I wanted them to keep the feelings they had when we were married, thinking I was happy. I didn't want to disappoint them."

Then she said something that shows the depth of sacrifice she was willing to pay to protect her parents. In words that haunt the most seared of consciences, she said, *"I wanted to keep the shame right here, where it wouldn't spread."* Those words reflect a depth of sacrificial love that even her anguished soul would not betray.

During the next few days, Sonny remained the same, never mentioning the incident that led Happiness to flee her own home in terror. Happiness did her best to cope, a difficult task made harder by the fact she couldn't tell her family. *I am trapped forever,* Happiness thought. She fed Queenette in silence and put her down for her afternoon nap. Then, as she had so many other days when she was alone, she wept.

After about an hour, her sobbing was interrupted by the phone. Happiness cleared her throat and tried to regain her composure as quickly as she could.

"Hello," she said hoarsely.

"Hello Happy, it's Ogu! What a joy to hear your voice! Listen, I have great news! The people at Howard University have agreed to give Sonny an internship here. He can begin this fall. How soon can the three of you get to Virginia?"

"Oh, Ogu, that is great news!" Happiness exclaimed. The thought of moving near her brother, someone who cared for her, seemed too good to be true.

"Great then! Well, tell Sonny to call me for the details, and start packing. I have to go now. Comfort wants to take the boys for a walk together."

Two thoughts clouded Happiness' mind as she considered this unexpected and wonderful development. First, she was fairly certain Sonny had not completed medical school as he had led everyone to believe. His paperwork from Mexico was taking far too long to arrive. Second, as badly as she wanted to, she knew she could never tell Ogu about how Sonny treated her. They were close friends, having attended the University of Alabama at Huntsville as roommates. She didn't want to spoil her brother's friendship. She would have to keep her silence. *Yet,* she hoped, *perhaps Sonny will be encouraged with this new career opportunity. Perhaps he will change.*

12

A BRIEF RESPITE IN VIRGINIA

※

It was late April or early May, 1984, when Sonny and Happiness packed up their belongings and made the 3,000 mile journey across the country to Alexandria, Virginia, where they moved in with her brother Ogu, his wife, Comfort, and their two little boys. Adding to the challenge of a cross-country move, Happiness was three-months pregnant with her second daughter.

However, the re-union with her brother was their first since he had left Nigeria six years ago and it was joyous for both of them. Happiness had always admired Ogu. He was smart, highly educated, and ambitious in a good way. Of course, he needed to be all that and more if he wanted to become a doctor. Ogu had always been a good brother to her and he reminded her of the family she treasured back home in Nigeria.

Ogu and Comfort's Alexandria apartment was a nice three-bedroom located on one of the upper floors of a modern high-rise. It was spacious for their family of three, but definitely cramped for two families totaling four adults and three children. Yet Happiness knew it would take them

a while to be able to afford a place of their own. Despite
the cramped quarters, she was secretly relieved. As long as
they were living with another family, Sonny would have to
keep his behavior under control.

Comfort welcomed Happiness like a sister, showing
her the ropes of the faster-paced city and getting her a job
at the home health care agency where she worked. The two
women worked alternative shifts, sharing childcare and
housekeeping duties. *Oh God, You have seen my suffering
and you have had mercy on me,* Happiness thought on more
than one occasion. Life was becoming bearable again, if
not outright promising.

Given the close living arrangements with Happiness'
brother, Sonny had to remain on his best behavior. It was a
protective environment for Happiness and, for the first time
in their brief marriage, she felt safe. She began to let herself
dream of a better life for she and her children, and to even
hope that Sonny might change into the husband he should
have been all along. Everything was going smoothly and
the two couples were meshing well together. That bonding
of the two couples was about to change.

SLAM! Sonny had returned from his clinical orientation
at Howard University, and his dour expression said that not
everything had gone well. Happiness' heart beat quickly: the
children were sleeping and she was otherwise alone in the
apartment. Why was he upset? She dared not ask.

Later that evening, she overheard Sonny and Ogu
talking in hushed tones. Sonny was still agitated, but under
control as he always was before his friend. What was going
on? It was a few days later before Sonny told Happiness.

*"The school administrators at Howard have messed up
my paperwork,"* Sonny began, doing his best to shift the
blame from himself. *"They insist that I have not completed
the requisite course work from the medical school in
Monterrey. They say I must finish that work, which will take*

at least one year, before they will allow me to resume my internship."

"Oh," Happiness replied. *I knew it!* she thought to herself. *I knew he was not studying. We left Mexico so suddenly and he never called anyone. He was never working that whole time.* "I have spoken to Ogu about it," Sonny continued. *"He agrees it is best that I return to Monterrey and complete my school requirements. Ogu and Comfort have offered to let you and Queenette stay here until I return."* Happiness' heart swelled with unexpected excitement. Living without her husband! She immediately envisioned a better life without him. Yet how could she impose on her brother and his wife this way?

The next morning, she approached her sister-in-law. *"Comfort, you have been more than a sister to me! I cannot possibly continue to take advantage of your kindness. You are working so hard, supporting Ogu through his internship and we will be in the way."*

"It is no trouble. Ogu will soon receive a stipend for his studies, and I will be able to stay home and take care of the boys," Comfort responded.

"But I will have the new baby soon," Happiness said tentatively.

"Of course you will. I will care for Queenette and your new baby. Nothing would please me more."

Was there ever a wife happier to say goodbye to her husband for one year so that she could work to support her two children alone? It is not likely. Upon Sonny's departure, life became peaceful for Happiness. For the first time since they left Nigeria, she would experience what it is like to make her own decisions, to function as a respected adult, and to walk in a freedom she once knew only through distant memory.

All continued well for Happiness while living with Ogu and Comfort until Ogu began receiving the stipend for his

studies and Comfort decided she could now afford to quit
working. That decision meant Comfort had less to spend
on clothes and other things she wanted. Compounding this
financial restriction, Comfort became frustrated watching
Happiness able to afford the nice clothes and other items
she enjoyed. The contrast between the two women became
more obvious with each paycheck Happiness received.
Even though Happiness would buy groceries for the family,
and brought home gifts for her sister-in-law, it wasn't
enough to eliminate the jealousy Comfort was feeling. Her
jealousy became even more pronounced when, after giving
birth to her second daughter Millicent in December, 1984,
Happiness found a higher-paying job.

Money was not the only reason for Comfort's jealousy.
She also resented having to watch Happiness' two girls.
No longer did she benefit from their prior arrangement of
taking turns watching each other's children when they were
working alternative shifts. Seeing the need to intervene, Ogu
suggested that Happiness seek to find herself a different
baby sitter. Unfortunately, even after Happiness did so, that
change was not enough. The damage in the relationship
between Comfort and Happiness seemed to be permanent;
a dynamic that noticeably changed the atmosphere in the
apartment. Even though Ogu enjoyed having his sister stay
with them, his wife was exhibiting greater hostility towards
Happiness. Happiness even began to hide in her bedroom to
reduce the tension, but that too failed to work.

The last straw came in March, 1985, about three
months after Millie was born. Happiness had to work late
one day and her child care provider was not able to watch
her girls. Comfort was filling in as the babysitter and she
became angry when Happiness was late getting home. By
the time Happiness arrived back at the apartment, Comfort
had reached her emotional limit. She could not maintain
any semblance of civility. Her emotions exploded with a

venom that had been building for months. Happiness felt
the full brunt of the tirade when she entered the apartment
and before she had even had a chance to hang up her coat.

"I want you to move out now," Comfort abruptly
announced, her face red with built up rage. *"Just get out!
Take your girls with you and get out,"* her voice rising in
volume. Happiness was stunned. This was no time to try to
discuss the issue rationally; Comfort had completely lost
her ability to deal with the situation. Happiness had no time
to make plans where she and her girls could go. Without a
word, she bundled her girls up in their coats, and the three
of them left the apartment as quickly as she could get them
out the door.

Outside, it was already getting dark and the air was
quite cold. Happiness had only one option. She walked over
to her child care provider's apartment, who lived a couple
blocks away, and knocked on her door. When Tamika
opened the door, she saw Happiness standing there holding
baby Millie, crying from the chilled air, while also holding
the tiny hand of her little girl, Queenette in the other.
Tamika had a small, unkempt apartment where she lived
with her two grown daughters. Whether it was sympathy
for the desperate plight they were in, or the thought of
getting more money out of her, Happiness would never
know, but regardless, Tamika agreed to take them in.

The situation was far from ideal. For the first time,
Happiness saw how her child care provider lived, and it
wasn't good. As they entered the house, the floor was still
covered with children's toys, and the couch and easy chair
were old and stained. The television was on, but the lights
in the apartment seemed awfully low. Happiness sat on the
couch with both children and awaited further instruction.

*"You gonna have to sleep out here, cause both my girls
be stayin here these days. I told 'em they grown and they
needa find a place, but you know, they know their momma*

gonna take care of 'em," Tamika explained. Happiness nodded.

Her first night passed less than peacefully. At 1:30 a.m., a man entered the apartment with a key, closed the door, went to the kitchen, ate a snack and went to one of the girls' bedrooms. After 3:00 a.m. another man banged incessantly on the door until one of Tamika's daughters opened it. They exchanged a brief but loud conversation and then the door slammed shut again. That time, Happiness had to get up and lock it herself. Naturally she was awakened each time the door opened unexpectedly, but her daughters remained mercifully asleep. *They must be used to these kinds of noises,* she thought with a shudder.

She awoke as she normally did at 5:45 a.m., washed as best as she could in the dingy bathroom, and dressed for work. She realized that the 7:00 a.m. to 3:00 p.m. shift that she worked meant that all the troublemakers had been asleep when she dropped her kids off and had woken up and left by the time she picked them up.

The next two weeks passed in similar discomfort. She slept with her children in the living room while men came and went at all hours of the night. Happiness later described it as a "typical ghetto atmosphere" with strange men coming in and out of the place as if they lived there. She bought groceries almost daily, which seemed to be consumed by anyone who happened to come by. She cringed as she saw the different men entering and exiting Tamika's and her girls' rooms. As if all that was not enough, Tamika also "milked" her for food money in addition to the child care money she was already paying, even though Happiness was buying her own food.

A few days after moving in, Happiness came home to find several men sitting around a coffee table where Tamika, along with her two teen-age daughters, were dealing drugs, specifically a white powder kept in small plastic bags. That was it. She and her girls could no longer stay in that place

The next morning she got up an hour earlier than normal, bought a paper and scanned the advertisements for apartments. *I will have to figure out what I can afford,* she thought. She calculated her monthly income after taxes, along with her needs for groceries, childcare and other essentials. *How much do they charge for electricity and water?* She wondered. Sonny had always taken care of the bills. After work that day she stopped by to visit an unfurnished, two-bedroom apartment that was available in a safer area of Alexandria. Finding it suitable, she completed the lease application, provided her proof of employment, and was approved for the apartment that very day. The same woman who could hardly cash her own paycheck just a year ago, now had found, negotiated, and signed the lease on her own apartment!

Of course she had nothing to put in that apartment but herself, her clothes, and her daughters. But it did not matter, at least they were safe. She purchased a pot and a few plates, they ate on the floor, and slept on a blanket together on the floor. She also found a government supplemented childcare facility that was clean and drug free.

Happiness continued to take the girls to church with her, even though she was often exhausted from working. Her days off were otherwise consumed with taking the girls to the laundromat on foot and by bus to the grocery store. Even little Queenette could hold a small bag of groceries on her own now.

Over time, and with the help of some local churches, Happiness was able to obtain some donated furniture and fix her little apartment up nicely. It became a place of refuge for her. It was both clean and safe, but there was a more significant reason this apartment meant so much to her. Happiness was finding out who she was as a person.

She now saw for the first time that she could take care of herself and her daughters and do a good job of it.

The next week, Happiness was balancing her bankbook when she realized that after just five months of paying rent, utilities, groceries, childcare, taxes and other bills on her own, she had saved up over $700. She started calculating her bus fare, plus all the hours it took her to wait for the bus, the extra trips to the grocery store and laundromat because she couldn't carry everything at once. Then she began to look in the classified ads for used cars.

Two days later, she arrived at the babysitter's house in an old Plymouth Volare. She smiled remembering how she bargained with the gentleman who was selling it, talking him down from $800 to $550. These were skills her father would never have dreamed his little Happy would have been forced to learn, but she had learned them successfully. Although her car was far from fancy, it was hers, and as she would laugh about it later, *"God kept it running."*

Happiness was also establishing a solid home life for herself and her daughters. Like her father before her, Happiness made sure she and her daughters regularly attended church, and she would constantly pray for God's protection and blessing over her girls. Happiness had not forgotten her "invisible friend" through all the things she had been through, despite some of the doubts she experienced in California.

Sometime in June, 1985, while her girls were playing in the living room and she was putting away the groceries she had just bought, the phone rang. It must be Ogu she thought, he was the only one who had her number.

"Hello Happy," said a familiar voice through a crackled connection.

"Sonny!" her heart stopped.

"I have finished my medical school requirements. I am coming home."

In the conversation that followed, she found herself telling him of the apartment she had obtained and a little about the life she and the girls were leading. Sonny actually sounded pleased. In a tone of voice she had rarely heard from him, Sonny uttered words she thought she would never hear; *"I am proud of you; you have done really well."* In that moment, Happiness allowed herself to believe that her marriage could be turned around, that all would be right again, and she forgot about all the abuse she had been through.

The day Sonny returned home was a blur to Happiness and the details of that day have faded. What she does remember about that time is the change of heart she had towards a man she had thought she hated. When he had left for Mexico roughly a year before, she had been secretly relieved and glad to see him go. Now that he was back, to her surprise, she was genuinely excited to have him home. For his part, Sonny was genuinely excited too. Why wouldn't he be? He came back to a place of his own, nicely furnished, decorated, clean, and in order. Happiness had done well; God had seen her through, and now she was experiencing a glimpse of marriage as it should be; as she had always hoped it would be.

13

"WHAT AM I GOING TO DO?"

The glimpse Happiness received of a complimentary husband and a normal marriage would not be sustained. Sonny acted the part of a normal husband for only a few days, just long enough for him to become familiar with his new surroundings. Then, empowered by familiarity, he re-asserted his abusive control. However, unbeknownst to Sonny, there was a new dynamic in the relationship. No longer was Happiness a naïve, unknowing young girl. Now she knew she could take care of herself; knew she was capable; and knew what it was like to finally experience some freedom.

As Happiness began to ignore his threats and verbal abuses, Sonny would grab her by both shoulders and force her to stand in front of him while he was speaking to her. If she dared to speak in her defense, he would yell at her to "shut up," push her away, then grab her and forcefully pull her back in front of him. Sexually, he continued his old method of brute force: she felt she had no choice but to submit to his demands on his terms and his timing.

After several more months of such abuse, Happiness became pregnant again. *Oh God, what shall I do? Still my husband shakes me, screams at me, and cares nothing for our girls. How can I bring another child into this house?*

As Happiness expected, the news was not well received by her husband. *"You are pregnant again?"* Sonny asked indifferently. *"I do not see why you are telling me. I'm sure it is someone else's child; I know it's not mine. Just get rid of it. The American women do it at the hospital every day."* He did not even look up from the television. Happiness' heart beat with rage. *How dare he accuse me of being with another man? It is he that stays out all night after work, and returns home smelling of drink and perfume.* Clearly his accusation of her infidelity was a calculated and cold-hearted means to attack her reputation and bring her added shame.

His attack affected her more than she expected. To hear such a ridiculous assertion riled her to the very depths of her emotions. She could not believe his arrogance and hypocrisy. She was being accused of infidelity by a husband who had already produced two children out of wedlock in Mexico and who had left a long trail of women he had fooled around with. Who even knew how many children he could have fathered had it not been for possible abortions or birth control that conveniently hid his numerous indiscretions. Beyond the anger though, Happiness recognized a consequence from his attack that left her feeling not just additionally burdened, but overwhelmed. She knew his response assured her she could expect to receive no help from him in raising another child.

Ordinarily, Happiness would recognize her baby as a gift of God. She would understand its precious destiny and purpose from the hands of a loving Lord. But Happiness was no longer the same woman to which the word "ordinarily" applied. Life for Happiness had long since ceased to be remotely "ordinary." She had reached the point where she could think of little else but her hopelessness.

Happiness had become worn down emotionally by the constant abuse, the lack of affection, and the pure hatred her husband exhibited toward her. As her husband, Sonny was the one person she most needed support from, especially now that he had gotten her pregnant. Yet she knew such support would not be forthcoming.

That realization brought her more fatigue and discouragement. She was in a vicious cycle of despair. Each morning sunrise failed to bring any new glimmer of hope or hint of coming restoration. Instead, it brought another re-run episode of emotional and physical hurt. The only mystery to her life was not knowing how bad it would become before darkness brought her day to a merciful close. This was not what she had dreamed about back in her college dorm room in Port Harcourt, Nigeria when she asked God for a husband and four children. Now she was just trying to survive each day, without joy, comfort, and certainly without love.

So it was that Happiness reached a decision she would not have made under "ordinary" circumstances. The next morning she dropped her children at daycare and, instead of going to work, she returned home after she knew Sonny was gone, calling in sick. She made an appointment with a Nigerian doctor, a gynecologist, and drove to his office that morning. Dr. Achebe welcomed her into his office with a warm smile.

"Well hello, Happiness Dike. Please sit down. The nurse tells me that you are expecting," he said.

"Yes, Doctor, it is so," she answered.

"You do not seem as happy as your name," he remarked kindly.

"My husband is a cruel man; he has said that the baby is another man's, but I assure you Doctor, I have known no other man."

He listened patiently as Happiness spoke. He sympathized with her plight since he understood the Nigerian culture where an accusation of infidelity was a serious assault upon a woman's reputation. *"Of course you have not,"* the doctor assured her. *"I can tell that you are a virtuous woman."* Happiness was relieved that he trusted her. From the moment she entered his office, Dr. Achebe was observing her closely. He suspected a woman who was being abused by her husband. He knew the tell tale signs.

"I do not think that I can have this baby, Doctor," Happiness said, her voice quivering.

"What are you saying Happiness? Are you asking me to abort your baby?" Dr. Achebe's use of the term "abort" made her uncomfortable. Happiness looked down at her lap. This is what she had contemplated once Sonny had accused her and suggested it, but she could not bring herself to say it out loud.

"I understand why you want that, Happiness. As you say, you are married to a mean man. This is your third child and you will have to work, clean and care for all the children by yourself. This is true. But I do not think I should take this new baby away from you." Happiness looked up at him in confusion. *"You see,"* he explained, *"I can look in your eyes and see that if I do this thing for you, you will cry many more bitter tears of regret than if you have this baby. I have seen it. I have seen women like you, and when I take the baby away, they are not relieved. Their lives do not become easier. Instead of only hating their husbands, they learn to hate themselves even more."*

Happiness shuddered. In her heart, she knew he was right. They talked for a little while longer, and he took down the rest of her medical history. On her way out, she made an appointment for a follow-up visit, still startled by what just happened. She hadn't expected the strong encouragement the doctor gave her. Nor was it typical behavior of busy doctors in the Washington metro area. In what can only be described as a divine miracle, orchestrated by the sovereignty of God Himself, this doctor, who routinely had no qualms about accepting a patient's money and giving them their requested abortion, was actually convincing his patient to forego such a procedure. Based on such an unusual consultation, Happiness re-considered her decision to abort her child, although she still had many concerns.

The next few weeks passed without incident. Happiness' days began early in the morning by fixing the girls' breakfast, braiding their hair, packing their lunches and snacks, dropping them at daycare and going to work. Then she would run errands, pick them up and prepare dinner. Sonny would occasionally come home for dinner, about which he complained incessantly, but more often than not he would be at work for an unspecified amount of hours and then "out." Sonny's paycheck now disappeared into the unknown abyss, but he once again demanded Happiness' pay as well, giving her small amounts for food, diapers and grudgingly for gas.

Happiness did her best to recall her doctor's words of encouragement now that she was confronted with the same abusive nightmare that sent her to get an abortion in the first place. But now she had an additional concern: as Sonny began to realize that Happiness was not going to terminate her pregnancy, he became more angry and violent towards her.

He began physically assaulting her without provocation; actions he knew could and should cause her to have a miscarriage. He purposefully tried to hit her in the stomach, while she curled up protectively on the bed, screaming for him to stop and doing her best to block his blows at her baby. When he wasn't beating her, he was piercing her with hate-filled eyes, staring at her like she was contemptible trash not worthy of placement in a garbage can. Such phys-

ical and emotional assaults were devastating. Happiness'
world was collapsing on her once again.

Despite the kind words of her doctor, she felt virtually alone, and her thoughts were approaching suicide. She
hated her life and wanted out. The worthlessness she felt
was like a heavy anchor, trying to pull her head beneath the
waves. She instinctively knew if she allowed her head to
slip beneath the water, she would not be coming back up.
She needed a life preserver fast.

She made an emergency appointment with her doctor.
He immediately discerned her dire situation and knew
he had a patient that was close to the edge. The examina-
tion revealed that Happiness was either further along in
her pregnancy than she realized, or she was carrying an
exceptionally large baby. The conception date she had told
him did not match her physical condition. Dr. Achebe was
convinced Happiness had the wrong date of conception, so
he sent her to the Alexandria hospital to get a sonogram.
This sonogram would produce yet another surprise at a
time when Happiness could not handle much more.

While Happiness laid on a table, the gentle hand of
a nurse slowly glided a sonogram instrument over her
enlarged belly. As the nurse expertly guided the instrument,
she watched the sonogram screen intently, squinting her
eyes to see more clearly. *"There's your baby, Mrs. Dike,"*
the nurse's voice was calm and assuring as she continued
to stare at the screen. It seemed that there was something
else the nurse was trying to see. She kept manipulating the
sonogram instrument over Happiness' belly. Then the nurse
smiled and nodded her head, as if to confirm what she had
suspected. With words that hit Happiness hard, the nurse
made a further announcement, *"Just as I thought; here is
another one; you have twins."*

As Happiness would later describe it, she felt as if
"they had drawn all the blood out of my body." Again,

had this been a situation where she was in a loving and supportive marriage, she probably would have been over-joyed with excitement. But that was not her situation. At first Happiness acted in denial, practically accusing the nurse of not knowing what she was talking about. Patiently, the nurse allowed Happiness to see the screen for herself, pointing out the two separate babies in her womb.

Seeing the disappointment on her patient's face, the nurse tried to encourage Happiness that everything would work out. She talked about how lucky she was and how special it would be, but Happiness was not listening. Happiness had already drawn into an emotional cocoon filled with frantic anxiety and fear. The remaining minutes on the sonogram table, her walk back down the hospital corridors, then her crossing through the parking lot to her car, were all a complete blur. Her body was now on auto-pilot while her mind emotionally paged through one disas-trous thought after another.

Physically she knew she was small, and she was afraid the delivery of twins would be dangerous. Coupled with the physical abuse she would likely continue to undergo, by her due date she could be gravely weakened both mentally and physically. Emotionally, she knew that even if she were able to survive the pregnancy and subsequent childbirth, she would be stuck with the responsibility of raising four young children on her own. Her husband would be of no help. She would be expected to raise these children on her own and to work full time, all while trying to dodge further abuses hurled her way.

Happiness had reached her breaking point. As she drove home from the hospital, she became convinced this would be how she would die; either through complications with her pregnancy or in childbirth. Either way, she figured she was at the end of her life. It was all too much for her to handle. The devil was attacking her ruthlessly; completely robbing her of the joy such an event should have produced had this been a normal marriage. What was worse, she was allowing her overwhelming circumstances to blind her to see or seek her invisible friend who had always been there for her in the past. She was unconsciously pushing God away where she couldn't hear Him.

Once she had returned home from the sonogram, what few emotional levies she had left, were completely breached by the flood of tears that poured forth. She couldn't stop the onslaught of rushing emotions any longer. God now came to her mind, but not in a soothing way. She was a woman with no answers, drowning in a sea of disappointment and hopelessness. Why, she wondered, did God allow her to keep experiencing such misery? Why would He not allow her to experience a normal life like everyone else? She knew God existed and she knew He was sovereign. What she didn't know was why this was happening to her. It would be several hours before she either ran out of tears or the energy to cry them out.

The next morning, still drained and dejected, she called her brother Ogu for advice. As he listened to his younger sister pouring out what was left of her emotions, he could tell she was dangerously distraught. In a torrent of words, all painted in defeat, Happiness finally blurted out what had been most prominent on her heart; *"Ogu, I don't think I can make it through this; I think I'm going to die."* Ogu assured her she would not die, with the calming influence that only a loving older brother could provide. *"But how can I do this?"* Happiness persisted, *"I already have two little girls and a husband who will not help me; how can I handle twins on top of all that?"* Ogu's next words had to have been of divine origin, for they instantly got Happiness' attention. In a sure, steady voice of faith, Ogu told her the words she needed to hear: *"God would not have given you twins if He knew you could not take care of them."*

To Happiness, God had never been just a theory or
a theological fine point; He was real and He had always
been real. She had been the frequent recipient of His love,
His compassion, and His protection. Even when she had
allowed herself to forget Him, He never forgot her. Ogu's
words touched her. They reminded her that God was in
control, even if she couldn't see it. Surely her Lord had a
purpose in all this, and His purposes were always good,
even if His ways were not always understood. From that
moment through the rest of her pregnancy, Happiness held
onto her brother's words and vowed to carry on as God
gave her the strength to do so. She said a silent prayer to
the Lord as she committed to go through with the pregnancy; *"When I go into labor Lord, if I die, that is okay; it
just means that you are taking me home."*

Throughout the rest of her pregnancy, Sonny did his
best to make things hard on her. He refused to lift a hand
to assist her with the children, with the housework, or with
the cooking, isolating himself in front of the television.
Periodically he would still physically abuse her, although
the worst of the beatings seemed to have subsided. She
was left to get the children to their day care, and forced to
continue working at her job up to the very latest stage in
her pregnancy.

Sometime during her eighth month of pregnancy,
Happiness and Sonny had a heated argument. Happiness
was no longer backing down to him. She had been through
too much. He could no longer intimidate her. Her response
Sonny viewed as insolence, an attitude which was too much
for him to allow. In a moment, Sonny had wrenched her
off the couch by her shoulders, and thrown her to the floor
so that she landed on her stomach. She cried out in pain,
and felt a warm liquid begin to trickle down her legs. *I am
bleeding or losing fluid. Oh God, the baby!* Sonny slammed
the bedroom door and did not emerge. Panicked, Happiness

called 911, notified them of what happened, and within
minutes was being whisked away by paramedics to the
hospital. Her doctor had been notified and when he arrived
and had a chance to examine her, he gave her the bad news.
One of her twins was about to suffocate with the umbilical
cord wrapped around its neck. The only way to save the
baby was to perform an emergency caesarian section.

There was no time to discuss the matter. The decision
was made and the doctors and nurses began preparing
Happiness for surgery. She was now at the point she had
previously feared; delivery of her babies. She recalled her
brother's words of assurance and she recalled her prayers
to the Lord. Her "invisible friend" would not let her down.
Understanding the seriousness of the moment however, she
re-committed herself to the Lord, and she committed her
twins and her daughter's lives to the Lord. She was in His
hands now; it was out of her control. Still she fought her
emotions, half expecting to die, half expecting to live. She
put her mind into "survival mode" as she had done so many
times before when facing unbearable pain and hardship.

Happiness lay in silence on the gurney as she was
prepped for surgery. She begged the Lord to spare her
babies, but prayed no prayer for herself. *I am ready to be
with You, Lord.* She felt her legs go numb and watched
them take her to the OR. *Who will care for my children if
I die? Esther would take them, I know she would.* A screen
was erected to prevent her from seeing the surgery itself.

The doctor and nurses busied themselves for the surgery
as if she wasn't even there. Her mind wandered, wondering
what would become of her and her children if she survived.
She soon lost track of time. Then, out of the fog of her
dream-like state, she heard the words, *"It's a boy;* as the
medical staff continued their work. Three minutes later
she heard, *"It's another boy."* The voice of the doctor was
calm and professional and it mingled with the babies' cries.

"Congratulations Mrs. Dike, they both look good. The baby with the prolapsed cord needs to go to the pediatric intensive care unit right away, but he looks fine. Don't worry. We're sewing you up right now." Sweet relief flooded over her. She heard the soothing cries from two healthy babies: God had answered her prayers twice over.

Then she heard another voice; that of her husband. He was gloating as he leaned over the hospital bed to tell her that "we" had male children. The word "we" struck Happiness as being completely inappropriate. After denying the children were his, urging her to have an abortion, beating her and trying to cause her to have a miscarriage; after refusing to assist her in any way, and after berating her without mercy, now he was telling her that "we" have twin boys. He hadn't even helped get her to the emergency room. Never had such a simple word sounded so twisted.

In a way, she marveled at how his shamelessness seemed to have no bounds. It was like a dagger stabbing her in the heart, except this time, she would not let it hurt her. She wanted to bask in the warmth and glow of what God had done. So as the medical staff wrapped up the surgery, Happiness ignored her husband and allowed herself to enjoy the moments of peace and contentment she was feeling. Her "invisible friend" had done it again. She felt so close to her Lord, she realized she had not experienced any pain in the childbirth. Even as she continued to lay in her hospital bed, God was busy pouring forth His love and affection upon her. She realized now that her doctor had been right; she was grateful she had kept her twin boys. These were moments she treasured in a marriage that to this point had contained so few.

It would be a few days before Happiness was strong enough to leave the hospital and she couldn't wait to take her two new baby boys home with her. She gave her first boy the name of Johnson, or JD and her second boy she named Charles Azundah, both born on October 10th of 1986. Of course, Azundah was her father's middle name. Although the boys shared her husband's last name of Dike, she didn't really consider them his, regardless of his gloating assertions to the contrary. These boys belonged to God and she merely had them on loan on His behalf. There really was no other honest way to look at them. When she considered all the efforts the enemy made through her depression to give them up in abortion, or through her husband's beatings, to take them from her, JD and Charles were truly miraculous gifts from God. Her gratitude to God was deep, for only He could have protected those two precious boys.

Due to the extra trauma JD had experienced with the umbilical cord wrapped around his neck, he was kept in an incubator for many days after his birth. Coupled with the extra days Happiness was also kept in the hospital to recover, the extra time became a temporary oasis, giving Happiness the chance to begin bonding with her boys. During those precious peaceful days in the hospital, Happiness nestled Charles close, treasuring his little toes and fingers, kissing his stomach and cheek to her heart's content. JD was still in an incubator, but she caressed his feet with her finger and gazed at him joyfully. She talked to them whenever they were in her care, telling them all the wonderful things they would do in their lives, how well they would do in school and what wonderful men they would become. This time in the hospital was such a blessing to her. She knew once she returned home, she would have no assistance. For now though, she experienced the relief of having others wait on her and attend to the needs or her and her boys.

Her heart ached when at last she and Charles were released to go home, and she knew she must leave JD in his incubator. The doctors had insisted that JD stay another week for observation to give him more time to gain his strength, but Happiness came to visit him every day. As she held her first-born son, she whispered words to him not unlike what her father had whispered to her almost 25 years before; that she would do all she could to protect him, his brother and his sisters. As this grateful mother spoke her gentle words to her son, JD looked directly into her eyes and smiled. It was as if he understood all that she was saying to him and was communicating back to her in the only way he knew how, with a trusting, innocent smile.

There was a special bond she had with her twin boys, and especially with JD, who she came so close to losing. They were the little babies she almost had aborted in a state of extreme depression and hopelessness. How glad she was for a doctor who encouraged her to keep them. As difficult as she knew it would be, she also knew these two boys, along with her two little girls, would now be the main source of hope and encouragement she would have to get her through.

In a special way, life had come full circle for her. Much like her father did with her in that small Nigerian hospital many years earlier, she had now done with her twin boys, dedicating them to God's ultimate protection and care, yet promising to do her part to protect them as well.

Life had come full circle in another way for Happiness. She now had, thanks to these twin boys, the four children she had prayed for as a young girl in the dorm room bunk-bed that day she "cut a deal" with God; specifically two girls and two boys, exactly as she had prayed. Although she would have one more pregnancy, Happiness would never give birth to another child, as God well knew. So for her prayer to be answered, this last pregnancy needed to produce twins, and her twins both needed to be boys! Thus, while Happiness had been initially overwhelmed by the news of twins, in retrospect, God was merely answering the prayers of a formerly distraught girl whose heart's desire was to have four children. God had given her the desire of her heart. He had never forgotten her prayer of those many years earlier. It was yet another way her "invisible friend" showed Happiness He would never leave her nor forsake her.

Dr. Achebe was right, she reflected gratefully. *And Ogu was right. And God has given me two girls and two boys, just as I had always hoped. So perhaps He has not forgotten about me after all.*

—

God certainly did His part, giving Happiness enough grace to care for the growing girls, peaceful Charles, and JD who continued to need extra help and attention. Their routine returned to the way it was, with Happiness rising early, caring for the children, working full time and returning home to do all the other things that needed to be done. Sonny continued to live his life as he pleased, oblivious to his responsibilities.

Only church offered a much needed respite from her weekly marathon of work, childrearing, and household duties. At church, she could relax, singing the hymns from childhood that reminded her of happier times. Her children loved it too, and many of the people at the church, despite the fact that most were white, gravitated towards her and showed her much kindness.

It wasn't long before not just her own church, but several other local churches heard of Happiness' plight and she began to receive several well-meaning visitors; some by prior appointment; some who would just knock on the door unannounced. All were welcome. One of them was an elder from the Woodbridge Seventh Day Adventist Church who offered them marriage counseling, but Sonny refused to cooperate with the effort, going so far as to accuse

Happiness of having an affair with the elder. Anyone who was pleasant to Happiness, Sonny resented.

There was a clear difference in the way Happiness was treated. While Sonny treated her like trash to be discarded; everyone else from church treated her with respect and admiration; a person of value. They saw what Sonny refused to see; a hard-working, conscientious woman who refused to give in to overwhelmingly difficult circumstances. Through it all, she remained a faithful mother to her four small children, and such strength of character was drawing people to her in a very genuine way. It must have been difficult for Sonny to hear so many church people tell him how blessed he was to have such a wonderful wife and family.

It was only natural that Happiness began to develop bonds of friendship with many church members who came to visit her, especially several who came from a local Baptist church in downtown Alexandria. One lady in particular, Mrs. West, took a special interest in Happiness, showing her a genuine love for Christ. This lady was an elderly Caucasian woman. That fact struck Happiness as odd, for Happiness had frequently experienced a quiet, yet unmistakable, resentment and discrimination from many Caucasians in her life. This was the first Caucasian to befriend her in such an authentic way.

Mrs. West wrote Happiness special greeting cards of encouragement at least three times a month, telling Happiness how much she loved her and how much God loved her. It was as if the Lord, knowing how much she needed encouragement, had brought this lady across her path at just the right time. Mrs. West always seemed to understand what Happiness was going through in a sort of unspoken bond. It was almost as if she lived with Happiness and saw with her own eyes the steady abuse that occurred behind closed doors. This unassuming elderly

Caucasian woman was demonstrating what Happiness knew, but rarely experienced, that in God's kingdom, skin color did not matter. It was also a much needed reminder, that regardless of how bad things can become in life, God's love always triumphs over evil.

14

SHELTERED FROM ABUSE

❧

"*Ah, my little Happy! You have done well.*" Mr. Emejuru nestled his grandchildren against his sides in a warm embrace. They were at Ogu's apartment, where her father was staying for his all too brief visit to America. Until now he had known his grandchildren only through pictures and letters. In their shining eyes he could see his legacy: their sharp intelligence, joyful laughter and love for their mother. Now he had a memory to treasure for the rest of his life.

Mr. Emejuru had been meaning to come for quite a while, but only since he retired had he been able to find the time to make the trip. He stayed with Ogu, as tradition would dictate, but saw his Happy everyday and the handful of weeks went by quickly. For much of her time with her father, Happiness' countenance once again reflected her name. She and Ogu showed him many sights in the nation's capital, but for this grandfather, he truly treasured his time with his beautiful grandchildren.

While seeing his grandchildren brought him great joy, this visit was difficult for Mr. Emejuru. Although he was not as strong or energetic as he had once been, his eyes were as

observant and his mind as sharp as ever. He saw first hand
what Happiness had tried so desperately to keep hidden
from him; that her life did not fit the serene and joyous
descriptions she had been giving him through letters back
home. Though Happiness was careful not to say anything,
Mr. Emejuru could tell her situation was not good.

There were many subtle, yet clear indicators. Despite
the money he, and the Dike family had been sending
throughout the marriage, Sonny and Happiness were
not living in the kind of place he had hoped they would.
Moreover, despite Sonny's best efforts to conceal his
mistreatment of Happiness, Mr. Emejuru perceived problems in the marriage as well. Even though he was too much
of a loving father to mention it to Happiness, she could tell
that he knew and that he was saddened by it.

Too soon, it was time for Ogu and Happiness to take
their father to the airport. As they walked him to the gate,
Mr. Emejuru's face betrayed his sadness. No matter how
well his daughter hid it, he now knew that he had failed
to keep the last part of his vow in that hospital room so
many years ago. He had protected her through war, famine
and genocide. He had seen that she was raised well and
had received the best education. He had married her into a
prominent and wealthy family, but he had married her off to
a terrible man.

"Goodbye, Papa," Happiness said with the same tender
smile she had always saved for him.

"Goodbye, my Happy." He said a little prayer to
himself; *"Oh God, have mercy on her. Give her the strength
that she needs to see this through."*

Following their goodbyes, Happiness watched as her
father walked through the security checkpoint and down
the concourse toward his departure gate. She observed
him closely as he walked away into the midst of fellow
travelers, fighting to seal the memory of the moment in

her mind, much like she had done when she was on the plane departing Nigeria as a new bride. Her tear-filled eyes tracked him until he was out of sight, then she too said a little prayer to the Lord, *"Please Lord, let me see him one more time."* It was more of a desperate plea than a prayer, for she was already sensing that this might be the last time she would see her father on this side of heaven. He meant so much to her. How would she ever handle his loss?

—

It wasn't long thereafter that Sonny and Happiness realized their six-member family had outgrown the original two-bedroom apartment that Happiness had obtained during Sonny's studies in Mexico. They began to save for a bigger place and in the fall of 1987, they relocated to a three-bedroom apartment, not far from their old apartment in Alexandria. Now there could be a separate bedroom for both the girls and the boys.

Their new surroundings did not change Sonny's disposition. For the most part, Sonny remained aloof, refusing to interact with the family or assist in any responsibilities. Sonny focused on Sonny and Happiness focused on her children, pouring her energy and emotions into their lives. In large measure, she was able to ignore her husband's selfish behavior, seeking contentment through her children.

When Sonny was not aloof, he was ridiculously controlling, often losing his temper over the most mundane incidents. One of those incidents occurred in early December, 1987. Upon returning home from work, Sonny barged into the apartment angry about something. When he saw the typewriter cover on the floor, it set him aflame like gasoline to burning embers. He became enraged.

"What is this typewriter doing on the floor?!" Sonny demanded. Happiness looked out to the living room from

the kitchen and saw that the veins in his forehead were already throbbing with rage.

"Charles put it there. He wanted to help me type some of my letters," Happiness answered calmly. *"I will put it away; it is I who uses it anyway—"* Sonny rushed past her to the boys' bedroom, and kicked the door open with a bang. A shriek let Happiness know that little Charles had been struck by the door.

The force of the blow was severe, splitting the little boy's head open at the forehead. Charles began crying hysterically, prompted partially by the pain of the blow and partially by the shock of seeing his own blood pouring down his face onto the floor. Happiness responded instinctively, pushing Sonny out of the way, grabbing her little boy, and carrying him to the car to get him to the emergency room. By the time they arrived, Happiness' clothes were covered in dried blood, her face and hands were blood smeared from holding her son close to her, and somehow, she even managed to get some blood in her hair. Of course her son looked even worse, the result of a deep wound that was slow in clotting. Even the ER nurse, by no means a novice at seeing blood, was startled by the sight of them as she handed Happiness the registration form.

"He will need some stitches, Mrs. Dike, but he will be fine," the ER doctor informed her. *"You can come and hold him for us if you like."*

"Of course," she answered numbly, too relieved to say much else. They walked down the hall together to a small operating room. Happiness held Charles as the doctor set to work with the stitches. A nurse handed the doctor what he needed and smiled at her kindly.

"How did this happen, Mrs. Dike?" the doctor asked. Happiness said nothing. The doctor finished his work and motioned to the nurse to cover the sutures with a bandage. He looked at Happiness directly and repeated his question.

Happiness again said nothing, but an urge to expose her situation began to rise up inside her.

Although Happiness would not realize it until much later, this traumatic incident would prove to be a breakthrough for her and her children. Though she knew God would never cause such a potential tragedy, He would use it to bring a release and freedom to a woman who had not known any since she had been free of Sonny during the one year he was completing his medical studies in Mexico. Now, for the first time in her marriage, she took the opportunity to inform a non-family member about the physical and mental abuse she had suffered at the hands of her husband.

She had never chosen to do so before since the abuse had always been directed at her. But this time was different. By attacking her child, Sonny had crossed an invisible, but definite line. She had already vowed to God to do all she could to protect her children. It was not a vow she had made lightly. Now that her little boy had been hurt, Happiness did not hold back.

"It was my husband, Doctor. He struck the boy with the door. It was an accident."

"I see. And how often do such accidents happen?" he inquired.

"Never before with the children."

"But perhaps these accidents have happened to you many times?"

"Yes."

"I see. Mrs. Dike, I know that this is a very difficult thing to discuss. I have a duty to report this to the appropriate child and social welfare agencies, but I do not want you to be afraid. They know how to handle such situations. They will not inform anyone whom you do not want to tell. They will not ask you about your immigration status or anything like that."

"Thank you doctor." Someone outside the family knows. There was no turning back now.

The next day, a social worker contacted Happiness to confirm what she had reported to the doctor. She asked a few more questions and then presented Happiness with a choice.

"Mrs. Dike, it is not safe for you and your children to continue to live here. The county can provide you with an alternative place to live. It is a homeless shelter for abused women and their children and it is not far. Your daughter can stay in the same school and your other children can remain in their current childcare facility. You will be safe there and the staff will provide you with the protection that you need." Happiness said nothing, but her mind was racing. Was this possible? Could she really leave Sonny?

"How many women live in this shelter?" she asked cautiously. It had never occurred to her that others may have experienced the marital abuse that was her daily lot in life.

"There are between seven and ten at any given time. I can assure you that many women have been in the situation you are in; too many. Yet we have been able to help a lot of them. There is nothing outside the house that makes it obvious who is living there. You will be safe, if we can get you out of here when your husband is not home. That way he will not know where you are. Will you go?" Happiness paused for a moment.

The social worker spoke in a way that made Happiness believe, for the first time, that she might actually be able to get out of her abusive situation. It also made Happiness realize that there were other women in similar abusive marriages and, best of all, there was a way to escape it all. Happiness grew cautiously excited.

"I will go," Happiness answered decisively.

They arranged a date and time for the social worker to come by while Sonny was at work so he would not be aware of her leaving, could not follow her, and would not

know where she was. As excited as she was becoming
at the thought of escaping her abuse, Happiness had to
pretend like nothing was different in front of Sonny. She
worked hard to control her emotions and remain cautious,
yet inside, she was giddy with excitement. She wanted to
scream with joy, she wanted to sing and shout, she wanted
to dance, but she could do none of those things. She had
to maintain her same demeanor at all costs. She didn't
want to blow this opportunity. *Oh God, can this be true?
Can I build a life away from Sonny? I am so excited! More
excited than I have been since I was a little girl.*

On the day planned for the move, Happiness waited for
Sonny to leave for work before doing anything. Once he
was gone, she hastily packed their necessary belongings
in a couple suitcases and hauled them out to her car. She
would have to leave most of her possessions behind, the
shelter had no room for them, and they had no time for a
protracted move. At the appointed hour, the social worker
arrived as promised, and Happiness and her children
followed her in their car to the homeless women's shelter in
Alexandria.

On the outside, the shelter was purposely incon-
spicuous. It looked like a typical house with no signs or
other markings that would indicate it was a shelter for
battered women. Inside there were separate rooms for each
woman and her children. The large living room served as
a "community room" where they held weekly counseling
meetings and various social gatherings. In the back was a
kitchen and near the front door, there was a reception area
where the house director worked and staff could monitor
everyone's comings and goings. Men were not allowed in
the house at any time.

*"You must never disclose the location of this house,
Mrs. Dike,"* the house director cautioned firmly. *"Not
even to your family members or friends. This is a tempo-*

rary place to stay until you can build a life on your own. Your oldest daughter will continue in school and you can continue working, but you must never tell her teachers or the daycare workers where you live." Happiness was more than eager to comply.

Life in the shelter was regimented, but to Happiness it was liberating. All meals were provided free which meant she could once again open her own bank account and begin saving her money. Following breakfast, mandatory meetings were held each morning in the community room at which time each woman explained the progress she had made in getting job skills, education, or a place to live. As long as the women were making progress, they were allowed to stay in the house, but their activities were closely monitored.

The weekly counseling meetings offered a glimpse into the lives of her new housemates. She heard the story of one woman named Linda who was beaten by her husband to the point of unconsciousness. He then tied her up in a trash bag and left her for dead on the side of the road. She was discovered by a jogger and needed six months of medical care and rehabilitation in order to recover. *I am not the only one. There are others who have suffered even worse than I have.*

The counselors were extremely helpful in attending to the women's deep and varied emotional needs and helping them to deal with what they had been through. Each woman's story was a tale of sadness and pain; but most of the women saw this shelter experience as a new beginning and a step towards independence. All of the residents were encouraged to obtain necessary job skills, find work, or go to school. Although a few of the women failed to embrace the challenge, most did.

Happiness was particularly excited about getting back to college. Given her father's emphasis on education, she could not imagine a life without going back to school. She decided to start part-time with computer classes at Strayer University while working two jobs; one as a nursing assistant and the other as a housekeeper. The opportunities at the shelter were endless, including information and free assistance to help the women apply for food stamps, apply for jobs or job training, and even legal help.

Happiness was in her element. She always thrived in a structured environment and she found the protective atmosphere was a "refreshing" change where she finally felt safe. This move into the battered women's shelter was exactly what she needed. For the first time since she left Nigeria, she felt as if she had allies in her corner who not only cared about what happened to her, but who had the authority and resources to make things happen. As she would describe it later, *"it was very powerful"* to realize that she and her children were now protected from abuse. Happiness eagerly took advantage of every opportunity the shelter provided.

Shelter staff provided her with her own attorney to go to court to obtain a legal separation and Protective Order against her husband, as well as a child support order. Two ladies from the shelter staff even accompanied her and her lawyer to the court hearing. The support she received was overwhelming to her. She had not experienced such support since she had been married. The court granted each of her requests and now, supported by the law, Happiness began to gain confidence that her abusive past was behind her. She was legally separated from her abusive husband, she had a protective order, and she would have court-ordered child support. Life was turning around for her at the shelter, and it was little wonder: Happiness was a model "tenant." The staff loved her enthusiasm for all their programs, and was thrilled to watch her blossom before their eyes.

Her shelter experience reached its zenith during the Christmas season. The shelter hosted a large celebration, with other local shelters joining them in the house. Shelter staff decorated a large Christmas tree and, with the help of community donations, provided an abundance of good food, and lots of toys for all the children. There were more toys for each child than any one parent could afford to buy. Each child was asked to come forward by age group and all the kids were visibly excited, many of them never having experienced such a celebration. Everyone was happy. For Happiness and her children, it was their first real celebration of Christmas. Happiness was even called up to receive a special award presented by the shelter: a round, gold wall clock in recognition of the Most Outstanding and Improved Resident.

As Happiness stood in the living room of the shelter, filled with the joyous sounds of laughter and Christmas carols singing in the background, she watched her children playing with their new toys. Everything was so beautiful; the decorations, the tree, the presents; the entire atmosphere overflowing in love and good cheer. This, she thought to herself, is the way Christmas is supposed to be. She basked in the relief of being somewhere she felt safe and she allowed herself to reflect on a better future. Such joy had been a fleeting and rare visitor in her life since she accepted Sonny's proposal for marriage. Now she hoped, it would be a more regular companion.

Her experience in the women's shelter was a turning point for her in so many ways. She was grateful beyond measure for a chance to escape her bondage, and yes, "escape" is the best way to describe her feelings. She had been trapped behind a wall of pain, emotional control, and physical intimidation for so long; she had come to assume she would never get out. She had resigned herself to just put up with it. Now, thanks to the protection and temporary refuge of the women's shelter, it was like watching the dark clouds parting to reveal blue sky and radiant sunshine after enduring days of dreary storms. She was exhilarated. The shelter experience had given her a second chance and it was a time of her life she would never forget.

15

UNHAPPY RETURNS

❧

B y March of 1988, it was time to find her own place. She located a nice three-bedroom townhouse in the Hybla Valley community just south of Alexandria, Virginia, and made arrangements to share it with a single lady she had met who would help pay the rent. Between Ogu and her savings, Happiness was able to pay the required security deposit and first month's rent.

She was still working as a nursing assistant at the health-care agency, along with her housekeeping job that included making the beds, scrubbing floors, and cleaning bathrooms. Yet even with her two jobs, it was difficult to pay for childcare for three children, along with rent and utilities. The fourth night in her new home, she made a terrible realization. *I have half a loaf of bread and three eggs. If I eat nothing, this will last my children a day. I cannot ask Ogu for anything more. Comfort is likely furious that he gave me $500 toward the security deposit anyway. I will not be paid for ten more days. What can I do?*

Happiness prepared half a piece of toast for each child the next morning, and hard boiled the eggs for their lunch. After dropping them at the daycare, from where Queenette would catch the bus to school, she began to consider what she was going to do for food. Her mind wandered back to the endless conversations she had had with her new friends at the women's shelter when she remembered Linda mentioning a church close by that had helped her with food when she was first out of the hospital.

After an exhausting shift at work, Happiness drove to where she thought the church must be. Unsure she was even at the right place, she parked her car across the street. She timidly entered through a side door that was ajar and saw an elderly woman seated at a table in what looked like a large kitchen.

"How can I help you?" the woman asked kindly.

"I'm so sorry," Happiness fumbled. *"I was told that you can help people who cannot pay for groceries. If I am wrong I will go now."*

"Nonsense!" the woman smiled, handing her a used cardboard box. *"Just come with me. I will need you to fill out a small form, but here is a box. You can go to our pantry and fill it with what you need."* Happiness filled out the form and followed the woman across the room. In the back of the kitchen was a large walk-in closet filled with canned and dry goods. Happiness' eyes grew wide. Beans, rice, corn, even macaroni and cheese! Her heart was elated as she realized that they would be okay; that her children would not go to bed hungry.

"Listen, sweetheart," the woman noted as she said goodbye, *"we get a lot of people with problems in here. Druggies, alcoholics and the like. I can see you are just a young mother who's going through a rough patch. The YMCA down the street gives out sandwiches everyday at 5:00 if you can get there. Church of the Redeemer in Northwest gives hot meals on Fridays and Sundays. There's a line, but if you can afford to stand there, they'll feed you real good. Just hang in there. Things'll look up, I promise."*

The woman's smile assured her that things would look up. Filled with that assurance and renewed hope, Happiness placed her "box of plenty" in the trunk of her car and went to pick up her children from daycare.

During her first few months in the new house, Happiness quickly learned the ins and outs of most of the homeless shelters and soup kitchens in the area. Many times it meant standing in line, often with all four of her children during the cold winter months, including longer lines at Thanksgiving and Christmas of 1987.

Yet it was not a time that Happiness felt sorry for herself or for her condition. Gratitude, not self-pity, filled her heart. Considering what she had been through with Sonny, standing in relief lines for food was a blessing she still cherishes today. It helped her to make a successful transition out of the shelter which had been her protective cocoon during the past few weeks. *Oh God, thank You for this food. Thank you for all these nice people, and for meeting all of our needs.* She smiled as she recalled how God had sustained her in similar lines with her mother at the refugee camp as a little girl. *Thank you that my children don't have to go hungry tonight.*

Although there hardly seemed time to continue her education while working two jobs, she knew that she would be standing in lines for free food for the rest of her life if she did not keep pressing forward. So press forward she did. Often, she fell asleep with her text books open on the couch, trying to get a little more studying in after the children were in bed.

On the positive side, classes were more interesting than changing bedpans and cleaning toilets, and Happiness soon made friends with other West Africans from the school. It was nice to converse with people who shared the immigrant experience, and even the same tastes in food. Often they would have informal pot-luck lunches after class, and the smells reminded her of home back in Elele, and the contentment and peace she had known there. Unfortunately, some of the students were not well-intentioned.

At a time when she needed to receive reassurance of her self worth, several men approached Happiness seeking to exploit her. One man she met at a fellow student's party approached her and, though married, offered to provide her with a "worry free" life if she would only agree to be his mistress. Another man offered to take her to Paris, but like all the others, this offer was not a benevolent one. These offers, and many others like them, were not complimentary or encouraging. Instead these men brought degradation with every sexual solicitation; chipping away at her whole being; challenging her personhood. They didn't care about who she was, what her dreams were, what her beliefs were, or anything about what comprised her identity. It seemed that her father's admonition she received as a young girl was being confirmed once again: "boys are bad news," especially big boys.

Although it sounds odd, at least the timing of these demeaning offers was a blessing. Since these attempts to exploit her came so soon after she had just left an abusive marriage; she was much less likely to be drawn into another abusive relationship. She rightly viewed the men as the potential trouble they were, saw each of their advances as a personal challenge, and was determined to resist each one that came her way.

It was therefore ironic that during this time when she was showing strength against the advances of various men, that she wavered with the one man that was most dangerous to her; her husband. Perhaps, she was now feeling so worthless, that in some distorted way, part of her might have felt she didn't deserve any better. Regardless of the reason, Happiness was about to make a decision she would later regret.

—

The next two months were an abundance of peace and contentment for Happiness. Outwardly, she still had to work both jobs, care for her home and her children, and endure the occasional rude proposition at school. Inwardly, she glowed with the confidence and joy of recognizing how God was taking her to a new level. She even felt new bursts of energy while washing clothes or cleaning the apartment. The most menial tasks felt purposeful, not arduous.

She went to great lengths to arrange her work schedule so that she and the children could attend church every week. As in her early school days, it no longer mattered to her what other people thought. She was content to be herself and accept what life brought to her. *Truly I have discarded the old and put on the new.*

After about a month of living in her new townhouse, Happiness had just picked up her children at their day care and they were driving home. On the way, she noticed Sonny was in the car behind her, following them. Her heart sunk. How did he find them?

Perhaps I can drive somewhere else so that he will not know where we live.

"*Mommy, when will be home? I am so hungry!*" Millie begged.

"*Me too, me too!*" Charles added.

She had no money to take them out to eat, and she could not think of anything else to do but go home. Her mind felt frozen. Before she knew it, she was in her driveway and Sonny had pulled in behind her. It was an awkward few moments as she got the children out of the car and Sonny called out to her children. Happiness had tried to shelter her children from all that he had done; she wanted them to remain innocent towards their father, so the children were excited to see their daddy once again.

"My children! It is Daddy!" he called out as if nothing was wrong.

"Daddy!!" the girls squealed as they rushed to hug him. Charles and JD toddled after him as fast as they could. Happiness stood helpless, watching her children embrace the man she had worked so hard to escape. She quickly calmed herself and walked toward them, closing the car door behind her.

"Hello, Happiness," Sonny said to her warmly.

"Hello," Happiness responded quietly.

"May I come inside? I think we really need to talk." I cannot turn him away in front of the children, she thought. Besides, he knows where we live now.

"I must make dinner for the kids. If you want, you can join us. We will talk after I put the children to bed." The words came out without a trace of emotion in her voice. The six of them entered the house and Sonny played with the children until dinner was ready. They sat and had a pleasant meal. After Happiness had bathed the children, combed and re-braided the girls' hair and put everyone to bed, she came to the living room where Sonny was sitting. To her surprise, a cup of her favorite tea also sat waiting on the coffee table.

"I want you to know that I am sorry," Sonny began. Happiness looked down at her tea and said nothing. *"I know that you ran away from me because of what happened with Charles. I did not mean to hurt him. I was angry because of working so many hours and getting so little sleep. It will never happen again."*

So many hours, she thought; *You have no idea what it is to work hard!*

Despite her hesitancy, Sonny's entreaties made a positive impact. After successfully rebuking the advances of other men, the tug from Sonny was stronger than she anticipated. She considered the excitement of her children in seeing their daddy again; she knew that divorce was not God's desire for a marriage, and she still longed for a happy family situation. Against her better judgment, Happiness allowed him back into her house.

Once back into her life, Sonny continued to work his charm. He talked about his desire for reconciliation and having a future together. He watched the children while Happiness attended school, and gradually grafted himself back into the heart of Happiness and the family. He knew how to "play" Happiness and he understood her weakness for family.

In retrospect, it is so easy to see the mistake Happiness was making. She had worked so hard to recover from what he had done to her before. She had been so resolute in her refusals of all the other men who she recognized as seeking to exploit her. Yet now, on the threshold of breaking permanently free from her bondage, she yielded and gave into compromise with a man who was seeking to exploit her more than all the others. Her desire for a family overshadowed her judgment, it made her forget all the stories of the other battered spouses she had heard in the women's shelter, and it subdued all the alarm bells and distress signals that God was trying to give her.

Counselors of abused women will frequently explain the strange phenomenon that causes a former abused woman to return to the man who abused her. It is a phenomenon the Bible refers to in explicitly graphic terms, akin to a dog returning to his "vomit." It is something that those who have not been in an abusive situation cannot relate to or fully understand. Happiness had worked so hard to move on with her life. She was so close to complete freedom from her abusive past.

It therefore must have been especially difficult for God to watch his special daughter, who He had worked so hard to set free, now give in to this trap. As He watched the unfolding drama below, from the perspective of His heavenly balcony, the Lord must have done so with tears streaming down His face and with a heart that was filled with grief. He had always been her "invisible friend," the one she turned to for comfort and protection. Yet now, she was turning away from all the comfort and protection He had provided her. For at this point, only God could know that the phenomenon that so often afflicts abused women was now afflicting Happiness, and it was leading her back into abuse, like a dog to his vomit.

16

RESTORING THE
FOUNDATIONS

Happiness was excited as she eagerly opened the letter marked with a familiar return address: "Elele, Rivers State, Nigeria." It was from her father. She had not heard from him for awhile, so the letter was like a priceless treasure. She unfolded its pages, almost trembling inside, and began to read.

My Dearest Happy,

Although it has now been awhile since my visit, I want to say again what a joy it was to see you and my beautiful grandchildren. So many days I find myself reflecting fondly upon that time with all of you. How I wish I could see each of you everyday! I want so much to watch my grandchildren grow up in strength and wisdom as I know they shall do. You have done well, my Happy. You have made me proud. Never forget that.

I am growing old now, and there is something I must say to you before it is too late. I know the doctors say my breathing issues are not that serious, but I can feel our Heavenly Father beckoning me home with each breath I struggle to take. So I must tell you that I am sorry and I ask for your forgiveness. I know you would have never married Sonny were it not for me. I assumed that he was like his father: an upstanding man and a strong Believer. I can see since my visit to America that it is not so. I thought a doctor in America would be able to give you everything. Now I see that you would have been better off staying home. I am so sorry.

Please do not grieve too much, my Happy. God has called you to be like your name: to be full of joy even as you have filled my life and the lives of so many others with joy. One day, it will be so for you.

Your loving father,
Papa

Oh, how many tears she wept over that letter! Her father's words touched her heart in so many ways. She must have re-read it a dozen times. Life had dealt her some serious blows, but what she had with her father was special. She missed him so much. Her father's health concerned her, but there was nothing she could do, that is except pray. *Oh Lord, please don't take my father home yet. Let me see him again. But if his time on earth is ending, please don't let him suffer.*

—

Many people believe there is no hell and there is no devil. Their denials are wishful thinking, which stand in stark contrast to the overwhelming evidence real life presents in the courtroom of history. No doubt a result of the special destiny God had for Happiness; the devil spent a lot of energy going after this woman. His mission was to destroy her heavenly destiny and his chief weapon was her own husband. If the devil could not bring Happiness to his eternal damnation, then he intended to bring hell to her on earth in hopes she would forsake her Lord. It was a plan birthed out of desperation, but it almost worked.

It wasn't long after Happiness allowed Sonny to come back, that he began to return to his same destructive tendencies of mental, physical and sexual abuse. His depravity seemed to have few limits. On numerous occasions, he defiled the marriage bed, ignoring the pleas of his wife and would overpower her against her will, using his force of strength to overcome her resistance to his advances. Inconceivably, Sonny's assaults upon Happiness would continue while she was literally praying out loud to the Lord for protection!

It is hard to fathom a greater incongruence. Anyone with even a semblance of a conscience would have stopped in such a situation. Even criminal rapists have been found to break off their assaults on a woman who cries out to Jesus or begins to pray out loud. Yet such prayers that often dissuade would-be rapists filled with disdain and hatred towards their victim would not deter her own husband. He would often say, as if it excused his behavior, "You are my wife." His insistence on raping his own wife while she was praying for him to stop, demonstrated the extreme hold the devil had on Sonny and how much he was being used against Happiness to destroy her.

Happiness was often close to her breaking point throughout this time. She had little strength left to fight, and she had no help from Sonny. Even though she was still married, she never had her husband's support. Instead of being her earthly shield and doing his best to protect her from evil, as a proper husband would at least try to do, Sonny was the source of the evil. Happiness described her mounting frustrations in this way:

"One of the things I resented so much was that he never embraced me, he never let me know he was proud of me. I always did my best. I took on so much for the family and for him because I didn't want God to have any reason to blame me for what was happening. While a person cannot earn their salvation, I still tried my best to be obedient to God. I wanted to make sure I had done my part, that I wasn't part of the problem or the reason I was going through this suffering. I was consumed with making sure I didn't deserve what was happening to me."

Her husband, who was supposed to "step in" for her father as her protector, was her greatest nemesis. Such a circumstance is one of Satan's most diabolical schemes, transposing the love of a husband or wife into hatred.

What made it worse was the feeling that her ultimate source of protection, the Lord, had seemingly abandoned her. As she described it; *"There were many times I didn't think God cared about me. God told me He would not give me more than I could handle; that there were blessings awaiting me in my obedience and devotion to Him; that He would protect me from evil. Yet while I obeyed, while I stayed faithful, while I remained devoted to Him, evil continued to hit me."* She would cry out to God so many times and ask Him, *'So why the evil, Lord?' 'Why does it continue?' 'Where are you in all this?'* The questions kept coming, but the answers never did.

—

In what was likely intended as the ultimate and final *"coup de grace,"* the devil hit Happiness with one more attack in this onslaught, at a point he felt she was at her weakest, and at a time when he hoped she would not be able to handle it. It was during this period of her life when Happiness received the news she had never wanted to hear, although she knew it had to happen sometime. On September, 9, 1988, her oldest brother Ogu called her to tell her that their father had just passed away in Nigeria. Of course she knew he had been sick for awhile with breathing difficulties, but Happiness had not expected him to die from it. At a time when she had no support from her husband, and she was having difficulty connecting with God, her last source of strength was taken away from her. Her father had always meant so much to her. He was the closest person she had to reflect her Heavenly Father's love. He was the one who gave her such a strong foundation in God and, in so many ways, had provided her the spiritual strength to have made it through life thus far. Now he was gone.

When she hung up the phone, she couldn't help reflecting on her silent prayer at the airport asking the Lord to let her see him one more time. Now she realized, having just spoken with Ogu, her prayer had not been answered, at least not in the way Happiness had hoped. Because her immigration papers had never been corrected from her nightmarish experience in Tijuana, she couldn't even return home to attend her father's funeral. To do so meant she could not return to the States. The pain and bitterness of such a restriction just added to her anguish. To not even be able to attend her own father's funeral or to see and console her brothers, sister, or mother in such a time when families are meant to be together, was almost more than she could bear.

How much can a human heart endure? It was a question Happiness found too painful to imagine. In fact, she did her best to avoid thinking about her father's death and the funeral she couldn't attend. To do so would consume her emotionally from the inside out. As it was, brokenness and heartache were the only companions Happiness could count on, or so it seemed. She knew God had not forsaken her, but it sure seemed like it.

During this time, Happiness had some pretty frank and candid "talks" with God and they weren't the cute little ones found in children's stories. These were real talks, motivated by the rawest of human emotions. At least she was still talking to Him, but quite frankly, she was doing more demanding than talking. In what sounds like near defiance, yet in words born out of a relationship only intimacy could produce, she made her declarations known.

"God, you owe me big time," she forcefully asserted, clearly having long since gone beyond the stage of sugar-coating her prayers; *"because I honored you, because I suffered. You said if we trust you and obey you, you would protect us, but you didn't do your part. You failed me."* She wasn't through. *"When do you step in and let me stop suffering? When do I get to cruise for awhile and enjoy the blessings of life?"* Her prayers could not have better reflected what all of us have wondered at some point in our lives if we are honest with ourselves. Maybe we didn't use quite such forceful language, but then, maybe we haven't reached the same point of despair that produces such emotion.

In any event, Happiness bared her soul to her life-long friend who she knew was real and she knew was her only hope. She understood that God owed her nothing; that He had created her life and He could snuff it out in an instant if He chose. She was aware that her God was sovereign over all things; yet she also knew He was merciful and that His mercies endure forever. Happiness understood, due to a deep relationship forged over years of prayerful intimacy, that her "invisible friend" saw her heart; her anguish. What she clearly did not understand were God's purposes in all of this suffering, but then suffering is one of those things that we will probably never fully understand until we get to heaven.

Following another one of Sonny's physical beatings, she called her brother Ogu. When he answered, she was crying, having trouble saying exactly what had happened. Ogu came over and was immediately shocked to see Happiness' face; it was badly swollen and bruised. He took a photo of her injuries to document it, and then he confronted Sonny, who had long been his friend. Up until now, to protect her brother's friendship, Happiness had tried to hide Sonny's abuse of her from Ogu. But she was weary of this continued abuse, and she was beginning to reach out for help.

Unfortunately, Sonny was not approachable, even by his friend. In no uncertain terms, he told Ogu to stay out of his business and to "mind his own family." The incident failed to affect Sonny, but it clearly affected Ogu. For the first time he realized his friend was not who he thought he was. He also realized his sister was not living the wonderful life he had hoped, or he had been led to believe. From this point on, Happiness began to share a few things with Ogu, although not all. Ogu began to support Happiness even more, sending her money when she needed it, and most importantly, as a new ally, encouraging her and giving her the moral support she needed.

—

During this same time frame, the early part of 1989, Happiness was confronted with a truth she had been doing her best to deny. Throughout their marriage, people had made comments, and some not-so-subtle insinuations, that Sonny was cheating on her. Of course, she had her own suspicions based on the lady in Mexico who had approached Sonny with the baby, and all the women who visited her in San Bernardino pretending to be her friend. But for her own sake, she felt she needed to "believe a lie." In fact, she badly wanted everyone making such insinuations, to be proven wrong.

One day, while Sonny was at work, Happiness was cleaning up around the house. Sonny had just returned home from a week-long business trip, or so he claimed, and he had left his belongings in a travel bag in the corner of their bedroom. The bag was left open and she noticed it contained a bathing suit and recreational clothes that he never wore around her. She began to examine the bag more closely, becoming more and more curious. Her search turned up more than she had bargained for.

Lying amongst his clothes were pictures of her husband with another woman, receipts from hotels, love letters, and condoms. Her artificial reality of denial ran square into truth like two powerful locomotives colliding on the same track. *"It hit me so bad,"* is how she described the emotional collision: such simple words to describe a devastating impact. Her shock was deep, for she had been extremely effective at believing the lies that Sonny was a faithful husband. Her last remnant of trust in him was now shattered, along with the broken shards of displaced hope. Everything she had wanted to be true, even the simple plea for faithfulness by her husband, was a lie. She cried tears of deep despair. Her world was rocked once again. How much more of this could she take? When would it end? She needed answers, and she needed them now.

Her husband's employer, Hazelton Laboratory in Vienna, Virginia, offered professional counseling as a benefit for their employees and their families. Even though Sonny refused to attend, and refused to acknowledge any culpability in the matter, she scheduled an appointment with Dr. Libovichi, a marriage counselor in Alexandria. The first two counseling sessions were spent explaining what she had discovered in Sonny's travel bag, the long history of abuse, and her efforts to keep such information from her family to protect them. She didn't want either her family or her in-laws, who she still greatly admired, to be disappointed. She had thought it was better for them to believe a lie, than to be saddened by the truth.

While nothing remarkable occurred in the first two counseling sessions, that changed dramatically in session three. As Happiness described it, *"it was on my third session that we had a breakthrough."* "Liberation" was another word she used, which might be even more accurate, for it was in this session that Happiness was able to see beyond her cultural veil that had shrouded her thinking. She received a revelation that had eluded her until now.

The counselor noted that Happiness was living in the U.S. now and was no longer bound to a Nigerian culture that had her sacrificing her peace and happiness for that of her family. Her family back home was living their own life and she needed to live her life. She needed to do what was best for her and her children, not what was best for a family that was living thousands of miles away. While Happiness was concerned with the reputation of her family and in-laws in Nigeria, her family in the States was suffering. The counselor asked her why she was sacrificing her life and the lives of her children for the sake of her family on another continent.

The words hit their mark. Her way of seeing the entire issue permanently changed from that point forward. No longer would she live for the sake of her parent's reputation; no longer would she hold back truth so loved ones would be spared, while living in a destructive lie. No longer would she be beaten, raped, and cheated upon and then write her parents and in-laws telling them how well she was doing. It was like being set free from the weight of other's expectations. The guilt she had worn since accepting the marriage proposal was finally removed and she would never be the same again. It was a revelation that pierced through the thickest part of her cultural cloud. God had spoken to her through this counselor and Happiness was now getting free.

With a renewed sense of truth and courage, Happiness confronted Sonny about his cheating; in fact, in her words, she did more than confront him, she "raised hell." When he denied it, she didn't back down. Instead, she showed him what she had found, the pictures, the receipts and the condoms. The evidence could not be denied. He was a liar and she knew it. Sonny left shortly thereafter, leaving Happiness and her four children in a home that was father-less, but at peace.

—

Soon thereafter, they received a much-needed change of environment. Happiness learned of, and was granted approval to rent, one of the church elder's vacant houses on Vermont Street in Alexandria, Virginia. It was less expensive and the move represented a fresh start. The change of environment and the absence of Sonny, combined to bring a renewed outlook.

She soon found herself dreaming of owning her own business. As she drove to her housecleaning jobs to scrub more toilets, she observed the nicely dressed business people going to work. She admired them and she began to desire her own office to work in like they had. She wanted to be the "decision-maker" in a business, the one in charge, instead of the one always being told what to do and how to do it. She was tired of cleaning houses for a living. She wanted more out of life. She began dreaming of a corner office, having a nice car and being a respected businesswoman. Sometimes her dreams were so specific and wonderful, they even startled Happiness. When that happened, she would ask God to take away any of her dreams that were too selfish.

Not only did she reflect upon such dreams, she began to act on them. First she took typing classes. Then she bought herself a computer with a word processor. She saw the need to help students type their research papers and other typing tasks. From that need, she decided to create her own business, Administrative Support, Inc.", incorporating with the help of a lawyer. She contracted out work to accountants, bookkeepers, and other professionals, while retaining a portion of the fee. She created a business brochure and began to market her business. Her business, though fledgling, was soon generating enough income that she was able to quit one of her two other jobs.

In late 1989 or early 1990, Happiness heard of a pastor who was visiting the United States from Ghana, West Africa. She had heard wonderful things about the power of God in his meetings so Happiness and a friend made an appointment to drive to New York to meet with him. When they met, he prayed with them and spoke a few words over them. He agreed to visit her house when he came into the Virginia area later that month, which, as promised, he did. He prayed over the house in a powerful and authoritative way that Happiness had never experienced before. As Happiness recalled it:

> *"He commanded, bound and loosed everything he could perceive in the Spirit. He challenged me to keep the faith and witness the handiwork of God almighty. He prophesied over me and spoke with*

unwavering faith and hope, telling me, 'Don't worry, all will change.'"

The presence of the Holy Spirit was so strong, that around midnight that evening, she felt as if the entire apartment was shaking. It was very powerful and Happiness sensed in her spirit that it was finally "over with the devil" and that she was getting her life back.

Her life was now being lived on a new spiritual level. She had been released from the grip of the devil on her life and had truly been set free. Her new apartment became a spiritual oasis, and both it and her heart were filled with the love, joy and peace of God. There was a new atmosphere that enveloped the entire place. In describing the emotions years later, she referred to that apartment as *"one of the most memorable places I ever lived."* She recalled a *"feeling of release"*, like she had *"won the lottery."* The bondage she had felt was now gone.

She experienced a deeper peace and contentment that drew her into a deeper intimacy with God. She fell "in love with God" all over again and He occupied her thoughts continuously. She remained "always in the Spirit" even when doing menial tasks like washing her clothes or cleaning her apartment. She renewed her commitment to attending church and she was baptized. She would meditate on the love of God *"like a woman during courtship."* She had made up her mind to obey God and to live her life to please God alone. She realized that she and her "invisible friend" had been through a lot together; that they were truly best friends.

The Lord had given her a freshly laid spiritual foundation, and Happiness had become "resealed." She sensed, as never before, that from here on out, no matter what would come her way in life, nothing mattered more to her than holding on to her core; her Lord who made her whole. She was complete in Him and in no other. It was an unshakable feeling. As God's word says, a thousand could fall at her side and ten thousand at her right hand, but the destruction of life would not come nigh her; God had her back.

In looking back on this time of her life, something remarkable had occurred in the spiritual realm that Happiness would only realize years later. Her earthly father had been the one who the Lord provided to establish a rock-solid love for God and His Word in her life as a young girl. He provided her with her original spiritual foundation. Her earthly father had been the one who had done his best to protect her, and to provide her with an unwavering support of love and acceptance that allowed her to get through all the twists and turns that a hard life had brought her way.

Now, just as her earthly father had passed away, it was like the torch was passed once and for all, to her Heavenly Father to complete the job in a way that her earthly father could never do. No longer would Happiness need to lean on her earthly father for support, for now she had a greater, more enduring support in God. God had re-established her spiritual foundation, setting her feet upon a rock that could not be moved or shaken by anything life would throw at her.

While life would not always be easy, and she had not yet sunk to her lowest depth, from this point forward, she knew that her victory was ultimately assured. She could have confidence that her new torch-bearer was one who had ultimate authority over everything. He had ultimate love for her, and He was bigger, tougher and more powerful than the devil who had been such a thorn in her side for so long.

Her earthly father had done well, especially given the inherent limitations of human frailties; but now Happiness had a new advocate on her side with no human frailties to limit Him. He had been there all along. He had been the one her earthly father had pointed her toward. He had been the one she had leaned on throughout. But somehow, now that the torch had been officially passed by her earthly father's death, there would be a new and deeper relationship between this daughter and her Heavenly Father. This Father would once again make sure that Happiness remembered the significance of her divinely-inspired name, as her earthly father had, only with a slight variation: instead of being "the daughter of her Father's joy," now she was "the daughter of her Heavenly Father's joy."

17

DARING TO DREAM

S onny always had a knack for showing up at the most
inopportune times. Just as Happiness was getting
her life re-established and re-ordered from the emotional
pain and messy twists he had created for her before, he
chose now to re-appear. Once again, he poured on the
charm. Once again, his charm somehow managed to cause
Happiness to hope that things could change between them;
that the nightmares of the past were behind them. Over
the course of a few days, Sonny successfully convinced
Happiness that they could make it as a couple again.
Moreover, they talked of combining their income and, with
the help of a realtor friend of Sonny's, they began looking
for a home to buy.

Not long thereafter, they found the house they were
looking for; an affordable, four-bedroom house in
Woodbridge, only about 20 miles south of where Happiness
was currently living in Alexandria. They signed a contract
to buy it on December 30, 1990, and moved in shortly after
New Years, 1991. The move to the new environment in
Woodbridge would require some adjustments.

One of those adjustments was finding a new church for her and her children to attend. Sonny was not part of this equation since he had never been much for church and he continued to be distant about the idea now. Since she had always had a Seventh Day Adventist background, it was only natural that Happiness began worshipping at the local Seventh Day Adventist church in Woodbridge. However, a new friend she had met, Debbie Patten, encouraged her to attend her church, Christ Chapel. She did so, liked it, and made it her new church "home." Happiness had met Debbie as a Day Care provider for Happiness' children and had quickly become close with her. They only lived a few houses away from each other on the same street, so the friendship naturally flowed from a shared faith and proximity of location.

During this time, Happiness continued to pursue college courses part time through Strayer University, while working her nursing assistant job and the business she had established while in Alexandria. Her dream of a college degree was strong upon her heart, and she was willing to make the difficult sacrifice of studying while working two jobs and being a full-time mother to four children. While her life was difficult to say the least, it was also exhilarating. Knowing that she was inching ever closer to realizing her desire for a college degree made it all worthwhile.

Sonny, as was his typical pattern, began to revert to the selfish, unsupportive husband he had previously been. Likely the result of a bad case of envy towards Happiness' success and ambition, Sonny began to put heavy pressure on Happiness to quit school. He had no desire for her to "outshine" him educationally, although he must have known she had long been "outshining" him in all aspects of life. Happiness had been driven by dreams and aspirations for a better life, and she possessed the ambition, fortitude, and persistence to push through the difficulties standing between herself and her dreams.

Since Happiness was a threat to Sonny's ego, he was determined to prevent her from continuing with college classes, let alone graduating. At first he yelled at her whenever he learned she was leaving for, or returning from class. Still she persisted in continuing her classes. Then Sonny began to intentionally leave the house minutes before Happiness had to leave for class, refusing to say where he was going. This forced her to either scramble for a last-minute babysitter, which was extremely difficult to do, or miss her class. Regardless of the outcome, the result was unnecessary stress and weariness upon her simple desire to make something of herself through a college degree. Nonetheless, she refused to give up.

The Bible says that without a vision, the people perish. She knew that she had to press on. Her emotional and spiritual well-being depended on it. Without a husband to share her dreams with, she had shared them with God, the one who had given her such dreams. She fondly recalled the countless nights in bed, before drifting off to sleep, she would picture herself owning her own business. She saw herself as a professional business lady, dressed in nice suits and working in nice offices just like the people she had seen commuting to work. She longed to be the one responsible for either the success or failure of the business. She was not afraid; she just needed the opportunity, and that opportunity started with a college degree.

During one of these late-night sessions of sharing her hopes with God, she thought of a way to pursue her classes and put a stop to Sonny's mischief. She would tell him she was quitting school to get another job. Of course, what he would not know is that the "other job" was her college classes, and her new "work hours" would just happen to coincide with her class schedule. While her plan was deceptive, it was also brilliant. Sonny would make sure he stayed home to watch the children since he would believe it was in his own financial interest to do so. Her plan actually used Sonny's greed for more money to assist her in pursuing her education. Although she realized her plan was premised upon a lie, she hoped that God would understand. In any event, her plan worked perfectly! Under the guise of working another job, Happiness was secretly able to pursue her dream, attending college part-time, while working two jobs.

In 1992, through her work with her Administrative Support, Inc. business, she met a printer, who in his application for print work gave the National Black Caucus of State Legislators (NBCSL) as a reference. As she questioned the printer about the group, she mentioned that she was looking for an office job. He told her they were looking for an administrative assistant. That is all she needed to hear. She wasted no time in submitting her application and almost as fast as she applied, she was hired.

The job required a lot of administrative planning, coordinating of conferences and board meetings, along with significant travel. Happiness assisted the Executive Director in planning the executive board meetings, and the meetings between legislative, corporate and labor representatives. She was also responsible for planning the travel, arriving early at the destination to set everything up, and preparing the agenda. After the meetings concluded, she took care of wrapping up the conference details, typing up the minutes, and drafting the final report. Fortunately, the job also gave her a significant increase in pay, allowing her to hire a live-in nanny to make sure her children were taken care of during her travels. She certainly couldn't count on Sonny since he refused to help with his own children.

Happiness was given a lot of responsibility in her new position, allowing her to display her strong organizational skills, and to travel to many of the big cities around the country. She was working with highly educated and ambitious people and the work was exhilarating. Rather than being intimidated by the many legislators, influential businessmen, and lobbyists, Happiness found herself enjoying the high-level, fast-paced environment. The experience and the atmosphere served to feed her now-growing appetite for going into business for herself.

Yet a nagging feeling in her stomach began to grow daily. Life had been so chaotic and exhausting for so long that Happiness had had little time to think about her immigration status since being unable to attend her father's funeral. Yet now she was working with high level businessmen and other people of influence. They listened to her and relied upon her. What would they do if they found she was not here legally, even if the problem was a mere technicality?

On September 30, 1992, she began seeking permanent residence status (her "Green Card"), the first step in obtaining U.S. citizenship. She contacted an immigration lawyer, was advised of the process, and began filling out the many documents necessary to commence the long and arduous immigration process. Like a college degree, Happiness understood that U.S. citizenship was another required hurdle in accomplishing her dream of becoming a successful business owner. While the hurdles were real and difficult, Happiness was determined to persevere.

—

I cannot believe the depth to which You have blessed me, Oh God. After standing in lines at soup kitchens in the cold winter with her four children, Happiness cherished the simple pleasure that she now had more than enough in her pantry. At that moment, however, a strong impulse gripped her heart. She longed for some confirmation to sustain her and, hopefully, propel her forward. She began asking the Lord for "a meeting," for Him to show Himself to her.

In what would be the first of many significant events of that year, Happiness determined to go on a three-day fast on February 21, 1993. That morning, when she prepared breakfast for her children, she did not fix a plate for herself. After the children were in bed that evening, she began reading her Bible, becoming more absorbed in what she read with every page. The first time she looked at the clock, she realized that she had been reading and meditating on what she was reading for over three hours.

During the course of those three days, Happiness sought the presence of the Lord; she prayed, she worshipped, she read her Bible, and she reflected on her relationship with the only one who had sustained her through her life. She still went to work and fulfilled all her duties, but inside she was a woman on a mission. *God, I need to hear from You. I need Your direction for my life. I do not want to gain the whole world and lose my soul. I do not want to gain riches and lose You. Tell me what it is You want me to do, and I will do it, Oh Lord.*

At the conclusion of the third day of fasting and seeking the Lord for a word of confirmation or direction, she went to bed having received neither. She tried not to be disappointed, for she knew that the Lord could speak to her anytime He wanted.

That night, when she no longer expected it, God answered her prayer for direction. In the most vivid and clearest of dreams, Happiness saw a brilliantly illuminated star, much like the Christmas star as often portrayed shining over the shepherds tending their flocks outside Bethlehem at the time of Jesus' birth. It was breathtaking to behold, sparkling like a true star of purpose and destiny. As she stared at the star's brilliance, she heard a distinctly audible voice say to her, *"Don't worry, don't worry; I will provide;*

feed my sheep." Happiness awakened with a start, sat up in bed, and looked at the clock. It was 7:00 a.m. She pondered with excitement the meaning of her dream. *Even as You fed me, day by day, as You provided manna to the Israelites, so I am to feed others who walk the path of hunger that I once walked!*

Happiness was overwhelmed with joy, realizing that the Lord had heard her plea to draw close to Him and to be His constant companion, and He had given her a word. To the natural mind, the word seemed so short and simple; but to the spiritual mind, the word had a depth of meaning that led to hours of joyous rumination.

She thought about that word and what it meant practically. In reflecting on how she could best serve God, she felt like she wasn't a good public speaker, let alone one who could preach about God. Yet now, as a result of this word from the Lord, she felt that God was telling her to use her finances to share with the homeless people and the less fortunate; to minister to His "sheep." So, as she described it, that is what she began to do, in earnest.

> *"For awhile, I fed the homeless on the street,*
> *trying to be obedient and to please my Lord. I went*
> *about doing good in obedience and honor to God.*
> *I wondered how I could feed His sheep when I did*
> *not have enough for my own family, but I remained*
> *faithful, trusting in Him. I paid my tithes and I was*
> *open to support people I believed God must have*
> *sent my way. God had a bigger plan."*

Happiness began seeing people's needs and trying to meet them. If she saw a person who looked hungry, she would give them food or money. Often, after seeing an apparently needy person, she would pull into the nearest grocery store, buy some groceries, and then give the groceries to the startled stranger. She began volunteering with her church at soup kitchens in Alexandria to feed the homeless. There were even times when she would see a forlorn or disheveled-looking young woman standing outside and she would ask the woman if she had a place to stay or needed anything.

On occasion, if the woman had no place to go, Happiness would take her home and allow the woman to live with her temporarily until she was able to get back on her feet. This latter act of "sheep feeding" sometimes resulted in Happiness having some of her personal items stolen from her house, but she didn't care. *It is all Yours anyway, Lord. You have given it all to me. Who am I to withhold it from those You want me to bless?*

Though she knew she needed to use discretion, she ultimately tried to follow the promptings of the Holy Spirit, refusing to stop blessing people and giving of herself. Her efforts were tireless. But, instead of it draining her, she felt invigorated, knowing God had given her a purpose in life. While not her focus, Happiness began to realize that God was blessing her new-found trust in Him with more abundant finances. Her annual income that year increased from $15,000 to $43,000. She also began receiving creative revelations on saving additional money, and through it all, she continued to grow closer to her invisible friend.

One of those "sheep" that Happiness was feeding with her patient care and tender love, was Mary Fisher, an elderly lady that Happiness was attending to as a private duty nursing assistant in Mary's home. Mary had become a patient of Happiness in 1989, after Mary's husband had passed away, leaving her with no children or family close by to care for her. Her husband had set up a trust for Mary, and the Bank, as trustee, had hired Happiness as Mary's permanent nursing assistant. Although Mary was old, her mind was alert, and she and Happiness would spend hours talking with each other. Happiness became like a family member to Mary, like the daughter she never had. She saw her as a special child of God, deserving of genuine love and affection.

It was a perfect blend of young and old, with Happiness soaking in Mary's wisdom, while Mary was invigorated by Happiness' youthful zeal. Happiness made sure she would get Mary out of the house, taking her out to lunch and dinner, and just "hanging out" together. The two friends stayed close over the years as Happiness continued to care for Mary. The relationship would set the tone for how Happiness would treat others who God brought across her path.

—

Happiness awoke on a bright June day in 1993 with a sense of excitement, for she was about to realize another of her dreams. She had worked hard for this; overcoming tremendous obstacles. In spite of working multiple jobs, raising four children, managing the home with no help from her husband, and dealing with the emotional torments of an abusive man, through it all, she continued to take two to three college classes a semester. You would be hard-pressed to find any examples of greater perseverance and steadfast-ness than that. Now, on a beautiful sunny day at the Patriot Center on the George Mason University campus, Happiness lined up in cap and gown with several other graduates to receive her degree. It was a bachelor's degree in Business Administration from Strayer University, and it is probably safe to say that no other person standing in cap and gown that day worked harder for their diploma.

Happiness had much to be proud of, and much to be thankful for. It was one of the best and happiest moments of her life. But for Happiness, she wasn't done. As she stepped across the stage and was handed her diploma, she was already planning on enrolling in a Masters of Business Administration program. She had been raised in a highly educated family where education was greatly valued and regarded. For the Emejuru family, a bachelors degree was good, but not really that big of a deal. Her parents had always expected their children to go further than that, and so that is what Happiness intended to do. Besides, she was in her element in college. She had always been a good student and she found learning to be completely rewarding.

In the audience that day, watching her walk across the stage and receive her diploma, was her brother Ogu who had supported her so much. Next to him was her sister-in-law Comfort, whose differences with Happiness years earlier had been overcome now. Missing from her group of family supporters was her husband Sonny, the one who did all he could to prevent this day from happening. Happiness had not invited him, or even told him she was graduating, keeping it a secret to the very end. It is unlikely he would have come anyway.

18

DREAMS PLACED ON HOLD

❧

"*I will not sign it.*" Sonny left the house for the thousandth time without saying where he was going. Yet this time Happiness was truly shocked and afraid. For years now, their marriage had been at a kind of stalemate. He did little to nothing for the household, but as long as Happiness kept her schooling secret he was happy enough to take free room and board in exchange for leaving her alone.

Yet now he was refusing to sign the INS paperwork she had finished preparing that would allow her to apply for her Green Card and lawfully stay in the country. Her mind raced through the various possibilities. After all this time, Sonny had once again found his way back into power. A phone call from Sonny reporting her to the INS as an illegal alien would send her back to Nigeria, permanently separating her from her children. She had dreaded this moment for ages, but she knew now that she had no time to lose.

Happiness found a lawyer who promptly filed papers with the court seeking a Suspension of Deportation. This meant she wouldn't be deported without a hearing, but it also meant she was officially out of hiding. She was on the INS radar screen now and if she did not win her case at the hearing, they would take immediate steps to send her away. It was now all or nothing. She had to win this hearing and convince the judge to allow her to stay.

Over the course of the next few months, Happiness, with the strong guiding hand of her lawyer, began to organize her evidence. In many respects, her evidence would be her life story up to that point. She gathered documentation of how she had held down numerous jobs while trying to raise her four children; she gathered documentation about the mental, physical and sexual abuse she had endured from her husband; and she gathered documentation showing how she had gone from a homeless shelter to a college degree taking classes part-time.

Little did she realize that she was gathering documentation that would provide the court with one of the most compelling and inspiring presentations the court had ever witnessed in its courtroom. Once the documents were gathered and organized, Happiness provided them to her lawyer and the lawyer presented them to the court by a detailed report filed in advance of the hearing. This would allow the judge and prosecutor to better understand the case, but there would be no way for Happiness to know how the court would react to the report. It was in God's hands now.

As the court date approached, Happiness spent many evenings in urgent prayer with her Lord, her friend who had sustained her through so many storms; through so many difficult times. *Oh Holy Spirit, you have always been my Invisible Friend, the One who has sustained me through so many storms and difficult times. Will You not have mercy on me now, Oh Lord, and grant me the ability to stay in America and raise my children in peace? Although I have suffered much, I see now that You have never forsaken me. Have mercy on me once again, Oh God!*

While Happiness and her lawyer were busy preparing their case, God was busy doing His part. His part, of course, was the most important. The Lord was setting the stage for Happiness to find unbelievable favor with the court by preparing the hearts and minds of both the judge and prosecutor. Although Happiness did not yet realize it, God was orchestrating one of His most dramatic victories on behalf of His beloved "daughter" who He cared for so deeply. If Happiness had understood what God was doing, she could have relaxed and saved herself a lot of anxiety.

On the morning of July 2, 1993, the day scheduled for her formal hearing, Happiness and her lawyer arrived in the courtroom. Happiness braced herself emotionally for what was about to occur. But with so much riding on the decision of the court, this morning found Happiness with a churning stomach, sweaty palms, and a mind contemplating the terrible things that would ensue if the hearing did not go her way. Her lawyer had warned her that if she lost, there was the possibility that she could be placed in immediate detention in preparation for deportation. Was this morning the last time she would ever see her children?

As the prosecutor entered the courtroom, Happiness thought of all the legal dramas on TV in which the prosecuting attorney bullies witnesses trying to get a confession. Her heart skipped a beat as she heard the judge enter from his chambers and everyone stood up.

The judge called the case to order.

"Okay, Counselor," he said, speaking to the prosecutor. *"Will you call the witness and examine her for the record?"*

"Certainly Your Honor," the prosecutor answered with a smile. Happiness went forward, still nervous, took the oath and sat down in the witness chair.

"Mrs. Dike, would you state your full name for the court?" the prosecutor asked in an almost unbelievably friendly tone.

"Happiness Wegwu Dike," she answered meekly, inwardly surprised at how kind and informal everything seemed.

"And you reside at 13846 Delaney Road in Woodbridge, Virginia?"

"Yes," she answered again.

To her shock, after a few more preliminary questions, the prosecutor sat back down and motioned to the judge that he was done. Then the judge began to speak. Now Happiness was about to receive the shock of her life.

"Thank you, Counselor. Mrs. Dike, I have reviewed all the documents submitted in the case, which were meticulously put together, all of which checked out perfectly. I want to say that I have rarely had the privilege of hearing the story of a mother who has worked so hard to provide for and take care of her children, and to take advantage of opportunities to better her situation. Yours is perhaps the most impressive case I have ever seen come before my court. I particularly want to congratulate you on your recent graduation from Strayer University. I can see from the record that you have had to overcome many obstacles including a very challenging domestic situation. In light of all this evidence, which is overwhelming on your behalf, I am pleased to grant your Suspension of Deportation which will allow you stay in the country."

When the hearing was over, Happiness sat in stunned silence. She was completely dumbfounded. The judge and prosecutor were the first people, other than her own lawyer, to have heard her story; to learn what she had been going through all this time. The effect on them was obvious. Despite all the efforts of her husband to lie about her, abuse her, demean her, and now to even refuse to assist her in staying in the country with her children, the judge saw the truth. The effect on Happiness was deep, yet reassuring. God had come to her rescue and brought her complete and total vindication in a way that would be humanly impossible to obtain.

—

Happiness was overjoyed: she had her college degree and her Green Card was being processed. She hardly felt like she could ask for anything more. Yet her appetite for progress had been whetted and, as she had already enrolled in an MBA program within days of getting her bachelors degree, she couldn't wait to get started. No difficulty seemed too great to de-rail her steady pursuit down the tracks toward a master's degree.

Despite all that she had going against her, Happiness performed at the highest academic levels in her MBA program, gaining the respect and admiration of her academic advisor. She received excellent grades the first two quarters, despite still having to hold down two jobs and care for her children with no help from Sonny. Even when her academic advisor expressed concern that she was spreading herself too thin, her excellent academic performance persuaded him to sign the wavers that permitted her to continue a full course load. All was set for Happiness to continue towards her dream of obtaining her MBA.

It was then that the bubble burst, and just like all bubbles, this one burst suddenly and without warning. In the middle of the third quarter of her master's program she returned home and was surprised to see Sonny sitting in the living room waiting for her.

"Happiness," Sonny said solemnly, *"I have been thinking a lot about finishing medical school."* Happiness could not bring herself to say a word. Sonny had begun medical school almost twenty years ago! Why now? *"There is a medical school in the Dominican Republic where I believe I can be accepted."*

"I see," she answered quietly. Of course, if he did so, she would have to quit her master's program and work to support him.

"Also, for me to go, you must co-sign the loan papers so that we can pay for the program." We? You would not sign my INS papers and you want me to co-sign for a loan?

Happiness could hardly believe what she was hearing. This was the same man who did all he could to prevent her from obtaining a college degree. This was also the same man who refused to sign her paperwork to prevent her from being deported and being separated from her children. He had abused her repeatedly in every way; he had failed to support her in any way; and he had been a source of continued emotional heartbreak from the inception of their marriage. Yet now, when he needed something from her, Sonny was willing to ask Happiness to put her dreams on hold and make a huge sacrifice for him; something he was never willing to do for her.

Silently she marveled at how selfish he was. Few people, no matter how rotten they might be, would have the gall to ask for any favors after treating someone the way he had, let alone such a big favor. His life was messed up because he had allowed it to be messed up. Had he not lied and fooled around in Mexico when they were living there, he would have already graduated from medical school. Then, he was given a second opportunity to return to Mexico for a year and complete his studies, after he had been kicked out of the internship program Ogu got him at Howard University. Had he not lied and fooled around in Mexico that second time, he would have again been able to graduate from medical school.

Now he wanted to put her dreams on hold to take care of business that should have already been taken care of. Essentially, he wanted her to pay the heavy price of his own irresponsibility. It wasn't fair and it wasn't right. Sonny should never have asked his wife to support him in this way. He would be reaping what he sowed if she said no; he would be getting what he deserved if she said no; and he would be receiving God's justice if she said no.

She also knew that he had repeatedly lied to his family back home about how little Happiness supported him. It was still important to her that she show in a real way that she was not selfish, as the small Nigerian community surrounding his in-laws now believed she was.

Only this time, her consideration of their feelings was not out of guilt or bondage, as it might have been earlier in her life. Now, perhaps there was a different motivation; a divine motivation, forged out of her dream from the Lord. She was a changed woman in so many ways. God had molded her into a much more caring, selfless individual who was keenly aware of her higher calling. If the Lord had asked her to "feed His sheep," who was to say, that Sonny wasn't the neediest of sheep that she was to feed. It was one thing to learn to feed strangers, but the ultimate test was to learn to feed those who had persecuted her, defamed her, and sought to destroy her on many occasions, over many years.

"I will sign," she said with a sigh. *"When do you need to leave?"*

With a heavy heart, in June, 1994, Happiness quit her Master's program, co-signed Sonny's loan papers as he requested, and took on yet another job to supply the extra money he would need to pay for school.

While Happiness did her part, Sonny failed to do his part. Over the course of the next few months, Sonny continued to miss deadlines for applying to medical school. When Happiness would ask him about it, he kept insisting he would do so for the next semester. At one point he told her he had to go to Mexico to get a copy of his transcript, even though such items are routinely requested

199

through the mail. It always seemed like he was taking steps to enroll, and yet, he wouldn't enroll. The reasons he gave were ones she could never verify. Still she worked to help him raise money and still he procrastinated. Not until his close friend at work enrolled in the program did Sonny ultimately enroll, three years after Sonny asked Happiness to quit her MBA program. Even then, she had to drain her retirement accounts, worth about $23,000 to make sure he could buy his plane tickets, pay his housing deposits, and cover tuition.

As a result of all his delays, it was not until June, 1997, that Sonny finally left for the Dominican Republic to finish medical school. In retrospect, Happiness could have finished her master's program by now and still had time to help Sonny go to school. It was therefore apparent, that part of Sonny's motivation was to prevent Happiness from achieving her dream of an MBA.

Once he had left, Happiness had much to deal with in his absence. The children were now getting older and involved in a myriad of school events which Happiness did her best to support and attend. Queenette was on the gymnastics and track team and both Queenette and Millie excelled in cheerleading. Later, when they reached high school, Queenette would become captain and both she and Millie would be selected for the varsity squad. Their team would even win the state cheerleading championship and Queenette would go to London to participate in an international parade. Charles and JD, who were now almost eleven years old were already showing a growing interest in sports. Happiness was grateful that despite having a non-involved father, her children were well-grounded.

She was also managing the household finances, sending money to Sonny, and working week-ends now to cover the extra costs associated with her husband's overseas education expenses. While she made a Herculean effort to cover all the expenses with additional work, she also sought to shield her children from her frequent bouts of discouragement.

Her work schedule was now nearly inhumane. At one point in late 1997 or 1998, her schedule finally caught up with her. The easier part of her schedule was from Monday through Thursday, when she only worked two jobs, starting at 9:00 am and finishing at 10:00 pm.

But on Friday's and Saturday's she worked a third job which required an even more murderous schedule. On Fridays, she left for her first job around 7:30 a.m. to be at work by 9:00 a.m. At 5:00 pm, she left that job to go to Potomac Mills Shopping Mall where she worked her second job at a retail store from 6:00 p.m. to 10:00 p.m. Once she had finished cleaning up at that job, she had to drive to Bristow, Virginia where she worked a third job during the graveyard shift as a nursing assistant at a Catholic Nursing Home from 11:00 p.m. until 7:00 a.m., Saturday morning. Caffeine pills got her through her shift. She would typically get home by 7:30 a.m. Saturday, where she would crash for a couple hours, then shower and get dressed to be at work at the retail store in the mall from 10:00 a.m. until 6:00 p.m.

It was during one of those hectic weekends of work when her children first saw her openly discouraged. After she had fallen asleep on the couch following her grave-yard shift at the nursing home, Happiness woke up crying uncontrollably, pleading for God to give her the strength to keep going. The children saw her crying, gathered at her feet and laid on her, trying their best to let her know they cared. It was the only time while Sonny was gone, that she let her guard down where the children noticed.

As if these challenges were not enough, a warrant for Sonny to appear in court was served on her. It seems that he had been involved in an auto accident a few weeks before he left the country and he failed to tell her. Now that he was gone, he was being summoned to appear at the Fairfax County Courthouse. To prevent a default being entered against him, Happiness had to appear in court and explain that her husband was currently in the Dominican Republic. It was then she learned from the court clerk that her husband had also been driving with a suspended license! She wondered what other matters her husband had neglected to tell her about.

Happiness was single-handedly keeping Sonny out of trouble, trouble that he brought on himself through his own irresponsibility. At times, the added pressures of providing for her family, while watching out for Sonny, seemed more than she could bear. She went through several sustained periods of deep despair and discouragement. It all seemed to wear her down and sap her of her strength. The only things that sustained her were her awareness that God was with her, and the thought it would all be over soon.

In July, 1999, after three years of absence, Sonny finally finished medical school. It is amazing to consider that when Sonny and Happiness were married in April, 1982, Sonny was already living in Mexico, supposedly attending medical school! Now, after all those years, he had finally finished, something he never could have done without the support of his wife. In fact, when it came time for his graduation, Happiness flew from the States down to the Dominican Republic to be with him for his special event. She didn't have to of course. Somehow she wanted to; maybe because she sensed that her husband was a "lost sheep" that God was calling her to feed, but regardless, the motivation was definitely heaven-sent.

That night, following the graduation, some of the students hosted a graduation party for Sonny and his friends who had graduated with him. There were about 20 to 30 people all eating, laughing, and sharing stories at a house somewhere in the Dominican Republic. At some point in the festivities, one of the students called the room to order and everyone got quiet to listen.

"Attention, everyone," the apparent emcee announced over the din. *"I have an announcement to make."* The room quieted down and everyone looked attentive. *"We have all labored much over the last few years and today represents a great accomplishment for each of us. Of course none of us would be here without the unseen support of our parents and the rest of our families. However there is one family member here today, all the way from the United States, who deserves special recognition. Would Happiness Dike please come forward?"*

Happiness was shocked and a bit embarrassed at the attention. She looked around the room and realized that everyone expected her to comply. She walked forward and shyly took her place in front of the room.

"Mrs. Dike, we have all seen how you have supported your husband in his schooling. We know that you are home in America with four growing children and that you worked three jobs to make sure that he could be here today. We would like to present you with this certificate recognizing you as the Most Supportive Wife in our 1999 class." Happiness smiled broadly and accepted the certificate to the applause of the room.

It may have been just a simple gesture, made in a simple setting, but the appreciation by Sonny and the students was real and Happiness knew it. On the outside, Happiness restrained the tears, but on the inside she cried; not out of sorrow by any means, but out of an empty well of emotions that was grateful to receive even just a few drops of appreciation. She had received so little of that over the years, despite all she had sacrificed for this man. So at least for a few moments, in the midst of students she didn't know, she allowed herself to bask in the warmth of a genuine thank you.

Sonny and Happiness spent the next few days together in the Dominican Republic before returning home. It was a time of reassessment of their relationship; it was a time of emotional restoration, and it was a time for two to become "one" once again. During that time, Sonny shared with her his gratitude and appreciation for how much Happiness had helped him. They began to talk once again about their future together, about how things would be different, and about how he was going to be a better, more supportive husband. Sonny promised that he would love her and take care of her and the children.

Whether it was the special Caribbean trade winds, the special glow of an island sunset, or just the relief of it all being done, we will never know; but for some reason, Happiness believed him.

19

HITTING BOTTOM

❧

Upon their arrival back home in Virginia, in June of 1999, the children were delighted to see their father again. It had been three years since they had been together as a family. The length of time apart, coupled with the renewed joy the children saw in their parent's faces, combined to produce an air of excitement amongst them all. There was a sense that finally, they were going to be a happy, loving family.

Sonny had a lot of re-adjusting to do. For the past three years he had been living by himself; now he was part of a family of six. During the three years he had been gone, his children had grown considerably. Queenette, his oldest daughter, had just turned 16; Millie was now 14 and the twin boys, JD and Charles were now 12 years old. Despite such a long absence, Sonny managed to quickly re-bond with the children, pumping them up with tales of the Dominican Republic and of his time there. He agreed to watch the kids and even did some periodic cooking; a welcome change from the Sonny that Happiness was used to.

Part of the re-adjustment period for Sonny entailed finding a job, which the family desperately needed to take pressure off of Happiness. She had pushed hard while he was gone, but now it was time for Sonny to pick up the slack. Regrettably, the job search revealed the "old Sonny" once again. To say that job hunting was not Sonny's forte would be kind. Actually, Sonny's efforts were less than stellar; ranging from extreme procrastination on his best days, to outright refusal to do anything on his worst days. In fact, had it not been for Happiness, he likely would not have found a job.

When Sonny balked, Happiness wrote his resume, wrote his application letters, and basically "held his hand" throughout the job search process. She mailed out what seemed like a zillion resumes and applications to various employers on his behalf. Her efforts resulted in Sonny receiving offers for interviews for two openings that looked promising; both as medical research assistants. Ultimately Sonny took the position at John Hopkins University.

With a job secured, Sonny still leaned heavily on Happiness to assist him in learning his new commute. Getting Sonny acclimated and adjusted to his new job and his new commute was almost like taking care of a small child; he demonstrated such little initiative. At first she drove him to Washington, D.C., and helped him find the right train to catch on to Baltimore. Later, she showed him how to use the infamous "Slug Lines" to catch rides into D.C, and even drove him to the commuter lots where the Slug Lines formed.

Once Sonny had secured a job and felt comfortable in his commute, rather than demonstrate gratitude to Happiness, he showed greater levels of contempt towards her and a desire to be left alone. He began to turn private, shutting himself off from family interactions. Although he was now studying for his medical board exam, he made no effort to mingle with the family, find out how the family was doing, or even trying to be a part of his family's world. It would have taken very little time or effort to ask his wife and children how their day was or what activities they were involved in, yet Sonny didn't even make that minimal effort.

Sonny was beginning to revert to his old habits and his recent openness with the family was now gone. It was as if he had used his family to get what he needed and now that he had it, they were of no use to him. He stopped helping around the house or interacting with the children. While he spent time studying, or appearing to study, the bulk of his home hours were devoted to his new faithful companion, the television. Maybe he should have been more devoted to his medical books than the television. When he took the medical board exam the first time, he flunked.

At a time when finances should have been in abundance, given Sonny's new job and Happiness' income from her two jobs, instead it was a period of financial disaster. Past due notices began to appear regularly in the mail and Happiness couldn't understand why they were always running out of money. She complained about all this to Sonny, but he just ignored her and brushed her off. She was at a disadvantage dealing with the family finances since Sonny always knew how much she made, yet Sonny would never reveal to her how much he made. So while she didn't know for sure, she couldn't help thinking that something was not right.

Her curiosity prompted her to go on-line and check their joint checking account statements, something she rarely did, having trusted Sonny to handle those matters. When she did, she was stunned at what she found. Sonny had been making daily withdrawals from the Baltimore and D.C. ATM machines, totaling at least $200 a week from their joint account.

Happiness asked Sonny about her discovery. When she did, Sonny was initially apologetic, and explained that the money was needed to cover his transportation expenses; but those were expenses his job was reimbursing. He was lying to her. She knew that he was hiding something.

Later while he was gone, Happiness went to the dining room table where he had laid out his medical board study materials. She looked through some of his papers, and in no time discovered the reason for the numerous withdrawals. There, hiding under his exam preparation outlines and papers, she found a huge quantity of used lottery tickets, lottery numbers, and a calendar he used to record his daily play of the lottery; along with recently purchased tickets from the D.C., Maryland, and Virginia lotteries. The tickets showed he was playing some games every day; the rest on a weekly basis, and his notes indicated a very sophisticated gambling operation.

Now she was really curious as to what else Sonny might be hiding. She decided to look in Sonny's closet, where she found more lottery tickets, condoms, pornographic magazines and materials from online dating services. *No wonder we never have any money! He is squandering it faster than we can earn it!*

For a few moments she just sat in the closet in silent rage. She thought of all the nights she had taken caffeine pills to stay awake through her shift at the nursing home, only to go directly to the mall for another eight hours of toil. She thought of Sonny gambling while she pinched every penny to buy the groceries and fished through boxes of donations to find school clothes for the children. She thought of how she had explained to J.D. and Charles why they must wear shoes that were a little too tight for a couple months longer while Sonny bought women expensive drinks at a bar. Trembling with rage, she waited for him to come home.

When he did, she laid into him, and she was not calm about it. She was yelling before he had even closed the door upon entering. *"Is this what you are doing with your time?"* Happiness demanded, while shaking some of the lottery tickets in his face. *"We thought you were studying; we left you alone. Is this how you treat us? We gave up so much for you. It's no wonder you didn't pass the board exam the first time."* Sonny stayed quiet throughout her blast of emotion. Yet, as quickly as her anger arose, it ended. She was done; she had spoken her mind and there was nothing left to say. But she knew what she had to do.

The next paycheck Happiness received, she used as a deposit to establish a new, separate account in her name. She was through with throwing her money away, feeding Sonny's habits of greed and lust. Although she could have, and it would have been completely justified, Happiness did not withdraw one cent from their joint account. She left it entirely for Sonny to consume. It was yet another act of mercy she showed him, yet Sonny never acknowledged it. Instead, he even lied about it to his family.

It was only a few days later when she overheard Sonny talking on the phone to his sister Evelyn in Gladstone, Missouri.

"No, you would not believe it. The stupid fool has cleaned me out," Sonny's voice was filled with all the moral outrage of a crime victim as he talked on the phone in the bedroom. *"I am nearly broke after working so hard all day, Evelyn. I cannot even get a hot meal. She badgers me constantly about why I do not cook and clean for her and treat her like the queen she was in her father's house."*

Happiness could not believe what she was hearing. She had entered the house quietly with a bag of groceries; obviously, Sonny had not heard her come in.

"Yes, and she is forever asking me for money. She has become like those American women who think they can order their husbands around like dogs. I told our father that Happiness was a spoiled brat. Her father was always

telling everyone in Elele that his little Happy was too good and too pretty for anyone. Well, I can tell you this, my sister; it has gone to her head. I don't know who she thinks she is."

Happiness was taken aback. After all the sacrifices she had made for him, he continued to use her to cover for his shameful conduct. It was as if he had no conscience. Again, she felt anger swelling up inside her. She had been through too much to back down now.

When Sonny hung up the phone, in a voice that was remarkably restrained given the circumstances, Happiness asked him why he had just lied about her. Now it was Sonny's turn to erupt into rage. He began yelling at her, accusing her of trying to leave him with nothing; she had wronged him, and it wasn't right. Clearly, he was trying to invoke his old methods of intimidation, hoping she would back down. He knew he was in the wrong, but maybe he could bully his way out of this.

Happiness wouldn't let him. He could not intimidate her any more. She gave it right back to him, yelling with equal fervor, yet without losing her reason. She laid out her case like a prosecutor in a closing argument before the jury:

> *"We have four children to care for. We looked to you for help. We gave up so much to get you through school and I promised the children that when you came back, we could have our lives back and slow down scrabbling to make money. Have you already forgotten your promises? Have you forgotten what you told me in the Dominican Republic that you would do better to support me and take care of the family?"*

He walked away and the argument was over. Inside, Happiness now realized that just as their argument was over, so too was their marriage. It didn't hit her right away, but over the course of the next few days, she was over-whelmed with disappointment and hurt. It seemed that what few hopes she had left for a life together were now dashed; splattered into little fragments of despair.

She reflected again upon those fleeting moments of joy in the Dominican Republic. He had been "Mr. Charming", the one who would be a proper husband to her at last; he would finally break the mold of old habits that had previously hindered their relationship. She had believed in him again; she had felt this was going to work this time; that it would all be worth the pain and suffering of the past. She had placed a lot of faith in that man. Now, it hurt to the deepest reaches of her soul watching him self-destruct once more, given all the chances she had given him; after all she had done to help him.

She began to reflect on the disappointment and, as she would later describe it, *"the disappointment consumed me."* Her focus turned completely negative, as she tortured herself with questions; *"What kind of life do I have? Why are all my friends doing well, but I never am? Everyone else seems to succeed; what is wrong with me?"* The hurt was as endless as were the questions.

Like an astronomer's Black Hole, everything was imploding in on her and it hurt more than words could describe. She felt like a complete loser. She had tried so hard to make her marriage work. She had scratched and clawed to succeed and provide for her family, she had poured every ounce of love and forgiveness into her husband, and yet it seemed to gain her nothing more than greater heartache.

After a week of trying to get through work, she knew she was in no condition to go out in public. She was an emotional wreck. She took two weeks of sick leave so she could be alone. At home, around her children, she did her best to pretend that everything was okay, but it was all an act. Once the children left for school, she let herself slide into an emotional abyss. Everyday for the next two weeks, she locked herself up in her room, shut the curtains and laid in her bed in complete darkness. It was here, day after day, that she went from living, to merely existing, and she existed in a world of despair.

It hurt to think, after all the promises Sonny had made to her in the Dominican Republic; after all the expectations she had of a new beginning, how Sonny so utterly failed to take his promises seriously. When Sonny would come home from work during this time, he just ignored her, like she didn't exist. Rather than apologize for how he had treated her, or failed to keep his promises to her, instead, he acted as if he was too good for her. As she described it, he refused to *"come down to my level because he was the man and I was only a lowly wife."*

Up to this point, she had always tried to give her children hope that when their Dad returned from medical school, everything would be alright. So all these failed promises hit her hard. *For all these years I have fought and fought. I built a life on my own and then I took Sonny back, believing that he could never hurt me again as he had once done. Then I allowed myself to hope that he would really change, that he would take care of us. I allowed myself to trust that he could actually love me, instead of use me and disrespect me the way he has always done.*

Opening her heart to Sonny again had set her up for a disappointment more devastating than anything she had experienced before. *I am old now. Who wants a middle-aged woman with four children? The only way I can survive is to divorce him, and what is a divorcee but a failure and a shame on her family? Who can comfort me now? I don't want to be comforted. I want to give up and die!*

212

Happiness allowed herself to plummet emotionally into that abyss of sorrow; to the point so deep, she couldn't feel anymore. She was becoming numb to it all; anesthetized to the pain that was cutting her so deep. She had always been a fighter, but she was tired of fighting; she had no more energy to battle.

She felt she was worthless; not deserving of anything good anymore. Sadly, given her relationship with the Lord that had been her steadying influence all her life, Happiness even turned away from God at this point. She didn't want to think about Him; she didn't want anything positive in her life right now. She just wanted to be left alone and she wasn't looking to come out of her sorrow.

Happiness had finally hit the emotional bottom of her life. Given what she had been through during the course of her marriage, that was saying a lot. Today she recalls this lowest point in her life with these haunting words:

"I was soaking in my misery. I would just lie there in bed thinking how horrible my life was; feeling sorry for myself. I had no strength to move; I couldn't get up; I was too mentally heavy. I didn't want to be comforted or encouraged. I just wanted to be left alone; I shut down completely."

Indeed she did. Soon she stopped bothering to get dressed, to shower, to put any make-up on, or even to comb her hair. She just lay in bed in the dark with the drapes closed, shut out from life and feeling. It may sound strange, but in a sense, Happiness had reached the point in her depression where it felt good to just lie there. She had shut herself off from responsibility, from decisions, from thinking, from everything that required any degree of effort. Emotionally, she no longer hurt. Like the paralyzed patient who is numb to physical pain, Happiness was numb to the emotional pain.

In so many ways, it seemed as if the devil had finally won in his quest to derail Happiness from her eternal destiny. He had destroyed her marriage, and with it, her hopes of having a happy home with a loving family. He had destroyed her dreams, and with them, her desire to pursue anything worthwhile. Finally, he had destroyed her remembrance of who she was in Christ; her true identity that marked her for greatness in God's kingdom. The devil must have been in a gleeful mood as he watched Happiness lying in bed in that darkened room, but if he was, his glee was premature. God had already been planning for the restoration of the daughter He loved so much. He knew what she needed, and He was in the midst of making all the heavenly arrangements to re-energize her.

Before she had taken her two weeks of sick leave, and upon completion of another day of work at which she was forced to wear her artificial mask of emotional stability, Happiness was standing in a "slug line", along with an assortment of other people she didn't know, awaiting a ride home. She watched as drivers would pull up to the front of the line, pick up two "slugs" (riders who got a free ride from the driver in exchange for giving the driver the required three people to drive in the high occupancy lanes that whisked cars past the snarled commuter traffic), and drive off toward the specially designated lanes between the congested freeway lanes.

The gentleman next to her in line engaged her in idle conversation as she waited her turn. She learned he was assisting people to get needed help in counseling. Up until now, no one knew what Happiness was going through. She had shared it with no one. Now, with this stranger that she sensed would not judge her, she shared a little of what had been happening, and before parting their separate ways, they exchanged business cards.

Now, in her final week away from work, during her deepest point of depression, Happiness received a call from that person, checking up on her. He had not seen her for a couple of weeks and wanted to make sure she was okay. That call, from a person she felt would understand where she was coming from, served to open the floodgates of her emotions. She poured out her story in detail, and in response, the gentleman encouraged her to seek professional help. With great hesitation and reluctance, Happiness took his advice and met with a psychologist.

Once home, having seen a "shrink" and now armed with anti-depressants, Happiness felt like she had nothing positive to show for her reaching out for help, except to be labeled as a "nut case." She felt betrayed by life, sought a temporary escape, and crawled back into bed.

Over the course of the next few days, Happiness continued to become more annoyed with how Sonny failed to help her with the household chores and the children even though he was aware she was battling with severe depression. She noticed that he never knocked on her bedroom door to see if she was alright, never asked how she was feeling, and never showed any care or concern for her welfare. She was confronting the lowest ebb of her life and her own husband could care less. She had always been there when Sonny needed help, yet he was not there for her.

It was time for another confrontation. When Sonny arrived home the next day, Happiness let loose with her anger. She was ashamed that she had been "forced" to see a psychologist and receive anti-depressant pills, and she placed the blame where it belonged; on Sonny. In her disgust with him, she showed him the pills she had been prescribed and told him of her visit to see "a shrink." She told him that his neglect of the family and contempt toward her had led her to this predicament.

As Happiness poured forth her frustrations, she noticed his curious response. He began smiling in amusement with an expression that conveyed he knew his wife was crazy and this just confirmed it. She had expected some type of sympathy. Instead, she was stunned to realize he wanted to use this information against her; to justify his behavior toward her, and to somehow affirm himself. He was almost gloating in an attitude of victory. He was not her ally; he was her enemy, seeking to tear her down. Even worse, she saw his intentions to get her committed to a mental institution where he would be rid of her without having to divorce her, the latter being an act that their culture and their families did not approve.

God's plan of restoration was now unleashed. Like a miraculous jolt of energy and renewed conviction, Happiness came back to life; real life with purpose. Her anger at his selfishness rose up like a spring of rushing water, refurbishing her as no anti-depressant pill ever could. Once again, the devil had overplayed his cards. Where once there was a broken spirit within her, now there was new life, new determination, and new hope. Up until now, she had avoided taking any of the anti-depressants, worried they might addict her. Now, she vowed within herself that she would never take a single pill or go to another counseling session. Never had she felt such strong resolve and determination. She was restored in an instant. *No. No. I will not let him crush me. I will not let him defeat me.*

Each day Sonny continued to neglect his responsibilities around the house, and each day Happiness would rise with new purpose and new energy in spite of him. No longer did she allow him to get her down.

As the morning sun dawned that next Friday, August 4, 2000, Happiness awoke with no premonition that this would be any special day, but it certainly would. While Happiness stood over the kitchen sink washing another set of dishes that Sonny refused to clean, Sonny was sitting nearby. At this point he was no more than an abusive room-mate who had overstayed his welcome. Happiness may not have realized it, but as she stood there washing the dishes, she was like a long dormant volcano coming to life. Years of built up emotional hurt began to build inside her, rising up from the deep underground of her soul. The pressure needed to be released and so she began to tell him off. The underlying anger rose slowly at first, then more steadily, the more she talked.

At first she told him how disappointed she was in him after all she had done to support him; that she was tired of living a lie in their marriage, and that he had deeply wounded her without remorse. Sonny just ignored her, but she continued to vent, the resentment rising higher inside her. She told him that his continued disrespect of her and obvious lack of any kind of love or compassion towards her gave her no further hope that their marriage could be saved. Still Sonny ignored her. Now, with her emotions rising further, she began to curse at him. She cursed the day she met him; she cursed the day she married him; and she cursed whatever it was that brought them together. The more she cursed him, the more liberated she felt. It was as if each declaration she made cut off another chain of bondage from her neck. Now she had his attention and he tried to interrupt her, but she wouldn't stop.

Then, in a rage that was rising in him, Sonny tried his old trick of physical intimidation. He started coming towards her with his fist raised to hit her, but she was no longer under his spell. Happiness did not flinch as she used to. Instead she grabbed a drinking glass, smashed it against the counter and held the jagged edges back in his face. Sonny stopped in shock.

"Don't you dare touch me, or I will kill you!" she
yelled, with all the force and fury of a cornered animal.
As she stood there ready to jam the glass into his face, her
voice was saturated with contempt.

"You will go to jail!" Sonny stammered, trying to calm
her down.

*"Oh really? You know nothing of American law! I will
tell the judge how many times you have struck me and I
will tell them that I feared for my life. It is called Battered
Wife Syndrome. It is on television all the time. One woman
burned her husband to death in his bed and she is walking
around free right now! They will never lock me up for
killing you!"* Every muscle in her body was taut, and she
raised the broken glass to strike. The outrage she felt had
overpowered both her depression and her fear.

For a moment, Happiness stood frozen, glass tightly
gripped in the air, her arm muscles taunt and ready to react
to any aggressive movement by Sonny. She meant business and her voice came across with authority. She wasn't
afraid; she was too full of rage for that. How dare Sonny
think he could raise his hand and threaten to hit her. If
he made even the slightest move towards her now, she
was ready to strike with all the force she had; whatever it
took, she was going to take him out. Sonny was looking
at a different woman than the one he so easily intimidated
during most of their marriage. He knew he was no match
for her in her determined fury. He wisely backed off and
walked out of the house.

Happiness, without hesitation, picked up the phone,
called a lawyer she found listed in the phone book, and
asked him to begin divorce proceedings.

Over the course of the next few weeks, Sonny made
life miserable for her; refusing to move out, eating the food
Happiness cooked, and continuing to "free load" off of her.
On August 25, 2000, Happiness was granted a legal separa-

tion, along with a court order for Sonny to leave the house. Yet Sonny stayed on; vowing to her that he would never leave the house. It was a test of wills, with Sonny confident that Happiness would back down as she always had before.

He was counting on the belief that Happiness would never have the fortitude to kick him out or go through with the divorce. He used her faith in God against her, and her awareness that God did not like divorce. He also counted on her being restrained by family reputation and Nigerian custom to not go through with a divorce or to kick him out.

He badly miscalculated. Happiness had already wrestled with the divorce issue with the Lord. In her heart, she knew the marriage was finally over. She had reached a point where God was just going to have to show mercy or understanding, both for her lack of forgiveness toward Sonny, as well as for the divorce. As she would say years later, *"This time, I had no forgiveness for him. If I have to go to hell, then so be it. I have done my best."*

Another month passed by, with no change in their situation. Happiness was growing in resentment toward him with each passing day; Sonny growing more confident he was winning this test of wills. Again, Sonny was underestimating the resolve and fortitude of his wife. Even though she was biding her time, she would not back down as Sonny had expected. According to her, *"he was in my way; a big block of evil sitting there."*

One day, Happiness reminded him, *"You're not supposed to be living here."* Sonny just ignored her, so when he left for work, Happiness went to the police station and asked for advice on how to get him out of the house. Once they learned she had a court order of separation, they advised her they could physically remove him. Arrangements were made immediately for a forced removal for that coming Friday.

On Friday, Sonny came home from work and found some of his bags were packed. Happiness told him that he had to leave the house now. Sonny scoffed at what he figured was another empty threat; called her crazy, and proceeded to eat dinner and begin watching television. He wasn't leaving. Happiness called the police as pre-planned and within ten minutes three armed police officers, with hands clutching their holsters, walked up to the door to remove him from the premises.

When the police knocked at their door, Happiness answered it, invited them in, and directed them into the living room where Sonny was watching TV. They asked him, *"Are you Sonny Dike?"* His affirmative reply was filled with arrogance. *"You are not supposed to be here,"* the lead officer continued in a calm, yet firm voice. Sonny tried to talk his way out of the situation. *"Why should I leave? This is my house and these are my children."* His contempt was revealed with every word. The officers would listen to none of his appeals to stay. *"Okay, you have to leave now,"* was all the lead officer said in reply. As one officer was posted at the door, another in the living room, the third one stood close to Sonny, waiting for Sonny to respond.

Happiness stood back out of the way, but watching as the drama unfolded. Sonny was playing his old games. He just sat there on the couch not moving for awhile, letting the police know that he was still in control of the situation, or so he thought. Finally, when the officers didn't budge, Sonny slowly stood up, walked to the bedroom and began to pack as slowly as humanly possible. The officers watched his every move while Happiness continued to stand back out of the way. Queenette, who had been watching Millie, Charles and JD downstairs in the basement, took them to a neighbor's house shortly after the police arrived, keeping them safely away from a possible violent reaction by Sonny. She had returned while her Dad was still playing his control games. After what seemed like an inordinate amount of time, the officers finally escorted Sonny out the door.

There was only one problem. He didn't have a car. Happiness had expected him to take a cab to a nearby motel, but instead, Sonny asked Queenette to drive him. However, rather than having Queenette drive him to a local motel, he had his daughter drive him all the way to Maryland where a friend of his lived, about one and one-half hours away.

While waiting for Queenette to return, Happiness couldn't help but reflect over her marriage that was finally over. Not once did she ever receive a birthday, Christmas or other holiday gift from her husband. He never recognized their anniversary and he never once even gave her a simple card on any holiday or other occasion. Although Happiness made sure the family celebrated Sonny's birthday with cards, cake, and gifts each July 5th, Sonny would not so much as even wish her a "happy birthday" when her birthday arrived roughly a week later!

Unlike other wives who received flowers, cards of love, gifts from the heart and simple, but vital words of endear-ment along the way, Happiness received little more than contempt. While other wives were receiving kisses and hugs of affectionate embrace, Happiness at worst was being raped and sexually abused, and at best, completely ignored. She never expected a perfect husband, just one who adored her, who loved her, who at least wanted her. She wasn't asking for much.

She had often dreamed of what it would be like to have a husband who reached for her hand in tenderness rather than selfish lust; who looked into her eyes with acceptance rather than disdain; who whispered words of adoration and encouragement, rather than yelled curses of hate. It had been a long journey since she had agreed to marry Sonny, seemingly far longer than the eighteen years of marriage she actually had endured to this point. Torment and despair have a tendency of slowing down time. Every time she saw a happy couple, it served as a painful reminder of what she never had, but always wanted. Such simple dreams, yet unfulfilled. It hurt. As she would describe it later, *"Life with Sonny was miserable. I gave and I gave and I gave. Yet, he hated to see me happy. He would always find a way to crush me."* Now the man who had brought her so much pain, was finally out of her life. It felt good; it felt really good. She was so glad it was over.

There remained one last order of business she wanted to take care of. Now that Happiness had her life back, she decided to do something she had wanted to do since late June, 1994. After six years of putting her dream on hold for Sonny, she re-enrolled in Strayer University's master's program. Sonny would no longer be able to stop her from getting her MBA.

20

CONFRONTING THE ENEMY

❧

"*L*isten, Happy. You'll have to act fast,*" Isaiah urged her in a static-filled call from Nigeria. Happiness could not imagine what the problem could be. True, Sonny was doing all he could to slow the divorce process, but a court commissioner had been appointed and things seemed to be moving along.

"What is it?"

"*Chidi called me last night. He told me his cousins would be furious with him if they knew he was calling me. But Sonny's father is very ill. They don't want you to know because they have been repeating Sonny's lies to their parents, trying to turn them against you and cover for him. They have said that you spent all Sonny's money and that you are angry with him because he can't give you a fancy enough lifestyle. They want to knock you out of the family hierarchy.*"

"So that is it," Happiness sighed. "*I have two sons with the Dike name, the children of their eldest son, and they want to disown us by deception?*"

"*I am afraid so. Their parents have always loved you. If you speak to them again, especially Mr. Dike, they are afraid he will know the truth about Sonny and know that his own daughters are liars. Sonny is in Nigeria right now making arrangements for Mr. Dike to come to America for treatment. Happy, you must find a way to see him when he is there. You must find a way to take the children to him. Chidi tells me that Mr. Dike often asks for them."*

"But surely he will stay with Sonny when he comes!" Happiness said, *"It is only proper that he should stay with his oldest son."*

"No Happy, they are taking him to Evelyn's house in Missouri, because it is so far away. This way they can make it difficult for you to take the children to see him, and they can tell him that it is you who doesn't want the children to see him!"

"Oh, the lies!" Happiness felt grieved. She no longer worried about her own reputation; that was in God's hands. But the thought of her father-in-law, ill and thinking that she did not love him or want him to see his grandchildren was almost too much to bear. *"I will call as soon as he arrives,"* Happiness promised Isaiah before hanging up.

Sonny's father, Mr. Dike was a very prominent man in Rivers State. In fact, he was a chief in his local community, a position of high authority and strong influence, deeply respected by all citizens. He had also been the friend and close advisor to the former Governor of Rivers State, and his connections with various governmental and business leaders were many. How Chief Dike was treated was there-fore a matter, not just of family concern, but of community concern as well.

Once she learned he was in the States, Happiness called him right away.

"Is that you, my Happy?" Mr. Dike's voice was notice-ably frailer than Happiness remembered it. He always called her "My Happy", the same pet name that her real father used to call her.

"Yes, Papa, it is I. I am praying daily for the full resto-ration of your health. Your grandchildren, too, call your name before heaven each morning and evening."

"Will I not see you, my Happy? They say that you will not come. Will I not see my grandchildren?" He obviously didn't know his family was intentionally preventing such a visit, and Happiness would not tell him; she didn't want to disappoint him. She wouldn't even tell him she and Sonny were legally separated and in the midst of a protracted divorce. She knew she held a special place in his heart and her children were the "apple of his eyes." As his only grandchildren, they were part of his legacy. The boys espe-cially brought him delight as they would carry on the Dike family name. While Happiness would not "spill the beans" about Sonny or the rest of the family, she did tell Chief Dike that she and the children loved him and she promised him that he would see his grandchildren.

"No, Papa, we will come. Just get well, Papa," she encouraged him, *"We will come there as soon as we can, we are making plans."*

True to her word, Happiness worked with her brother-in-law Daniel, one of her few allies in the Dike family, to arrange a visit with Chief Dike. As she did so, it became apparent the family would never permit her to see him, and perhaps not even the girls, but she remained hopeful they would allow his grandsons to see him. By pre-arrangement, she put her two boys on a plane to California to stay with Daniel and his wife with the understanding that they would make sure the boys got to Kansas City to see their grand-father. Sadly, the plan did not succeed. The grudge against her, likely intervened in the plan, because Happiness' boys spent two weeks with Daniel before returning home, and they were never allowed to visit their grandfather.

—

Shortly thereafter, in August, 2001, her father-in-law passed away. Thanks to his vindictive children, he did so having never seen his beloved grandchildren that bore his name, nor the daughter-in-law he cherished so deeply. Now, the obvious intention of Sonny and the other Dike children was to prevent Happiness from learning of Chief Dike's death so she would not be at the funeral. Her absence at the funeral would perpetuate the lie back in Nigeria that Happiness was selfish and didn't care about them. Given the status and wealth of the Dike family, the funeral would be very formal, with a large crowd and many dignitaries in attendance. The absence of Happiness would be a big deal. So Sonny and the Dike children made arrangements to send Chief Dike's body back to Nigeria for the funeral and burial, but no one told Happiness, not even Daniel, her former ally within the Dike family. It was a set up from the outset to make her look bad.

But God was with Happiness and He was super-naturally working out arrangements for her to be vindicated of all the lies spoken over her to her community back home. Her brother Isaiah, who still lived in Nigeria, was the first of the Emejuru family to learn about the death and upcoming plans for burial. He immediately called Happiness once he heard the news, although several days had already been lost and she had little time left. Sonny's plan to withhold this information from her to prevent her from appearing at the funeral had put Happiness in a difficult bind. Had it not been for her brother Isaiah and Sonny's cousin Aaron who confirmed it, she wouldn't have even known about the funeral and her fate in the community would have been sealed. Even as it was, she discovered it was too late for her to book a direct flight to Nigeria through normal channels. She desperately needed God's miraculous intervention to avoid missing the funeral, and that is exactly what she received.

First, Happiness remembered a friend in Nigeria who happened to be a government official in charge of all airports in Nigeria! Through his inside connections, she was able to get a flight that arrived in Nigeria in time for the funeral, but even then, the flight would arrive only hours before the funeral was to commence. It would be a race against time, with no room for flight delays, or traffic jams. With her flight secured, Happiness made arrangements with her brother Isaiah, to pick her up and transport her to the funeral as soon as she arrived in country. Time would be of the essence.

The long transatlantic flight offered Happiness a rare moment to reflect. Here she was, returning to Elele, the home that she had been so reluctant to leave, yet now unsure whether anyone but her nearest family would welcome her. She had spent nearly as many years as Mrs. Sonny Dike than she had ever spent as the joyful, hopeful Happiness Emejuru. She wondered if that Happiness was still inside her. For years she had toiled and wept, trying to hold life together for herself and her children. Yet now she was returning to a village that thought she had abandoned her husband and in-laws out of selfishness. It was outrageous, insulting, and unfair; yet a strange peace seemed to saturate her heart. *It doesn't matter. God will vindicate me!*

When the flight touched down in Nigeria, Isaiah was waiting for her as planned and they rushed to his apartment so that she could shower and change. They pulled up to the funeral and instead of parking behind the large cluster of cars; Isaiah drove his black Mercedes to the front and opened the door for her as if he were her driver. Happiness, stepped out of the car wearing a stunningly stylish black silk suit, black high heels, and a pair of large Gucci sunglasses. She looked the part of a Hollywood movie star. As they walked up toward the canopy-covered area where the service was taking place, all eyes had turned their way.

227

Jaws dropped as the crowd tried to ascertain who this trendy American was that was joining the funeral service. The casket was already lying in state in front of seated family members and dignitaries, along with numerous onlookers standing outside the rows of chairs.

A quick scan of the crowd revealed that not only had no place been reserved for Happiness in the front as it should have been, but that the Emejuru family members were standing in the back as if they were nobodies. Anyone with an understanding of Nigerian customs would realize that this was far more than an oversight: it was an intentional insult of the highest magnitude; just as it was intended to be. Happiness kept her cool.

Instead of cowering in the back, Happiness took her brother's arm with confidence and walked past all the rows of seats in the back. *Who is the American?* The whispers were audible as all eyes began to follow her to the front where ushers scrambled to provide Happiness a special chair directly behind her mother-in-law. As she took her seat, the crowd of people began to realize who she was. *They said she did not want to come! They said she prevented the Chief from seeing his grandchildren. Look at her! She looks like a celebrity!*

Now God was bringing her vindication. All the lies spoken about her were being exposed by this heavenly prepared "grand entrance." Truly, God had "prepared a table" for Happiness "in the presence of her enemies." Following the ceremony, the family walked to the grave site for the burial. It was common practice for the eldest son and his wife to head the procession. To save face, Sonny walked side by side with Happiness as a couple, and Happiness played along, no one knowing they were legally separated and in the process of getting a divorce.

Following the graveside ceremony, family members and guests began to console and talk amongst each other.

Happiness approached her mother-in-law, discreetly gave her some money to bless her, as she had done periodically throughout the last few years, and then offered Mrs. Dike a traditional greeting of respect, leaning forward to embrace her.

"Mother," she said with deep concern, *"I am so sorry. Your husband was a wise and great man and I was blessed to be called daughter by him. May God comfort you."* Mrs. Dike said nothing and did not return the embrace.

Unfazed, Happiness proceeded to greet and talk with the other relatives and guests. Immediately the attendees could see that she was the same Happiness they all remembered: the cheerful, respectful, and kind girl that had been a joy to know and the pride of Elele. Many extended family members embraced her as they saw with their own eyes that the stories they heard could not possibly be true. There was no selfish ambition, no disregard for traditional ways, no disrespect in this woman's demeanor or countenance. By virtue of her presence there, and the gracious manner in which she carried herself, Happiness began to win over the hearts of nearly everyone in attendance, a victory of no small measure. She was openly embraced by all but the immediate Dike family, who had tried so hard to perpetuate the lies about her.

Nonetheless, as she tried to make her way up the outside steps to the upstairs area of the Dike family residence where the immediate family was gathering, it was clear that the Dike's did not want her up there. She noticed an unspoken, yet distinct message that she was not welcome. As the wife of their eldest son and mother of their grandchildren, Happiness could have insisted on attending, but to do so would likely have created a scene. So, consistent with her true character, she chose not to create a disturbance. Happiness graciously made her way back down the stairs, and left.

The following day Happiness went to visit the family of then Speaker of the House for Rivers State, and now the current Governor, who knew her through her brother Isaiah. He and his family were also friends of her brothers, Isaiah and Ogu. They were delighted to see Happiness again. The former Speaker offered her a government car and driver who would also serve as her bodyguard during her stay in Nigeria. She graciously declined his offer as she had previously accepted a similar offer from a Rivers State assemblyman, the Honorable Hope Ikiriko.

Her first order of business during her stay was to attempt to pierce the lies the family had told her mother-in-law. She went to visit Mrs. Dike who she still deeply respected and cared for. She wanted the opportunity to tell her side of the story and seek to mend the obvious rift between her and the mother-in-law who used to adore her.

The government car and driver pulled into the entrance of the compound, parking near the front of Mrs. Dike's house. The driver let Happiness out of the car, and she was escorted into the house to Mrs. Dike's room. As the mother of the only children that bore the Dike family name, Happiness held a high place of honor and authority under Nigerian custom. She was entitled to enter that compound and their house without appointment.

The door was open as Happiness announced herself to Mrs. Dike. As soon as she saw Happiness at the door, Mrs. Dike became enraged in a spontaneous fury of venomous and derogatory words. Before Happiness had a chance to show her any love or affection, Mrs. Dike demanded that she leave at once. Happiness had clearly been wronged. She had been falsely accused. Justice said she didn't deserve such treatment. Happiness was stunned. She thought that her mother-in-law would at least give her the courtesy of listening to what she had to say. Yet, without trying to defend herself, Happiness respectfully walked back out of the house into the compound, got into the car as the driver held her door, and left, never to see Mrs. Dike again.

The full impact of this tirade by Mrs. Dike cannot be overstated. Chief Dike and Mrs. Dike had always loved Happiness, so much so that many of the Dike children were envious of the attention shown towards her. It was a love without reservation. Happiness meant everything to them. Mrs. Dike had seen Happiness as the chosen wife for her son, much like Rebekah had been for Isaac in the famous Old Testament account. Yet envy and vindictiveness in a family is a powerful component of hatred. Though not justified or deserved, Happiness was feeling the full brunt of years of lies told about her that she was not allowed to contradict.

Sadly, the poison of its venom would serve to create a deeply scarred barrier between Happiness and the people she loved and admired. How ironic that the love and respect she had for the Dike parents was one of the primary reasons she ignored her better judgment and married their son. Moreover, while Happiness had spent years trying to shield the family from Sonny's horrific actions at her own expense, Sonny was telling lies about how terrible of a wife and mother she was. The combination of her merciful withholding of truth, coupled with his selfish and deceptive accusations, led to her, rather than he, being seen as the enemy. Life, which is rarely fair, can sometimes be downright cruel.

Over the next few days, Happiness visited relatives and walked again in the old places of her childhood. She was greeted warmly by everyone, the news about her triumphant appearance at the funeral having quickly spread. She was amazed at how much things had changed in Elele, and not in a good way. The roads and houses that used to be kept repaired and well kept had now noticeably deteriorated. She too had changed. She was no longer innocent or

untouched by life's tragedies. Life's storms had strengthened her in ways even she was not aware.

As she was departing from one of her last visits, she
was presented with an unexpected encounter. She noticed
Sonny, his sister Evelyn, and Daniel, her brother-in-law
coming out of their father's well-known hotel and restaurant. She approached the three of them, but she directed
her attention only at Daniel, the one who had been her
ally, but who failed to tell her about Mr. Dike's death or
funeral. Without any preliminary pleasantries, she came
right to the point: *"You didn't tell me; you lied to me."* She
had been wounded by his disloyalty and deception more
than she realized.

Without giving him an opportunity to respond, she
continued on, *"You could not call to tell me he died and
when they were bringing the body back home? Well, despite
all your efforts, I made it,"* she said defiantly. Daniel
looked down at the ground, ashamed. She sensed he had
wanted to tell her but the family had precluded him from
doing so. Daniel had no words to say. As she had said what
she wanted to, she turned and abruptly walked away.

Happiness had just one last matter to take care of.
The pastor and elders of the local Seventh Day Adventist
Church that she and her family had attended when she
was growing up, had requested a private meeting with her.
They too had heard many rumors about how Happiness had
refused to visit or allow her children to visit Chief Dike,
her father-in-law, before he died. Chief Dike, as well as
Happiness and her family had all been prominent, long-
standing members of the church and the leaders wanted to
determine the truth about what had been going on.

Happiness arrived at the local pastor's two-story house
which served as his living quarters as well as the church
office. She was ushered into the living room where the
pastor and four elders sat in a semi-circle in front of her.

She greeted them respectfully and accepted their invitation to sit down.

"Ah, Mrs. Dike! It is hard for me not to call you little Happiness anymore! But you are indeed a grown woman now," the pastor remarked in a fatherly tone.

"It is a joy to see you, Pastor," said Happiness, relaxing. The mood was friendlier than she had anticipated.

"I will be direct, since I know you must soon return to the States and we have many things to attend to," the Pastor continued. *"Your father's family and your husband's family are two of the most honorable and important families in Elele and in our church. Never have we had cause to doubt the integrity of any member of either family, but we must be honest and tell you that for years now we have heard many rumors about how you changed when you went to America. When you didn't come to your father's funeral, of course your family said you could not get a visa, but others said you did not want to bother. Then some have said that you refused to visit the Dikes or allow your children to visit Chief Dike before he died. Until now, we have had no opportunity to ask you ourselves, but today we do."* The other elders in attendance nodded in agreement.

"Thank you, Pastor," Happiness responded calmly. *"I am so glad that you have asked me these questions today, because for years I have longed to tell the truth about these matters. I considered writing, to my family, to my in-laws and even to you, Pastor, many times. Yet I did not because I did not want to cause pain for anyone. I see now that this allowed the lies my husband and his siblings told about me to continue unchallenged, and I must trust God to vindicate me."* Again the pastor and elders nodded for her to continue.

This was a God-ordained opportunity for Happiness to finally explain her side of the story to church leaders who had heard many of the same lies and rumors that Mrs. Dike had been told.

Given the opening they provided her, Happiness told them everything. She started by answering their direct question, letting them know she had tried to send her children to see Chief Dike, but the Dike children prevented the visit. Then she proceeded to tell them about her marriage with Sonny from the time she left Nigeria, through the episodes in Mexico, the beatings, the lack of support, the lies, and everything else. These church leaders thus became only the second group of people, after the court personnel in the deportation suspension hearing, to hear her complete story. As she spoke, she saw the pastor and the elders looking at each other and nodding their heads, as if she was confirming what they suspected, but had no knowledge of until now.

Now they were hearing the truth. While they were not surprised that Sonny had been neglectful in his marriage with Happiness, the extent and duration of his actions they found shocking. They sat before Happiness dumbfounded. For a few moments after she finished her story, they couldn't even speak. They were not sure what to say. Finally, the pastor broke their silence: *"Mrs. Dike, what you have said is grievous indeed. We heard rumors of his irresponsible behaviors, even before you were married. However, we had no idea that his depravity had sunk to such a level. It seems clear that you have done a remarkable job suffering through such behavior. Thank you for sharing this with us."*

As the church leaders regained their composure, they began to encourage Happiness to remain strong and to keep up the great job she had done in raising her children. For another twenty minutes or so, they reminisced about old times and the pastor told her news of other people in Elele that she had known. When the meeting concluded, they again thanked her and they offered her their undivided support.

As she left the pastor's house, she marveled at how God had allowed her to be heard before the church leaders of the community that meant so much to her; how He had made sure that Happiness would be given a proper hearing to set forth the truth, even though she had been denied that opportunity by Mrs. Dike.

With that, after a two-week stay, her trip to Nigeria was over and she flew back home to Virginia. She had been vindicated by God to her entire community outside the Dike family. As for the Dike family, they had allowed their minds to be saturated with lies to the point that precluded any hope that truth would prevail over them. It was so sad to see how innocent people and relationships had to be needlessly destroyed for the sake of covering up the shameful life that Sonny had lived.

But God knew the truth; a truth that said, Happiness had conducted herself uprightly, with integrity, and with honor. Unlike the Dike family, she had nothing to be ashamed about. *Oh God, You have vindicated me! You have prepared a table for me in the midst of mine enemies! Oh, may Papa rejoice in heaven to know that his little Happy is Happy once more.*

21

SNATCHED FROM THE CLUTCHES OF DEATH

❧

"*Thank you, Queenette,*" Happiness uttered weakly from the couch as her daughter brought her a cup of tea. She had been back from Nigeria for over two weeks, and still seemed to be jetlagged. For a moment she had worried that perhaps her depression had returned, but she soon laughed away that thought. Emotionally, she felt freer than she had in two decades. Her heart was fine; it was her body that seemed to be permanently run down.

Unfortunately, the common sense treatment of plenty of fluids and rest didn't seem to be working. Soon, she developed a fever which didn't respond to over-the-counter medicines. Later, her body began shaking uncontrollably and she experienced bouts of dizziness. Finally, she realized something was seriously wrong and she needed to see a doctor.

"*Mrs. Dike,*" the nurse said to Happiness as she sat in the waiting room of her doctor's office, "*I have all your lab work here and there is nothing in particular that the doctor can find wrong. I'm afraid there is nothing we can do. Try to drink lots of fluids and get plenty of rest.*"

I have been doing that for five days and I am getting worse! Now she was both perplexed and mildly irritated that the doctor couldn't find anything wrong because she still didn't feel any better. Happiness was extremely weak as she made her way out of the medical building and to her car. As she was driving home, she began to feel as if she might pass out and lose control of the vehicle. *I wonder if someone tried to poison me while I was in Nigeria. Oh God, am I going to die?* She knew something was seriously wrong, and she was concerned that the doctor could not figure out the cause. She decided to call her brother Ogu.

"*What did your doctor say?*" Ogu asked after listening with concerns to her symptoms. He and his family were living in Virginia Beach now, but he still called to check up on his sister on a regular basis.

"*Nothing. The nurse said my tests were normal.*"

"*Did they draw blood? Take urine?*"

"*Yes, they did all that.*"

"*If you contracted a virus in Nigeria it would not show up. Did you tell them you had just been abroad? Did they test you for malaria?*"

"*I did tell them, but I don't know if they tested for malaria,*" she said. It was exhausting just trying to get the words out.

"*You must check yourself into the hospital,*" Ogu declared. "*You are probably dehydrated at a minimum from so many days of fever. Call me when you are checked in.*"

Fortunately, the children were old enough to stay home on their own, and Queenette could call her if anything was wrong. "*Don't worry, my children,*" she said as cheerfully as she could, while gathering up some personal items to take with her to the hospital. "*I will probably just stay the night. I will be better and back home before you know it!*" It was Tuesday, the week of Thanksgiving, 2001 and the cold November air bit at her cheeks as she stumbled back to the car and, although she was still extremely weak and in no condition to drive, she made it to the emergency room. She had been praying and crying out to God for help during the entire 30-minute drive to the hospital.

After being admitted, Happiness saw her nurse bring in a smaller IV bag to add to the larger one that was hydrating her. From her background as a certified nursing assistant, Happiness had some experience with IV infusion therapy. She knew this type of IV bag meant they were putting her on a broad spectrum antibiotic since they couldn't identify the cause of the infection. That was not exactly good news, but she rested easier knowing that doctors and nurses were watching her closely. Throughout that night, the nurses continued to monitor her, periodically coming in to replace the IV bags of potent medicine. *Surely by morning, with the aid of such aggressive amounts of antibiotics, I will be feeling better,"* she thought, as she drifted in and out of sleep.

The next morning, despite the large volume of medicine that had been infused into her weakened body, Happiness felt no better. That fact was mildly alarming to her, but she still had faith the doctors would soon figure out the cause of her illness. She still had her peace, and still believed the medicine would eventually begin to have a positive impact. *There is still time yet for the antibiotics to work. I must not panic. They will find out what is going on.* That afternoon she received her first doctor's report since being admitted.

"Mrs. Dike, I have reviewed your updated lab work from the time you were admitted and we still cannot identify any cause for your illness," the doctor on duty said apologetically. *"Based on your recent visit to Africa, we have done a test for malaria as well, but we won't have those results for a while."*

Happiness wanted to cry, but instead thanked the doctor and promptly called Ogu to relay the message. Her confidence that the doctors would find the answers was beginning to yield. For two more days, Happiness laid in bed growing weaker by the hour. She had plenty of time to contemplate what it could be that was attacking every cell in her body. *Can they make poisons that don't cause you to react until weeks later? Papa said God would protect us from the curses of the witch doctors. Oh, how I wish Papa was here!*

When she realized that her children would have to spend Thanksgiving alone, she could not help but cry. She called Queenette to assure them that all was well, that she was just being kept for observation. She did not want to worry them. Then she called her close friend Debbie Patten, who had been so helpful to her through the years, and who lived right down the street. She explained that the doctors could not figure out what was wrong and that she was getting weaker. She asked Debbie for her prayers, and asked her to look in on her children, since it now appeared that Happiness would not be released from the hospital for several more days. Debbie and Happiness's brother Ogu, were the only two people who knew about her situation.

Throughout the rest of that Wednesday and that evening, nurses continued to replace her IV drip with new bags filled with potent antibiotics. Still she grew weaker.

Oh God, will I ever see my children again?

Thanksgiving came. The doctor on duty stopped by while making his morning rounds. He apologized to Happiness that they still had no definitive answer: the results of all her tests were normal but the malaria test was still pending. Understandably, Happiness was beginning to feel very lonely and helpless. Being in the hospital on Thanksgiving was bad enough. Not knowing if she would ever go home again, or see her children again, was much worse.

With the latest doctor's report, Happiness fully realized she was in serious trouble. Her façade of confidence that the doctors would be able to turn her condition around was now eroding rapidly. As she lay in her hospital bed that Thanksgiving Day, she could overhear from down the hallway family members visiting their relatives, laughing and talking in animated tones, sharing at least in a small way, the Thanksgiving holiday with loved ones. In stark contrast, Happiness remained alone with no visitors or family to comfort her; only the periodic interruption of a nurse coming to check on her IV bag. Happiness passed the time frequently staring absent-mindedly at the IV drips slowly, yet rhythmically, dropping down the tube into her weakened body. She began to feel as if she was dying. All her hopes for living and her emotions began to shut down. She was tired of fighting. She knew she was giving up, surrendering to what now seemed inevitable.

She began to sense she was transitioning to her "death bed." This would be where and how it would all end for her, dying alone in a hospital room far away from her children and everyone she loved. She reflected upon her life. All she could see was sadness, pain and suffering. All she had trusted God for would never come to pass. She had so many things she had wanted to do, so many dreams she hoped to accomplish. She had always wanted to shine for God and make a difference.

Have I come so far only to die here alone? Oh God, for so long I have fought; I have clawed and scraped and toiled. I cannot fight anymore, Lord. My strength is utterly spent. Lord, I am not afraid to die if only You will take care of my children. Always I have wanted to shine for you and make a difference, but if it is time for my light to go out, I am ready.

She sobbed into her pillow as she realized that she never had been able to enjoy this world and the life God had given her. She had never been appreciated; she had never had the opportunity to have a loving marriage and a husband who adored her. She had always wanted to be the ideal wife, one that her husband would be proud of. She wanted so badly for her husband to see how special she was and to experience a relationship where there was no marital cheating, no major fighting, and where they just enjoyed spending time with each other. Indeed, no one really knew who she was as a person; she had always been timid and stayed in the background of every social occasion.

Her tears continued to flow without restraint. She recalled a vision she once had that was so real, she even spoke it out to Sonny during one of their many arguments in which he tried to silence her. She had told him, *"I am like a candle, a light that will continue to shine even when you try to cover my light. Like a lampshade covering the light inside it, my light will still shine forth from below. You can never blot me out,"* she had boldly proclaimed to Sonny that day. *"I will always shine, I can never be blacked out."* That vision now seemed so far away; so distant, and so impossible. Now she felt her light was fading and becoming more and more dim with each IV drip dropping down the plastic tube connected to her. Her moistened pillow case, saturated by tears, was a reminder of her hopeless and lonely condition.

As morning drifted into afternoon, she noticed that even her communication with God began to change. She spoke to God as one who had given up, as one who had fought the good fight of faith, hoped in God and His mercy, but now just wanted to have His peace and die painlessly in her sleep. It wasn't that she was afraid to die; she had too much assurance in God to doubt her heavenly destination and allow fear to grip her. Yet she was extremely disappointed that her life was ending without really having a chance at happiness. After all, wasn't that her name? Wasn't there to be some happiness in her life? Anyway, it was too late for all of that.

With her last remnants of coherency, she began to love on God and to praise Him. She meditated on His presence. She thought of all His promises, all she knew about Him, all He had spared her from. She thanked Him over and over as she prepared herself to be ushered into His eternal presence. After awhile she even began to question if she had already died and didn't know it. *"Do people always know when they are dead?"* she wondered. *"Could I already be dead?"*

She was busy in deep meditation on the throne room of God when she suddenly sensed a presence in her room by her bed. She was startled to open her eyes and see *"this tall, thin, white man"* standing at her bedside. He didn't look anything like the nurses or doctors she had seen. She quickly closed her eyes to get re-oriented as a strange thought came to her, *"Is this how they usher you into heaven?"* *"Am I alive or dead?"* She wasn't sure as she re-opened her eyes. She was truly baffled at who this stranger was in her room when the man introduced himself.

"Hello, I am Pastor Tony Hall from Christ Worship Center down in Woodbridge," he began, his voice firm, yet kind. *"I came to visit a church member who was in a motorcycle accident and Debbie Patten asked that, while I was here, I come by and see you."* As soon as the man said he was a pastor, Happiness knew he was a person of God and the barrier of a stranger being in her room was immediately broken. That title bridged the gap with her and she knew this stranger had been sent by God.

When Pastor Hall asked her if he could pray with her, she readily said yes, returning back to her senses for one last attempt to let God do what He pleased with her. Hope, faith, and a small remnant of courage began to rise up inside her. Then, from the moment Pastor Hall uttered the first word of his prayer, Happiness broke down in uncontrollable tears once more. This time her tears were not

birthed from despair, but came from a deep well of hope.
It was spiritually and mentally overwhelming being transformed from a state of despair to that of divine expectation
in virtually an instant. Her tears became sobs, and her sobs
wouldn't stop throughout the duration of the prayer. God
had not taken her "home" yet. Instead, He was bringing her
back to life!

How long the prayer lasted Happiness could not say; she
didn't hear a word of it until he said "amen." All she knew
was its power was strong and it impacted her immediately.
It was like receiving an injection of strength and vibrancy
and everything pertaining to life. The sensation ran through
her veins and she sensed she had been healed instantly.
What the antibiotics had failed to do over the last two days,
this pastor's prayer accomplished in a moment. At the end
of his prayer, Pastor Hall chatted with her for a short time,
and pronounced her healed. Then, just as quickly as he had
entered her room, he said goodbye and left.

Happiness was filled with peace and a sense of renewal.
She felt as if God had spoken to her, that she now had a
reason to live because God had shown up. She knew she
had been miraculously healed. As she described it later,

> *"Faith and hope overtook what I felt. I didn't feel*
> *hopeless anymore. I was in the Spirit. I had my faith*
> *restored and I wasn't listening to my body anymore*
> *because I knew I was okay; I had received healing.*
> *It was like I had been brought into the presence of*
> *God; I felt His touch in me, close to me, and even*
> *coming through me. It was like God was saying to*
> *me, 'It is finished.' I knew it was over and that I had*
> *been delivered."*

The rest of that Thanksgiving afternoon until the
doctor showed up, Happiness held onto that prayer and

the promise it brought with it. She returned to her meditations with God, only now they were not about preparing to "come home" to Jesus, but instead, they were about expectation for the plans God must have for her. A feeling that her life wasn't over, that she had more time, and that there was a reason to hope again. A revival seed had been planted in her and her faith had been re-ignited.

When the doctor came in with the lab results that evening, she calmly announced that Happiness was doing much better and that she could possibly be discharged "tomorrow." The immediate contrast of prognosis was dramatic, yet the doctor had no explanation. They still didn't know what had happened. Happiness knew the explanation; she knew that what she had just experienced was way beyond the human limits of medical science. She had been supernaturally touched by heaven and she was going to live.

The next day Happiness was discharged as expected, with the doctors never having determined what it was that had almost killed her. In reality, the cause didn't really matter, only the result. Happiness knew that whatever it was that tried to take her life was no match for God. Still, as she waited for her discharge papers to get processed for her release from the hospital, she couldn't help wondering about the stranger who God had sent to pray for her, the one who God had used as His instrument to save her life. Truly he was more than just a pastor; he was a messenger of the Lord. She had known many pastors before, but this one was much different.

Unlike so many other pastors who prayed *hoping* their prayers would be answered, this pastor *knew* his prayers would be answered. When Pastor Hall prayed, he prayed with assurance, and he prayed as one who had engaged in spiritual warfare many times before. He showed confidence in the promises of God to heal and he merely invoked

God's truths. His approach was simple, yet bold, as he took spiritual authority over the situation. She knew God had spared her life through the instrumentality of Pastor Hall, and she sensed that God had more for her to learn through this righteous man that God had used so mightily.

At that moment, while still sitting on the edge of the bed in which she had almost died, Happiness decided she would be attending Pastor Hall's church effective immediately. She may have been on death's doorstep on Thursday, but she was determined that come Sunday morning; she would be alive and well, and on the doorstep of Christ Worship Center.

22

NEW BEGINNINGS

True to her commitment, that next Sunday morning, the first one of December, 2001, Happiness was in worship services at Christ Worship Center. Inside she was filled with eager anticipation. She couldn't wait to hear what God would speak to her through this pastor who had prayed healing over her so confidently and successfully. As soon as she walked into the auditorium at Gar-field High School where the church met, she knew this was where she was called to be. She felt such comfort and peace; an overwhelming feeling of being "home." She was filled to overflowing in her spirit with excitement and anticipation of what God was going to do.

The details of that service are a blur to her now. She vaguely recalls Pastor Hall announcing to the congregation that she had just been healed and that she was now in attendance, but that was about it. Her only impressions were general ones; a powerful message by Pastor Hall and a "strong sense of purpose and a sense of belonging." When the service concluded and the preaching was finished, Happiness just sat there for a few minutes soaking it all in. All she could think about was returning for the next Sunday service.

Happiness made it a point to fully and quickly connect with this body of believers. She learned about a home Bible study the church had in one of the elder's homes during the week. She immediately began attending those studies as well, soaking in the teachings and the fellowship with every ounce of her being. She couldn't get enough. The Lord was pouring strength back into her as never before and she longed for Him to just keep "pouring" more of His Spirit into hers. God, His Word, and being with His people became her life. All else was a distraction. She continued to go to work, but now work seemed like such an unwelcome diversion from the main event of Jesus in her life. She couldn't wait until the next Bible study or church service.

God was also placing key spiritual figures into her life to encourage her and build her faith in God even stronger. In so doing, the Lord was quietly, yet effectively protecting her. One of those figures was elder Fred Rundell, who taught the home Bible study she was now attending. To her, Fred was remarkably self-assured as to who God is. He was strong in his faith and his convictions and he spoke from experience. He spoke from the life he had lived, from an assurance that Christ is real. He came as a timely messenger of God into her life, not realizing he was speaking God's truths that related exactly to what Happiness was going through at that period of time. Fred's teachings were helping Happiness feel secure in her new "journey."

Two other key figures for Happiness at this time were elders Rick and Charlotte Findley. She marveled at how the two of them, when teaching Discipleship Training classes at church, walked in one accord, demonstrating how a husband and wife should be united with God. At times Charlotte would start an idea or even a sentence and

Rick would finish it, as if they were one person teaching the class. Their teachings on the Holy Spirit solidified her understanding and spoke to her so personally; it was "like they held that class just for me." Charlotte especially became close with Happiness. They would talk on the phone about various circumstances Happiness was going through and Charlotte would pray for her, extending an invitation for Happiness to call her at any time of the day or night. Charlotte became an example for her of a "true woman of God."

Her friends, Bob and Debbie Patten, continued to be extremely supportive of her, often praying with her and counseling her as she went through so many trials. There were many evenings Happiness spent at their house just crying and releasing pent up emotion with friends she could trust. Over the years, when times were financially tight and difficult, Bob and Debbie gave her food, helped her with her children, and provided whatever support Happiness needed. They were always there for her as true friends.

As for Pastor Hall, he remained more at a distance, yet he was always watching and observing. He seemed to sense what she needed spiritually, like a spiritual father, and he made sure other church leaders were surrounding Happiness to meet her needs. Yet he was faithful to counsel her and bring her out of all her prior hurts and wounds. He was patient with her, yet never let her off the hook. He steered her towards spiritual maturity as he assisted with her spiritual healing. Indeed, he was so spiritually strong, it took Happiness a long while before she could see him as a real human! God had used him so significantly in her life, she saw him as a man of great honor; a leader whose authority she deeply respected. She knew she would be forever grateful to him for his coming to visit her and pray for her that Thanksgiving day.

The more Happiness observed how selfless and genuine her new church family was towards her, the more determined she was to embrace them. She was grateful to finally be a part of such a close-knit and caring group who shared her deep love of God. As she plugged into this new church body, she was able to begin dealing with major spiritual strongholds that had taken root in her. One of those strongholds was fear.

At the time, she was facing some serious problems at her job with a local health care agency. She had been serving as the Director of Administration over a staff of 13 employees. However, she worked for a female owner, Joan Bridges, whose boyfriend felt that Happiness had too much access and influence over the boss and wanted his girlfriend to get rid of her. While he began trying to sabotage Happiness in various ways, attempting to make her look bad, the entire staff saw through it. Even Joan saw through what her boyfriend was doing. Although she apparently had no ability to control her boyfriend's under-handed actions, the owner repeatedly assured Happiness that she was doing excellent work and her job was guaranteed.

Yet problems remained, with the conflict becoming much more serious when Joan's boyfriend directly intervened to set her up. When Happiness arrived at work one morning, she found a medical record laying out on the floor, a clear violation of privacy rules and laws. The boyfriend of the supervisor just happened to be there to witness the file on the floor. He accused Happiness of leaving it there overnight, yet it was obvious he had placed it there to falsely accuse her. None of the other employees had seen the file when they came in earlier. Happiness began to fear the possible repercussions of such a false report being made against her, including possible criminal charges and negative coverage in the local papers. Despite knowing she was innocent of the accusation, her fear began to grow almost exponentially until it was consuming her. She knew she needed to deal with it.

The next Wednesday night at elder Fred's home Bible study, Happiness got the courage to ask the group for prayer to overcome her fear. She had been convinced that "what you keep to yourself will hold you hostage." She had already been hostage to this problem long enough. It was time to get free of it. In response to her simple request, that small, but faithful group of Christians laid hands upon her and started praying with force and conviction. They bound the spirit of fear, they loosed peace over her, and they generally waged spiritual battle on her behalf. When they were done praying, she had a new sensation that God was in control and that she had no need to fear any longer. She gained a strong sense of security, walking in confidence that God would take care of her no matter what happened. She had a complete release from fear that night that brought her assurance and empowerment.

Equipped by those prayers, Happiness returned to work the following day and drafted a resignation letter. In it she quoted from the book of Ecclesiastes: *"To every thing there is a season."* Despite not having another job to go to, she was leaving the job in faith that God would provide something else for her. She delivered the resignation letter, which was effective immediately. Joan, who typically exhibited confidence and a bit too much pride, was immediately affected by the letter. She tried to call Happiness but Happiness did not return her phone calls. She didn't want to allow this door to re-open. It was over, and Happiness knew she had to move on.

Happiness would later learn from her co-workers that the owner, who rarely displayed emotion or weakness, called a meeting after Happiness had left in which she was crying in front of everyone over their loss of Happiness as an employee. She recognized the tremendous blessing her business had just lost, all because of the pettiness of a boyfriend. Even in this departure, the Lord's hand of protection was upon Happiness, preserving her reputation. Unknown to her, this same owner would several years later be investigated by the FBI, convicted of fraud in her business, and sentenced to jail. When it happened, thanks to God sovereignly moving her out of the picture, Happiness was never implicated. Had she stayed, being so close to the owner, she likely would have been accused of knowing of the criminal activity, even if she was completely innocent.

It was now summer of 2003 and Happiness needed another job. She had met a registered nurse who she had worked with before who was now the owner of another nursing care service. Happiness called her up to see if there was a possibility of working for her. When she went by the office to discuss the possibility further, there were boxes scattered everywhere. The owner explained that she was deeply in debt and was getting ready to close her business. Despite such grim circumstances, Happiness offered to help the lady get her business back up and running. They decided to form a 45-55% partnership with the former owner holding the controlling percentage.

With Happiness' now a part of the business, God began to show immediate favor upon it. Happiness was instrumental in bringing in new contracts, getting advertising started, and restoring the reputation of the business. Within four months of their partnership, the business was out of debt and profits were coming in. Times should have been good and the relationship between the two partners should have been flourishing, but they weren't.

Though a business partner, Happiness was being treated like a volunteer. For the next four months, Happiness was not paid a single cent, while she spent money out of her own pocket to buy office supplies, used her own gas to drive to visit clients and continued to invest what little funds she had into the business. Meanwhile, Happiness was unable to pay her mortgage; she was falling into a deep financial pit, while the business she was a partner in received income she never saw.

She shared her frustrations with her partner on several occasions, telling her of her financial bind and that she would not be able to continue working there much longer. None of her attempts to persuade her partner to pay her had any positive impact. By Thanksgiving, 2003, after only five months together, Happiness had reached her limit. She decided not to return to work after the holiday. She called the partner and told her that she would not be coming in anymore.

Happiness had truly been sacrificial in her efforts towards resurrecting the partner's business, yet she was never paid, nor treated as a partner. Happiness had placed her trust in the promises made by the partner, yet none of them came to pass. She had been used and now she was left with nothing. She was angry, yet even more; she was deeply hurt by the broken trust. Had it not been for Happiness, this lady would not have been able to continue her business. Happiness had almost single-handedly restored that business, bringing it from hopeless levels of debt to promising profits! She began to struggle mightily with feelings of bitterness and unforgiveness.

Her heart was broken by this affront to all her efforts on behalf of the business. Making it even more difficult was the fact that now Happiness had to deal with the reality that she had no money, and no way to pay her mortgage. Anxieties began to rise up inside her as she wondered if she was about to become homeless again. She had been homeless before; she didn't want to go through that again. As she reflected upon all that had happened, and where she now stood in life, second thoughts at leaving the prior job circled through her mind, tormenting her with regret and despair. She went to Pastor Hall for counsel; he had always given her wise advice in the past. She knew she could count on his advice now.

Through several counseling sessions, Happiness began to get re-grounded. She needed to officially terminate the partnership to limit any further liability she might be saddled with and she deserved compensation for her efforts with the partnership. Yet as she prayed and sought God about it, she decided she didn't want the compensation to be paid to her. Instead, she wanted it to be a sacrificial gift for God's kingdom. She knew that she could trust God to get her through, and she wanted to demonstrate to Him how much she trusted in Him to provide. He had never forsaken her before and she was convinced He would not forsake her now.

With her mind fixed on trusting God, she drafted up a letter, asking to be removed as partner of the business, requesting $10,000 of rightful compensation to be paid to her church, and then she relinquished all other rights she was entitled to as a partner. The letter served to formally terminate a relationship that had gone terribly sour, but the letter was not accusatory in any way. In the meantime, Happiness began working for temp agencies doing any kind of work she could to pay the bills.

There was still a major issue that she needed to be resolved. The partnership resignation letter may have freed her from the business relationship, but it did nothing to diminish her growing bitterness and unforgiveness. In fact, the more Happiness thought about it, the more those related emotions began to grow. They spread from her former business partner, to rekindling thoughts about Sonny, who thanks to his intentional efforts to hinder the divorce process in every way possible, had prevented her divorce from becoming final, more than three years after she had filed!

Each day brought greater anger. She found herself
rehearsing in her mind all the wrongs that had been done to
her. She repeatedly reminded herself she had done nothing
wrong; that she was a victim of injustice and unfairness.
She would even engage in impromptu arguments in her
head, responding with devastating rebuttals to every alle-
gation against her. She was clearly going down the wrong
path that bitterness was taking her.

Sometime in March, 2004, that would all change. God
was about to re-direct her back to His path, for the fulfillment of her destiny depended upon it. It happened one
Sunday morning at church, when Pastor Hall was preaching
on forgiveness. His preaching hit a nerve with her.
Everything he said was exactly what she needed to hear.
The most difficult part of the message, she immediately
embraced: even if you are right, or feel you are right, you
must forgive in order to be released yourself. Pastor Hall
noted that absent forgiveness, it is you who ends up paying
the price through bitterness and anger. You lose your peace
and your joy all for the sake of "being right." Rather than
holding on to your anger and resentment, you need to
be released from the growing bitterness, and that release
only comes through the act of forgiveness. As Pastor Hall
continued to preach, Happiness was being transformed with
a sense of renewal. She was being given a practical way to
get rid of all these negative feelings that were weighing her
down like excess baggage.

By the time church services ended, Happiness was
swelling with boldness and a need to take action on her
new revelation of forgiveness. It would require a two-step
process; first forgiving the other person in her heart, and
second, seeking the other person's forgiveness. That latter
part was clearly the most difficult and the barrier most
people are unable to cross because for them, being right is
more important than being free. Any act, such as this, that

requires that we die to our pride, is always a difficult task
in a society that fosters such a selfish focus. What made it
all the more challenging was that the seeking of forgiveness
from a person you felt had wronged you, had to be more
than empty words. For it to work, it had to be genuine and
come from the heart.

After leaving church, Happiness knew what she had
to do. She drove directly to her former business partner's
house. While driving there, Happiness was praying and
rehearsing what she would say. With tears of repentance
streaming down her cheeks, she forgave the former partner
as trust between her and God grew inside her, even before
arriving at the house.

Once at the house, she took a deep breath, said one
more short prayer for a right attitude, then she walked up to
the door and knocked. This was not easy for her to do. She
wanted to turn around and leave, but she knew it had to be
done. When the door opened, it was her former business
partner looking at her in surprise. After a quick greeting,
Happiness got straight to her point. *"I'm here in the name
of Jesus to ask for your forgiveness about whatever I may
have said or done that hurt you,"* Happiness blurted out
before the lady had a chance to utter a word. *"I don't know
what I did or said,"* Happiness continued, *"but I forgive
you and I want to know if you will forgive me. I just want
everything to be right between us."* She didn't try to justify
herself or lay blame on the other person. The preaching she
had just heard had warned her not to do so.

Her former partner seemed dumbfounded by this
unusual request. *"I forgive you,"* she said after a short
pause to collect her thoughts. *"I don't know where things
went wrong,"* the lady continued, as if she had nothing to
do with the fallout. To her credit, Happiness did not take
the bait of temptation to point out the other persons' fault
in the matter. The ladies' husband walked up at this point,

evidently having overheard what was going on. *"We always liked you"* he said; *"we didn't understand what happened."* Happiness responded perfectly. *"Whatever it was,"* Happiness continued, *"I repent. Please forgive me."*

Both of them accepted her request, assured her that they forgave her, and that was it. There were no fireworks, no trumpets blasting, nor any dramatic music playing in the background to mark the occasion. This was no Hollywood script; just real life. Happiness simply turned and left. She had done what needed to be done to remove the bitterness and unforgiveness she had been harboring up until this time, at least against her former business partner. Through that act of forgiveness, Happiness had let go and released all that built up bitterness, and now she was basking in a new-found inner peace. It felt so good.

Now she needed to address the source of even deeper bitterness and unforgiveness; that which was caused from all the years of hurt from Sonny, her husband from whom her divorce was still not yet final. Even though it would take every ounce of fortitude she could muster, Happiness realized now was the time to seek his forgiveness. Now, while she still had the boldness and conviction to take action, she needed to act. She reminded herself of the preaching from Pastor Hall; that seeking forgiveness has nothing to do with whether you are right or wrong in the matter. It was solely about getting a spiritual and emotional release from the bondage that bitterness and unforgiveness carries with it. For her to be able to move forward towards her destiny in Christ, she had to get right with Sonny.

The following Monday, Happiness called Sonny at his job. When Sonny answered the phone, Happiness got right to the point of her call. *"I'm calling to apologize to you and ask for your forgiveness,"* she began. *"Please forgive me for whatever I have said or done that hurt you,"* she continued. She could have stopped there, but she needed to really seal this the right way. With a large dose of humility, Happiness uttered the words she had never been able to say before; *"I take full responsibility for whatever I did to cause you pain; please let me know you forgive me."* There was a short pause on the other end of the line as Sonny, no doubt, was caught by surprise. Then he said it, *"Yes, I forgive you."* That was it. No offer to request her forgiveness; no apologies on his part for what he had done to her. Yet, none of that really mattered. Fault-finding and finger-pointing was not what this call was all about. Happiness had received what she had sought; his forgiveness. Happiness closed out this significant, yet simple call by merely saying, *"Thank you, I appreciate it."* With that, she hung up.

As she hung up, she immediately felt good; really good. She began crying to the Lord, overwhelmed by a feeling of complete release from the heavy bondage of bitterness that she hadn't realized she was carrying. She was free of it now. For so long she had carried the grudges and the anger, but it had only served to weigh her down. Now, that weight was gone. She felt a sense of accomplishment as well. She had heard God's message of forgiveness and she had acted upon it in faith. She was excited that the pettiness of who was right and who was wrong was all behind her now. None of that garbage mattered anymore.

She didn't need vindication from Sonny; she needed and had received vindication from the only one who truly mattered; Jesus Christ. Waves of peace came over her, while the guilt and the shame of a ruined marriage were being washed away. She now had a new beginning. She felt ready and equipped to move forward in what God had in store for her. Her past would no longer hold her back. Now she could focus on what lay ahead; she could dream again without restraint. She could soar again in her imagination and in her vision for her future. There was no better feeling in the world than what she was experiencing right then in being released from the bondage of bitterness.

23

PURSUING HER DREAMS

ye

Happiness may have received forgiveness, but she still had no job. The pressures from that reality remained, yet Happiness would not allow them to divert her attention from her true priority. She knew what God's word promised in the book of Matthew: *"Seek first the kingdom of God and His righteousness."* If she could keep her focus on the Lord, any and all other needs in her life would be met. With that assurance, her quest for God's presence was about to get very serious. She needed direction from the Lord; she needed to hear from Him in a mighty way, and she needed to hear from Him soon. The only way to hear from God would be to seek Him with everything that was within her.

Her mind became fixed and determined to enter into a period of prayer and fasting that would not end until she had God's answers. Much like Jacob's desperate plea from the Old Testament, Happiness too cried out to God: *"Lord, unless you bless me and change my life, I will die."* To the cynic, such a cry sounds overly dramatic, but to a desperate believer in Christ, such a cry reveals the absolute conviction necessary to pursue God at the deepest level. She was tired of compromise in her life that kept her in a rut of stagnation. She needed a transformed life and she needed it quickly.

As she continued to seek the Lord, her circumstances at first remained unchanged. No one had a job available for her and every job opportunity she pursued shut in her face. While some might conclude that God was not hearing her prayers, let alone answering them, God was actually moving mightily to turn Happiness in a different direction.

In February, 2004, as she completed her period of fasting, she attended a winter camp meeting at Church on the Rock in Stafford, Virginia. There the teaching seemed to speak directly to her needs. She continued heavily in prayer. When she couldn't sleep, she would get up in the middle of the night, turn on a Christian channel at 1:00 or 2:00 in the morning and allow the Lord to minister to her through more teachings, along with praise and worship music.

Gradually, through all this seeking and basking in the Lord, her dream of owning her own business began to be rekindled within her. She remembered how she had longed to have her own office, to dress like the other professionals, and to be her own boss. She recalled how she observed the various business professionals walking to work with a sense of purpose. She had wanted to be like them.

Still, the reality of her desperate financial situation without a job was a constant lure toward panic. She was behind on her mortgage payment, she had already received foreclosure notices, and she was collecting unemployment as her only source of funding. The devil wanted to hinder her focus, but to her credit, Happiness kept her focus on the Lord and what He was beginning to birth into her spirit. Through a temp agency, she obtained work at a residential housing development called Four Seasons working in their warranty department. It brought in some money, but not enough.

Despite such overwhelming financial pressures, Happiness remained unmoved and unshaken. God was birthing a dream of a home health care business into her mind with remarkable clarity. She would lie on her bed in the evenings after work writing down the ideas God was giving her.

She applied to the state for a start up home health care business packet that set forth the minimum requirements for her to open her own business. Through that packet and her prior experience, she knew she would need to have written policies and procedures in place before she could get licensed. She methodically began putting them together. The more she wrote, the more creative ideas God gave her.

Of course, sufficient capital was a key item necessary to start her business; specifically $50,000, according to the state start-up packet. Although that amount of capital seemed out of reach, she pressed forward. As she did so, she felt drawn once again to God's earlier command to *"Feed my sheep."* The words resounded in her heart day after day as she prepared her paperwork and she knew that her profits would not be spent on fancy clothes and vacations: whatever the Lord did to prosper her, she knew that she would share it with others.

Undeterred by the lack of finances to start a business, she entered into a covenant with God for the business. She had been burned by the earthly partnership she had previously entered into, but she was excited by the spiritual and heavenly partnership she was making with her Lord. She committed the business to Him, and vowed to not take a single step of preparation without God being a part of it. It was at this point that God gave her five books in the Bible to claim as her own: Isaiah, 1st and 2nd Timothy, Revelation, and the book that was most dear to her, the book of Deuteronomy. She read these books with renewed purpose and attention. Deuteronomy especially came alive to her; it was like reading an intriguing novel that she couldn't put down. It became a roadmap to her, a reminder of the blessings of her special covenant with the Lord that brought her greater intimacy and closeness to Jesus.

Her unusual business covenant with God would serve to protect her as she entered a service industry that was fraught with danger. Happiness had worked in the home health care arena for many years. She was personally aware of many such agencies that had been investigated, found to have violated one or more of the myriad of administrative state regulations, and either been fined or had money recouped from them. In one particular case, Medicaid was administratively reclaiming several hundred thousand dollars from a private agency because their paperwork was incorrect. As she continued her business preparations, Happiness did so knowing that God's hand of protection would need to be upon her.

It wasn't long thereafter that the Lord began to reveal His direction in some very real ways. First, she was encouraged to write down her business vision through a powerful teaching by Mark Ramos, another elder at Christ Worship Center, who taught on the scriptural admonition in Habakkuk 2:2 which reads:

> *"And the Lord answered me, and said, 'Write the vision, and make it plain upon tables, that he may run that readeth it.'"*

Through the revelations from Deuteronomy and the other four books God had given her, she was impressed to focus on meeting the needs of people, specifically the orphans, the fatherless, the widows, and the strangers. They became the center of her business "ministry," and a clarification of her earlier vision to "feed" God's "sheep." Indeed, it was clear from the beginning, that her business would not be any ordinary business with an ordinary purpose of making money. Her business would be a means to provide for others, to minister God's love, to "feed His sheep", and to glorify God in everyway she could.

As she was drafting up her business brochure and struggling to find the boldness to honor God, the Lord provided her further insight, through another teaching at Christ Worship Center that gave her the boldness to cite to scriptures and timeless principles of God. She heard a teaching on the faith of America's Founding Fathers, and how they boldly sought to build a nation based on God's timeless Biblical principles. That teaching gave her the courage to boldly proclaim God's truths in her business. *If the Founding Fathers were brave enough to establish a nation upon God's principles,* she thought, *then surely I can establish my business upon God's principles.* She would no longer be intimidated by what others might think. Like the business God was creating through her, her business brochure would not be any ordinary brochure.

Even financially, God was moving on her behalf in a mighty way. One night, around midnight, after having received another notice from attorneys that her house was being foreclosed on, Happiness was prompted to call her bank and find out the exact amount in her account. The automated message informed her of her balance, but she couldn't believe it was correct. She hung up and re-dialed, convinced it was a mistake. The automated message repeated the same amount, the same amount that her mortgage was in arrears! The next morning, she drove to her bank, withdrew the money, and sent the full amount of her arrearage by express mail to the attorney for the mortgage company. There was no earthly way such an amount of money should have been in her account. It was a miraculous provision from God and she knew it.

Before her new business would be licensed by the state, Happiness also needed office space. She began driving through the local area looking for vacant offices that would be suitable and affordable. As she did so, she came across a small office in Dumfries, Virginia near where she lived, currently occupied by the Prince William Airport Shuttle. She knew of someone who said they worked there, so she pulled in to talk to the owners. When she explained she was looking to open a business and was needing office space, her timing couldn't have been better. She didn't know it, but the business had been struggling to pay the rent on the building. Having another tenant to assist in the rent was exactly what they needed. They offered her a choice of one of four office spaces they had in the building for $300 a month that could be paid at the end of the month. She accepted the office in the front with a big window, trusting God to provide her the funds by the end of the month when the rent would be due.

She quickly found some used furniture to place in her office and with that, she was ready to have the state licensing agency come to inspect her office in hopes of obtaining her business license. She made an appointment for her initial inspection for June 23 and 24, 2004. She had already prepared her policies and procedures required by the business start-up guide and she was confident that the Lord would give her favor with the inspector. Then, while awaiting her inspection date, God moved again on her fledgling operation. The owners of the airport shuttle service offered her four more offices for an additional $300 a month, an incredible price made from their position of desperation to pay the rent. She again accepted though she didn't have the funds.

Her actions were far from reckless. She was operating in faith borne out of confidence gained in seeking first the kingdom of God. She knew all of this was being orches-trated by her heavenly Father. She was seeing first-hand a truth she had long heard; that faith will take you to places you can never go on your own. God had given her office space and had prepared her for the inspection coming up.

God had provided for every need to open her business, with one apparent exception: He had not provided her the $50,000 of reserve financing the state business start up package listed as a prerequisite for licensing and state approval. As her license inspection date approached, Happiness quietly trusted that God would somehow make a way for her, even without the requisite funding. She was neither afraid nor anxious. Instead, she was filled with a knowing deep inside that she would be approved for business.

On June 23, 2004, the lady from the state licensing authority arrived. Happiness greeted her warmly, sat her down in her front office, and handed her a neatly organized binder of all her policies and procedures set forth exactly as the state business start up package had recommended. Happiness was very prepared for this meeting and it showed.

Quietly, yet methodically, the inspector read each page of the policy and procedure manuals, turning the pages without a word. It was readily apparent that Happiness had her act together. Everything was covered that was required to be covered, and it was done with quality. Though she had tried, over the course of the two days, the inspector had been unable to find a single discrepancy, a rare occurrence in the licensing process. Happiness had everything so well put together that the inspector finished early on the second day.

After giving Happiness the good news that her license was approved, and while engaged in conversation, the state inspector's curiosity prompted her to ask a personal question, *"Happiness, you are a single mother and an immigrant in a new country, yet this is the most thorough and impressive plan that I have seen in years. How did you possibly have the confidence and fortitude to put this business together? Weren't you afraid?"*

"Thank you for your kind words," Happiness replied modestly, recognizing that this was the opening the Lord had given her to brag about what He had done for her. *"Well, actually I knew I couldn't do this by myself, so I fasted and prayed, and I sought the Lord for help. In doing so, He prompted me to make a covenant with Him for this business."* The inspector appeared intrigued; it gave Happiness the confidence to continue sharing. *"I asked Him to be my business partner, to give me the courage and assurance I needed to move forward, along with the creative ideas to make it special. So I can tell you with all honesty, that it wasn't me, it was the work of my covenant business partner, Jesus Christ. Through all my struggles, He has sustained me, and when it came time for me to start this business, He gave me the wisdom, courage, and favor that I needed to put everything in place. Without Him, I would have been too afraid, too timid to even try!"* The woman's eyes lit up with delight to see such rare assurance in God and the practical ramifications it had upon her business. The two ladies spent the rest of the afternoon talking about the goodness of the Lord!

Amazingly, the lack of $50,000 in start up financing never came up! God had ensured that such a lack would not hold back Happiness in realizing her dream of her own business. Although the official business license would not come in the mail until a few weeks later, on June 24, 2004, Happiness counted this as the day she realized her vision to own her own business. With only one used desk, one used computer, one phone, one used chair, one used bookcase and a pencil holder with some pencils she brought from home, Happiness, with the huge assistance from her covenanted business partner, was now open for business!

Only God could provide so much from so little. Happiness had dared to walk in the faith her Lord had given her; she had dared to dream big, do all she knew how to do, and then stand back and let God do the rest. Ordinarily, this would be the time to sit back and reflect on all that God had done for her, but this was not an ordinary time. Happiness was moving in the momentum that God had given her. There was still much to be done, and now, exhilarated by clearing this huge hurdle, Happiness continued to "press toward the mark" in the race that God had set before her.

24

FULFILLING HER DESTINY

As Happiness moved forward with the details of setting up her business, God continued to show her favor. The requirements were daunting: she needed to secure a $3 million malpractice insurance policy, worker's compensation insurance and a separate bond needed to protect against damages caused by employees. Then there was the small issue of letting people know she existed. *I suppose I should put some sort of sign outside my building!*

In the absence of a marketing budget, Happiness began to notify all her old clients about her new business and get in touch with many former coworkers to explain what she was doing. Within a couple weeks she had seven clients, which was enough to cover her basic expenses!

As Happiness gained patients to serve, she made sure she treated them in a special way. To her, clients were not just sources of money for her business; they were human beings with special needs. Each one was a gift from God and she wanted to bring God's love to each one of them. Her vision had always been to establish a ministry through her business; a ministry that honored God mightily, and served as a means to "feed" God's "sheep." Her home

health care agency was unique in that it would bring
Happiness face to face with the "widows," the "fatherless,"
and the "strangers" that God had impressed upon her to
minister to.

She made a point to physically visit with each patient,
and when they wanted it, she would pray with them and
speak to them about God. She wanted to get to know them
as individuals, and she wanted to make herself available to
them if they needed anything. Happiness bought booklets
on God's power to heal and she made them available free
in her office as clients and others stopped by. Most importantly to her, she made sure she posted a framed copy of
the Ten Commandments on the waiting room wall of her
offices. She wanted to give a special place of prominence
to the Lord's commandments that had held such a special
place in her heart since she was a little girl growing up in
Nigeria. On her business checks, right above the signature
line, as well as at the bottom of her official business letter-
head, Happiness had printed the reference to Luke 4:18,
a scripture with particular importance to her vision of her
business. That scripture reads as follows:

> *"The Spirit of the Lord is upon me, because he hath
> anointed me to preach the gospel to the poor; he
> hath sent me to heal the brokenhearted, to preach
> deliverance to the captives, and recovering of sight
> to the blind, to set at liberty them that are bruised."*

Her silent Business Partner held up His end of the
bargain and her business grew rapidly, allowing her to hire
more nursing assistants and other staff. She prayed daily
over her staff and began to hold monthly meetings with
them called "My Brother's Keeper," where she encouraged them to care for one another and cultivated a sense
of community. These meetings then developed into two

monthly newsletters: one for her employees called "My Brother's Keeper," and a separate one for her clients called "Compassionate Care."

She continually looked for creative ways to honor God as her business partner. *Lord, You have blessed me so far beyond what I have earned or deserve! Never will I forget what it was like to be employed by an uncompassionate boss, nor what a blessing it was to find sympathy with the ones who controlled my schedule and signed my paychecks. Never will I forget what I felt when I was homeless and had to go to the shelters to find food for my children to eat. You have given me a taste of Your compassion through all these sufferings You have brought me through. I will never forget Your kindness and mercy. Oh God, help me show that same kindness to those that you send to me!*

One of the creative ways the Lord gave her to honor Him in her newsletters, was to combine important health care information for her patients along with numerous scripture verses and quotes from the Founding Fathers about the need for God in the nation. Everyone who worked for Happiness understood that she worked for the Lord and that the business was a partnership between her and God. She was determined that God would receive honor and glory in this business He had blessed her with.

Happiness was also very attentive to her employee's needs, spending hours counseling some of the young women who worked for her about everything from finances, child care, and boyfriends. Whatever was bothering them, they knew they could talk to Happiness and she would listen. Considering all that Happiness had been through in life, she also brought great perspective and volumes of wisdom to the discussion. Happiness had clearly found her niche. She flowed easily in business leadership and ownership.

Happiness continued to expand and grow her business, almost at an exponential pace. As she did so, she began to also expand her influence in the community. She started attending meetings with the mayor, chief of police, and other business associates. She worked closely with state social workers and various others throughout the medical establishment. Though typically shy and unassuming, Happiness was becoming a community leader; one sought out for her wisdom and perspective. Through years of grounding in the word of God, coupled with the experiences of a life in pursuit of God, Happiness had much to offer local leaders. It seemed as if God was blessing her business in new and more remarkable ways as Happiness continued to dedicate her efforts to the Lord.

On September 6, 2004, Happiness was presented with a new opportunity to honor God through her business.

"Can you speak up, Ma'am?" Happiness asked, straining to hear the faint voice on the other end of the line.

"None of the other agencies will take me," the old woman whispered. *"My son John is taking the insurance money and I don't know what to do."*

"Why is your son taking your money?" Happiness asked in mild alarm and sympathy. She had seen a good many things in her life, but the willingness of someone to leave an elderly parent in need never ceased to dismay her. She could only think of her father and what she would have given to have been by his side in his last days.

"He...he..." the woman ventured weakly, *"he is not himself."* Happiness took down the woman's name—Elizabeth Atkinson—and information, and made inquiries with some of her staff.

"Oh yes," one of her young nursing aides said. *"I remember her. Everyone knows her. Her son is a crack head. He blew through the $70,000 her husband left her when he died and now she's getting older and sicker. He*

*insists that the insurance company sends him the reim-
bursement money for her care, and then he keeps the money
for his drug habit and never pays the agencies providing
the care. All the agencies have stopped treating her because
they are never paid."*

*"Doesn't she have other children or a sister or a
nephew to look in on her?"* Happiness asked in horror.

*"Not that I ever heard. We all said it was a shame that
the only person she has in this world visits just to steal from
her,"* the aide said, shaking her head. *"But don't you take
her on, Miss Happiness. She is terribly neglected, but she
can't pay. It's not her fault, but she'll leave you hanging."*

"Yes, I know," Happiness said, as much to herself as to
the aide.

The next day, despite her busy schedule, Happiness
went to visit Mrs. Atkinson herself. When she entered
the house, it was a mess. Happiness called out for Mrs.
Atkinson and heard a weak voice in the back of the house
answer her. She carefully stepped around the piles of papers
and animal waste and found the old woman in a little
bedroom lying in a bed. The bedroom smelled worse than
the rest of the house, and a wheelchair collecting dust in the
corner told Happiness that this woman was unable to even
take herself to the bathroom. The old woman looked as
frail and small as she sounded. Her nightgown was stiff and
stuck to her skin, and her hair was matted against her head,
having not been combed for weeks at least.

"Mrs. Atkinson," Happiness said gently. *"I am
Happiness Emejuru. We spoke on the phone. I am here to
see if I can help you."*

*"Oh thank you, my dear. I'm sorry about the house.
Nobody else came."* Mrs. Atkinson tried to sit up to greet
her, but fell back on her pillow from the effort.

"No, no, that is fine," Happiness said calmly. *"But
there is the matter of your insurance. You must tell the*

company what your son is doing so they can stop him. Otherwise you will have no way to pay for your care."

"I can't," the woman said, beginning to sob. "I can't. They'll lock John up. He doesn't mean to be bad. He's not himself. You should have seen him when he was a little boy, Happiness. He had bright curly blond hair and freckles. The sweetest child you would ever know. He used to sit in my lap for hours while I read to him..." her voice trailed off as she sobbed. Happiness' heart sank. There would probably be no payments from this woman, of that she could be sure. Her business, though strong, was very new and not immune from being taken down by one or two patients who defaulted. What could she do?

She knew Mrs. Atkinson should rightly turn her son over to the authorities; what good was she doing him by allowing him to pay for his drugs with her money? Yet was her unwillingness to press charges against her son a reason she should die alone in her own filth? *Lord, I endangered myself and my children by taking Sonny back, and yet You delivered me. Can I help this woman without bankrupting the business You have given me? I want to help her but I must feed my children and pay my employees.*

The ladies' condition reinforced the extent of the risk that Happiness was taking in accepting her case. In a moment, Happiness sensed the answer in her heart. *You feed My sheep, my Happy, and I will feed you and yours.* She remembered her dreams and remembered again that her Father had more than enough. She also knew that this task she was taking on would involve far more than providing home nursing care. Serving this woman would mean cleaning her house, making sure she had food to eat and clean clothes to wear. With a drug addicted son in her life, it would be no easy task.

Regardless of the dangers, risks, and difficulties, Happiness made the decision to do her best to meet this

273

woman's every need no matter the cost. It was a commitment that came from deep within her spirit. Happiness' heart went out to this woman and compassion rose up in abundance. She knew that one of her callings was to "the widows" and here was a widow in need. Happiness would serve this woman in obedience to God.

Initially Happiness and her aides performed regular care and also brought hot meals or donated food with them. Happiness procured used clothing for her from local charities and did Mrs. Atkinson's laundry for her. Over the ensuing weeks, Happiness quickly developed a deep and abiding relationship with Elizabeth Atkinson, becoming the elderly woman's daughter she never had. Whenever Happiness came by to visit her, which was often, Mrs. Atkinson's face would lighten up and she never wanted Happiness to leave. Happiness would talk with her as she tirelessly rubbed Mrs. Atkinson's aching shoulders, back and legs. She also brought special surprise "gifts" for her. Mrs. Atkinson loved junk food and chocolate in particular, so Happiness would bring her chocolate and hamburgers and an assortment of other treats. A special bond developed between them, generated by the simple, yet powerful effect of genuine love.

"You are like my angel, Happiness," Mrs. Atkinson said one day. *"You are the only one in the world who cares for me."*

"Jesus cares, Mrs. Atkinson," Happiness said confidently. *"He cares more than any person ever could. I could not be with my own father when his health began to fail, but God has granted that I can be with you."*

Still, the challenges were great. On one occasion, the nurse's aide found that all the utilities had been turned off, including the water, a direct result of the bill not being paid. The aide brought Mrs. Atkinson some water from her own home. When the power and water had not been restored within the week, Happiness tried to get Adult Protective Services to intervene. They explained they were unable to help, although they were very sympathetic. They had tried several times in the past to intervene, yet each time Mrs. Atkinson was uncooperative and refused to allow them to go after her son.

Happiness pleaded with them, *"Should we let her die like this?"* Still, Happiness was not able to get the government agency to act. In an act of utmost desperation, despite not having sufficient resources to do so, Happiness told the Adult Protective Services representative, *"I will be willing to take on this woman; I will pay her utilities and take responsibility for her."*

Happiness quickly explored alternatives to provide for Mrs. Atkinson. She couldn't bear the thought of seeing her friend living in such squalor. At this point, she didn't have a power of attorney or any other legal relationship, so she was limited in what she could do. Still she did what she could. With the little extra money Happiness had she would spend on food and cleaning supplies for Mrs. Atkinson. She also contacted Stan, who had been the families' financial advisor and who was well aware of the ladies' situation. She told him she was caring for Mrs. Atkinson and needed his advice. Stan too became a good Samaritan to this woman, albeit on a much smaller scale. He bought Mrs. Atkinson $200 worth of food and took it to her, yet sadly, the food didn't last four days. One of Happiness' aides cooked her a meal designed to last three days, but the next day the food was gone. They soon discovered that Mrs. Atkinson's son, John, was coming and eating the food and groceries for himself and taking what he didn't eat with him.

With Stan's help, and with the agreement of John, and the social worker, Mrs. Atkinson gave a power of attorney to Happiness so she could assist her in much greater ways.

Happiness even tried to reach out to John, realizing he needed to break free of his drug addiction and several other issues before he could turn his life around. She made arrangements for John to receive counseling and even gave him a gift certificate to help him, yet he chose not to attend the counseling provided for him. Unable to help John until he was willing to help himself, Happiness turned her attention back to her friend, Mrs. Atkinson, helping her to pay her bills, ensuring she never lost her power or water again, and making sure that her house was clean and tidy.

It wasn't long though, that Happiness was presented with yet another challenge. Mrs. Atkinson's health was continuing to fail and she became in need of 24 hour nursing care. Up until now she had only needed six hours of care a day which her long term care insurance covered. Stan, the financial advisor, recommended she sell the house and use the proceeds to cover the medical bills, since there was no money to pay the mortgage anyway. Yet Mrs. Atkinson wanted to stay in her own house until she died.

Happiness searched her heart for answers, and it was from the heart that an answer came. Happiness went to visit Mrs. Atkinson and made a sacrificial offer that demonstrated her true commitment to this lady. *"You stay in your house until it sells, then I'll take you into my house,"* Happiness told her friend, *"so that you will always be with me."* Mrs. Atkinson immediately agreed to this assurance.

Shortly thereafter, Mrs. Atkinson's health deteriorated more rapidly. She had been holding on while she could, but her ability to do so was now gone. Happiness got her admitted into Potomac Hospital where Happiness visited her almost every day for the one month she was there. The physical and emotional toll on Happiness during this time was great. She was trying to run a business, yet every spare amount of time she needed to devote to Mrs. Atkinson.

Following discharge from the hospital, a short stay in a rehabilitation facility, and the sale of Mrs. Atkinson's house, Happiness kept her promise and brought her to her own house at Delaney Road where she received the 24 hour medical attention and care she needed. Happiness took the proceeds of the house sale, gave them to Stan to deposit into a restricted account managed by Stan, where only a fixed amount was released to pay for the health care expenses, although it wasn't near enough.

John continued to be a leach upon his own mother. He never came to visit her. Instead he would come to Happiness and ask for money for himself and his son. John and his son would often sleep in the nearby woods, looking tired and unkempt, when they came to ask Happiness for more assistance. Happiness, consistent with her compassionate heart, would buy them food, since they were Mrs. Atkinson's family. John would periodically ask how his mom was doing, but it was apparent to Happiness his inquiries were not motivated by a concern for his mom, but a curiosity as to when she would die so he could get whatever money she had left. Once he learned that there was no extra money for him, John stopped calling. But sometime during his last visit at the house, he took from his own mother, what little jewelry she owned and pawned it, taking the money for himself!

When the money to cover the 24-hour care began to run out, Happiness and her daughters Queenette and Millie, took turns staying up all night with Mrs. Atkinson to save the costs of a nursing aide. The three of them would take turns changing her clothes, cooking for her and cleaning up after her, as well as taking her to all her doctor's appointments. As Happiness would explain it later, *"She became like a mother; whatever you would do for your own parents, became my responsibility."* While not literally so, it certainly was true in its essence. When

Mrs. Atkinson's condition required a special hospital bed for her to sleep in, Happiness bought a hospital bed for her as well. Whatever she needed to stay comfortable as her medical condition grew worse, Happiness did her best to provide it. Now, more than three years since she became her client, Happiness knew her time with her friend Mrs. Atkinson would not last much longer. The dementia was beginning to overtake her, and everything in her body began shutting down.

On December 1, 2007, Happiness' nursing assistant found Mrs. Atkinson slumped over in her chair, almost unconscious. Paramedics were called and Happiness, when notified, rushed to meet her at Potomac Hospital. Though hospital doctors were able to resuscitate Mrs. Atkinson, she was clearly dying. When Happiness arrived at the hospital, the attending physician explained to her the condition of Mrs. Atkinson and informed her that the prognosis was not good. Happiness was told she likely would not make it through the week.

Knowing her friend had little time left; Happiness began a frantic search for Mrs. Atkinson's son in hopes that she could see him before she died. She checked with all his old girlfriends, the homeless shelter in town, and any other place he was known to go. She even asked the police chief, who she knew, if he would look for him. Finally, Happiness went back to Mrs. Atkinson's neighborhood to inform her neighbors in case anyone wanted to go see her one last time.

On December 10th, Happiness came to see her special friend for the last time. When Happiness entered her room, she was not sure what to expect. Mrs. Atkinson was hooked up to an oxygen machine, asleep, looking weak and tired. Happiness knew her friend didn't have much longer to live. Though Mrs. Atkinson awoke when Happiness came into the room, she was too weak to communicate with her friend who had so faithfully and lovingly met her every need since she became her patient. The bond of love between these two women was strong, and it had been forged by the loving God who had brought them together.

Happiness began praying for Mrs. Atkinson out loud as she sought to bless her friend with God's peace and gentle hand in her waning hours of life. She sang worship songs to her and spoke words of love and encouragement to her. Happiness was comforting Mrs. Atkinson as she had done so many times before; being there for a lonely widow, when no one else was. Without Happiness, Mrs. Atkinson would have spent her dying days alone and unloved. God had brought them together and God had knit their two hearts into one.

When it came time to go, Happiness knew this would be the last time she would see her friend alive. She leaned down and whispered into her ear, *"You are a trooper; you did well; It's okay now to let go."* Happiness fought back her emotions, knowing that she had to be strong, yet also knowing if she allowed herself to shed even one tear, her emotions would break into uncontrollable tears. She couldn't let that happen. Happiness spoke again, as she re-gained control over her emotions. *"Rest in peace, it is well with your soul,"* she said with as much encouragement as she could muster. *"Jesus is going to take care of you now,"* she whispered, knowing she could not hold her emotions in check much longer.

She would have to end this visit quickly before she lost it completely, so she closed this last visit with one last word of friendship: *"Its okay, we've done well together."* After Happiness uttered those last words to Mrs. Atkinson, she turned and began to walk out the door, but before leaving, Happiness turned back for one last look at her friend. When she did, she saw that Mrs. Atkinson had opened her eyes and that she was looking right at Happiness.

Their eyes locked and Happiness saw on her friend's face a faint smile and even fainter gleam in her eyes, as if to say, *"Thank you."* When their eyes met, Happiness' heart broke completely. She knew there was nothing more she or anyone else could do for her. Both women understood they had shared something special, that only a pure love can provide, but now they also understood it was over. Happiness turned and walked out of her room, not looking back again. She wanted to retain the memory of that last faint smile from her special friend.

As Happiness drove from the hospital back to her office, she couldn't get Mrs. Atkinson out of her mind. She prayed in the spirit, while fighting the emotional crush that was engulfing her. All the way to her office, she kept praying, and then she began talking out loud to her friend as if Mrs. Atkinson could still hear her: *"You're okay, you will be better off; God is good; He will take care of you."* Happiness recalled many of the fun times they had shared, some of the funny things that had happened between them, and a flood of memories they had shared together. She pretended that Mrs. Atkinson was physically with her and sharing those same memories. She even pictured herself massaging Mrs. Atkinson's back like she used to do for her so often. Amidst the swirl of emotions and memories, there was also a sense of closure; that she had done what God called her to do. It was as if the Lord was telling her, *"It is finished."*

On December 17th, the Hospice Director called Happiness with the news that her friend had passed away. That she had lived 17 days from entering the hospital is probably more a testament to a mother holding on in hopes of seeing her son one last time, than to anything else. Yet her son had not been found, and a lonely mother had to surrender to her last hope. While the news was not a surprise, it still hurt. At the end, Happiness was the only one Mrs. Atkinson had.

With no one else to do it, Happiness took it upon herself to make the funeral arrangements. She had come too far to stop now, and besides, she wanted to ensure Mrs. Atkinson had a proper and decent burial. The details proved emotionally difficult. When it came time to choose a casket, and flowers, and all the other things necessary, Happiness couldn't do it; it hurt too much. She merely asked the funeral director to do what was appropriate. Happiness also still needed to find John and let him know his mother had died. She asked both the Mayor and the Chief of Police, approaching them with the request as a personal favor to her. She told the neighbors, she left voicemails with his ex-girlfriend and she delayed the funeral a few days in hopes John would appear in time to attend his own mother's funeral. Sadly, despite their best efforts, they were unable to find him.

The funeral was set for December 26, 2007 at the Quantico Cemetery. Happiness had made arrangements to meet with the other persons who said they wanted to attend, at the front gate. When the morning arrived, it was cold, rainy and dreary. Only three people showed up; Stan the financial advisor, and two of Mrs. Atkinson's neighbors. They made their way to a small covered spot near the burial site where the hearse was waiting. When Happiness saw the attendants rolling the coffin out of the hearse, she began to weep small tears, again fighting back the torrent that wanted to come. Then, as the four of them walked behind the casket, she cried a little more. At the temporary place near the grave site, the four of them stood around the casket, and informally took turns sharing their thoughts about Mrs. Atkinson. Each spoke from the heart about what this lady had meant to them, and how she had impacted their lives.

After making her comments, Happiness stood there watching the rain falling around them, reflecting on all she had been through. While the others were making their remarks, Happiness was busy talking with God, checking with her Lord as to whether she had succeeded in the mission He had given her. *"How did I do?"* she asked in prayer. *"Did I fail you, or did I pass the test?"* As the rain continued to fall around her, she felt the peace of God come over her and the Lord say simply, *"You passed."*

Her peace quickly turned to joy and gratitude at Her Father's approval that meant so much to her. Just like she had been as a little girl, desiring to please her earthly father, now, as a grown woman, she had that same strong desire to please her heavenly Father. She began thanking God for the love He had put in her heart that enabled her to overcome what others said was undoable. Through the love of Christ, she had been able to bear what others said was unbearable, and she was able to do it in joy, gaining a special friend in the process. Who was she, she asked herself, to have been able to take on what others could not? Where had she received the courage to do what others had been afraid to try?

As she stood in the cold and pouring rain at that lonesome gravesite, Happiness knew that God had given her a business for a heavenly purpose. She saw clearly His hand in all of this now. The vision to "feed His sheep," the purpose He placed on her heart to reach out to the "widows," and the "strangers," and now the special assignment He had given her with Elizabeth Atkinson was all part of God's plan. Even her prior hurts and heartaches earlier in life had given her a soft and tender heart that was attentive to the needs of others who were hurting. While the devil had been trying to destroy her life and rob her of her destiny through all the trials he put her through, God had been turning each of those trials into reminders of His sustaining love. As fire removes the dross and purifies the underlying gold, the fires Happiness had been through had forged a strong, faithful, and beautiful woman of God who could be used mightily for God's loving purposes.

As the rain continued to fall, Happiness now understood her calling and her God-ordained purpose. Up until now, she had thought that her name was God's reminder that He would bring happiness and a joyful heart to her. It had been an immature focus upon herself. Now, she realized God had bigger plans. Her name would more appropriately signify the joy, love, and happiness that she would bring into the lives of others; and in so doing, she too would be blessed. There would be one more reminder about her name that God would give her as she stood there on that dreary and rainy day, but it would have to wait a few more moments.

It is funny how we as God's children so frequently try to put God in a predictable box. When we expect a great heavenly revelation of our life's purpose, we often picture it coming while standing on a majestic mountain peak with rays of sunlight pouring through the clouds in some artistic masterpiece of beauty. Yet God has His own ways, His own timing, and His own mighty purposes. So for Happiness, she received a great heavenly revelation of her life's purpose, but it came when she least expected it, during circumstances far from the stereotype. Happiness met her calling of bringing God's priceless treasure of love to the hurting and the forgotten while standing at an inauspicious, rain-soaked, gravesite in northern Virginia.

As she and the three other people stood around Mrs. Atkinson's casket, it became clear that Happiness had been able to bring God's love to a lonely lady whose family and the world had abandoned. God had not forgotten that woman, and He loved her enough to send her Happiness; His special emissary. As she pictured that last faint smile on the face of Elizabeth Atkinson before she died, Happiness recalled the last words she had spoken to her special friend, *"We've done well together."* Now it was time to speak

283

those same words to her special heavenly friend who had always been there for her.

Through all she had endured in her life, the stresses of being a refugee in the Biafran War, the arranged marriage to a husband who never loved her, the abandonment in Mexico and being smuggled across the border, and yes, even all the physical, mental and sexual abuse during her marriage, she now could see God's hand in all of it. It had given her a heart focused on the needs of others. It had changed her in ways no amount of counseling could have. It had built her trust in her heavenly father who had sustained her through it all. She would never be the same.

It had been a long journey together, she and her Lord, from the innocent days as a little girl in Nigeria when she prayed to her "invisible friend." Now they were true and close friends. Her Lord was no longer just a childhood buddy. He had become much more. He was her sustainer through all the storms of life. He was her provider through all the droughts of finances. He was her ever, constant companion, who assured her that she would never be alone. As she had tried to be there for her friend Elizabeth, when no one else was, Jesus Christ had been there for her, through every trial and tribulation when no one else was. He had taken her through all the vicious attacks that the devil had thrown at her, and brought her from an unknown school girl living in a small African country, to a strong and successful business woman sought out by community leaders as a citizen of the most powerful nation on earth. Only her one true friend, the God of all creation could do that.

Yes, it was indeed time to speak those same words to her heavenly father that she had spoken to Elizabeth Atkinson; *"Father, we've done well together, haven't we?"* She couldn't help smiling at the thought. Then, unexpectedly, she heard a still, small, voice respond back to her through the wind, the rain, and cold of that December day. *"Yes we have, . . . Happiness."* When He spoke her name like that; she sensed a special significance that she had forgotten about. It now made sense why her father had given her that name. Now she had truly become what her name had meant all along, *"the daughter of her Father's joy."*

RESOURCES

ঙ৹

A round the globe, approximately one in four women has been physically abused by an intimate male partner. In the U.S., according to the U.S. Department of Justice, a woman is battered every 15 seconds, and approximately 1.3 million women are physically assaulted by an intimate partner annually. If you find yourself in a situation of such abuse in the U.S., the resources below are available to assist you.

National Domestic Violence Hotline
1-800-799-7233 (1-800-799-SAFE) TTY: 1-800-787-3224

National Sexual Assault Hotline
1-800-656-HOPE (4673) available 24/7 for the nearest rape crisis center.

National Stalking Resource Center
1-800-FYI-CALL (1-800-394-2255) M-F 8:30 AM - 8:30 PM EST

To contact either Douglas Anderson or Happiness Emejuru, you may write them at:

P.O. Box 224
Dumfries, VA 22026

Alternatively, you may e-mail Douglas Anderson at dsanderson56@yahoo.com and Happiness Emejuru at happyeme@yahoo.com

Breinigsville, PA USA
14 October 2009
225836BV00001BA/2/P